W9-BPS-720

Table of Contents

Appendixes

List of Illustrations

Acknowledgments

Sarah Baird, David Cherney, Kelly Freeman, Jeanne Gosselin, Daniel Klaus, Holland Lincoln, Elizabeth Jensen, David Juiliano, Christopher Lloyd, Erin Mastagni, Lisette Singer, Ryan Wingo, and Maxwell Woods, all students in the Claremont McKenna Colleges, worked with me in the Roberts Environmental Center to score, analyze, and extract data from corporate environmental reports. Without their effort, this book could not exist, and I am deeply grateful that they stuck with an often difficult and time-consuming task. My wife, Sia Morhardt, helped with the initial organization of the book and joined me in interviewing many European corporate environmental executives during an extended trip in 2000 prior to the ISO TC 207 annual meetings in Stockholm. Her insights were very helpful indeed, and her edits to the final draft helped to clarify many of its points. Our daughter, Camille, a writer at Stanford University also reviewed initial draft chapters and was quite helpful in establishing the final style. I also wish to thank the many corporate executives and financial analysts who have been willing to discuss the issue of corporate reporting with me, and delegates from around the world at ISO TC 207 meetings in Stockholm (2000) and Kuala Lumpur (2001) and a GRI meeting in Washington DC (2000) who shared their opinions and sharpened the focus of this book. I also thank three anonymous reviewers for helpful comments and suggestions on the proposal for this book and on its penultimate draft. Finally, it has been a distinct pleasure working with Annemieke Koudstaal, Craig Powell, Jennifer Czajka, and Denise Cawley at ASQ Quality Press; and with Leayn and Paul Tabili at New Paradigm, who edited and typeset the book. They have all been uniformly supportive, informative, and prompt.

Preface

More and more large companies, particularly manufacturing companies, are making their environmental and social performance public. As they do, the public is coming to expect similar transparency from all companies it does business with. At some point in the future, environmental and social reporting may be as commonplace and standardized as annual financial reporting is today, but it's not there just yet. This asymmetry provides a unique opportunity for proactive, forward-thinking companies that are smaller than the largest corporations or outside of the manufacturing sector to take leadership positions and differentiate themselves. Such differentiation does not necessarily require any change in environmental or social *performance*—many companies are already committed to acceptable levels of performance, and are systematically improving such performance because it saves costs, reduces risks, and seems the ethical thing to do. And if a company's current performance happens to be substandard, it ought to be rectified anyway . . . if only to save costs and reduce risks. But companies cannot be differentiated by stakeholders on the basis of performance, unless that performance is revealed. Hence, the opportunity of voluntary environmental and social reporting. (The combination of the two along with some financial reporting is the usual definition of sustainability reporting.) This book tells you everything you need to know to take advantage of this opportunity.

WHO SHOULD READ THIS BOOK?

This book is written for corporate leaders who are seeking to take credit for, and maximize the benefits from, their firms' responsible environmental and social performance. It is also written for the staff people and consultants who will write the reports and design the Web pages, and for the attorneys who will review them. Financial analysts and risk managers will get a perspective of what they should be able to expect from well-conceived environmental reporting, and regulators and environmental activists will be able to use the material herein to establish benchmarks for good reporting. Would-be corporate leaders still in undergraduate or business school can also use this book to inform themselves of an important aspect of the behavior of the best managers and corporations. This is good information to have on tap for job interviews and for conversations with the boss. Not all job candidates and aspiring managers will be so well informed.

MY RESEARCH INTO CORPORATE ENVIRONMENTAL AND SUSTAINABILITY REPORTING

In 1996, the year the ISO 14001 guidelines on corporate environmental management were introduced, I was managing a division of a national consulting firm that specialized in strategic environmental management. Our clients included the largest companies in the American automotive, petroleum refining, and energy sectors as well as the U.S. Department of Energy and the U.S. Air Force and Air National Guard. I supervised staff across the country from Washington DC to Honolulu and from Seattle to Houston, helping companies and military commands meet their environmental regulatory obligations, devise pollution prevention, waste minimization, and community right-to-know strategies, and decide whether and how soon to adopt the ISO 14001 environmental standard or to implement proprietary environmental management systems. Almost none of the companies or the military commands were producing voluntary environmental reports at that time, but we were intimately familiar with their environmental thinking, planning, and performance.

After returning to academia in late 1996 I began, along with my students in Claremont McKenna College's Roberts Environmental Center, a research program into corporate environmental performance and reporting. We have now been analyzing corporate environmental reports for several years and I have read hundreds of them. I have also interviewed many corporate environmental executives who produce them in Asia, Europe, and the United States. Our first academic papers involved analyzing reports by scoring them using some extant scoring systems, and with new scoring systems of our own devising (Morhardt 2001, Morhardt et al., submitted for publication). In this book I present a new scoring system, the Pacific Sustainability Index, that has been thoroughly tested at the Roberts Environmental Center and is superior to all of the existing systems in two ways: it separates environmental and social components of sustainability reporting and grades them independently, and it separates scoring of reporting comprehensiveness (transparency) from scoring of performance. We are continuing to conduct academic research into corporate environmental and sustainability reporting.

OVERVIEW OF THE CONTENTS

Part I is an introduction to environmental and sustainability reporting and to guidelines for writing and scoring systems for evaluating them. Chapter 1 describes the concept of sustainability and the idea behind sustainability reporting as an extension of environmental reporting. Chapter 2 develops a business case for active management of corporate environmental and social matters, and for periodically reporting on them. Chapter 3 describes and critiques the guidelines and operating standards that are currently available for environmental and sustainability reporting. Chapter 4 analyzes the content of the Global Reporting Initiative 2000 guidelines and the ISO 14031 guidelines, as well as the three best-known existing scoring systems, including the SustainAbility/UNEP system, and the new Pacific Sustainability Index. Chapter 5 critically reviews 11 quite different environmental and sustainability reports from large companies, and comments on four Web-based reports.

Part II is the heart of this book, consisting of 10 chapters corresponding to my 10 rules for writing highly effective environmental and sustainability reports. These chapters deal individually with how to report on your company's environmental and social (1) profile, (2) vision and commitment, (3) stakeholders, (4) policies and management systems, (5) aspects and impacts, (6) performance indicators, (7) initiatives and mitigations, (8) performance, (9) costs and investments, and (10) goals and targets. Each chapter explains the basic principles for effective reporting of its topic, then describes or gives examples from actual company reports that do good jobs of reporting that topic. Occasional examples from not-so-good reports are also included for comparison. Thus, not only do these chapters explain how to write an effective environmental or sustainability report, they tell you which reports to look at on the Web and to obtain for reference—they are all free.

Part III describes the previous scoring systems and introduces the Pacific Sustainability Index. Chapter 16 describes the existing scoring systems in detail and critiques them. Chapter 17 describes the new Pacific Sustainability Index and illustrates, with data from 30 corporate reports, how much attention is paid in existing reports to each of its topics.

Appendix A is the Pacific Sustainability Index scoring sheet. It will be useful as a checklist while preparing your own report, and can be used as a scoring system to evaluate your competitors' reports. By following it carefully you can be sure of writing a comprehensive environmental or sustainability report that will be scored highly by any of the scoring systems.

Appendix B presents scores for the 10 largest companies with environmental or sustainability reports, in each of four industrial sectors: electronics, motor vehicles and parts, petroleum refining, and utilities (gas and electric). It, along with two charts in Chapter 4, shows normalized scores and how the scores were distributed among the topics of the 10 rules for five scoring systems: GRI 2000, ISO 14031, SustainAbility/UNEP, Deloitte Touche Tohmatsu, and Davis-Walling & Batterman. These data show how much information the writers for these large companies devoted to the various possible topics in their own reports, and give a sense of how different sectors approach environmental and sustainability reporting.

Appendix C is the list of corporate environmental and sustainability reports used by the Roberts Environmental Center to compile the lists of metrics and performance indicators, and goals and targets contained in the next two appendixes.

Appendix D is a long list of environmental and social metrics and performance indicators from the reports listed in Appendix C. It is sorted by the environmental and social metric categories of the Pacific Sustainability Index and is intended to be used as a source of ideas for performance indicators you might choose to use in your own report.

Appendix E is a list of goals and targets from the 73 corporate reports listed in Appendix C, also sorted by Pacific Sustainability Index metric categories, and also useful for getting ideas on what sorts of goals and targets should go in your own report.

Appendix F is a list of the many corporate environmental and sustainability reports that are discussed in the text of this book, and in which chapters you can find the discussion.

J. Emil Morhardt
Claremont, California
March 2002

Introduction

An annual corporate environmental or sustainability report represents an opportunity to capture the moral high ground and the loyalty of employees and customers, not to mention the interest of financial analysts and the money of investors and lenders. It is also the best way to publicize the success of corporate environmental management systems. The largest companies are making the most of it, but the opportunity is there for any company. And the World Wide Web makes publishing an effective environmental or sustainability report economically feasible even for small companies.

This book is about how to write a highly effective corporate environmental or sustainability report. Such reports are entirely voluntary, required by no statutes or regulations, with no fixed or established content, and no necessary periodicity. In other words, they only exist because companies want to let their stakeholders—employees, investors, the public at large—know that they care about environmental and social issues and are doing something about them. What began as voluntary corporate environmental reporting is increasingly referred to as *sustainability reporting,* as health, safety, social, and financial components are included. Such reporting has become very common in the largest companies in many industrial sectors, at least with respect to the environmental components, and is poised to expand rapidly to other sectors and to smaller businesses. Four things drive this expansion:

1. The rapid worldwide acceptance of the ISO 14001 environmental standard (and in Europe, the EMAS standard) and consequent accumulation of environmental information by corporate environment, health, and safety departments and a desire to publicize it.

2. The desire (and probably soon-to-be requirement) of large corporations already certified against the ISO 14001 standard that their smaller suppliers and contractors become similarly certified. When they do, they too will feel ready to report the results.

3. An increasing tendency by financial analysts—legitimized by Dow Jones/Sustainability Asset Management, the Investor Responsibility Research Center, and Innovest, among others—to equate investment quality with sustainability.

4. Strong public reservations about the social and environmental effects of globalization and free trade, and increasing concern about subtle industrial effects on the environment and public health, all exacerbated by evidence of the hormonal effects of tiny concentrations of some industrial chemicals, and the possible negative ecological and health effects of genetically modified organisms.

As a result, many corporations are becoming convinced that visible evidence of environmental and social responsibility is important to their success. Environmental reports provide a forum to publicize the improvements in environmental performance associated with the adoption of an ISO 14001 (or similar) environmental management system. Adding the social and financial information that transforms an environmental report into a sustainability report allows firms to advertise other corporate initiatives for sustainability, and to document the socially beneficial effects that a company's globalization is having.

On first becoming aware of such reporting, many companies jump to the conclusion that the costs will be high and the amount of trouble not worth it. It is true that some companies spend a great deal producing and printing their reports, but lengthy and expensive reports are not necessary, or even necessarily the most effective, and the data collection may already be essentially complete; all but the smallest companies collect environmental, health, and safety information on their operations, and the information you already collect is the very information that is likely to be most appropriate for an environmental or sustainability report. It is perfectly reasonable to start small, using data you already have, and perhaps using a newsletter or Web page format to minimize costs.

This book tells you what other companies are reporting and how they are reporting it, and summarizes that information into 10 rules that will greatly simplify the writing process. It will give you a good idea how to proceed, with whatever level of detail you are comfortable. This book discusses 100 of the best corporate environmental and sustainability reports (see Appendix F for a list) with direct quotations from many of them. It also provides detailed scores for 40 of them using five different scoring systems, and analyzes 30 additional ones based on the 140 topics contained in the Pacific Sustainability Index.

In short, this book is a complete guide to writing a highly effective environmental or sustainability report.

I

An Introduction to Environmental and Sustainability Reporting

Part I begins with a description of the evolution and development of environmental and sustainability reporting (Chapter 1), and examines the business case for improving performance and reporting on that improvement (Chapter 2). It then surveys (Chapter 3) and analyzes (Chapter 4) the guidelines and operating standards that are currently available to aid report writers. Finally (Chapter 5) critically reviews 11 corporate environmental and sustainability reports and several Web sites.

1

What Is Environmental and Sustainability Reporting?

Voluntary environmental reporting began around 1989, coinciding with publication of the Coalition for Environmentally Responsible Economies (CERES) principles. The promulgation of the ISO 14001 environmental management system standard in 1996, and its rapid adoption by large corporations, increased the amount of environmental information companies had on hand, and the newly obtained information usually reflected improved environmental performance. Improvements are good news, and managers began to seek vehicles to disseminate that news—voluntary periodic environmental reports were the vehicle of choice. Meanwhile the CERES principles spawned an offspring, the Global Reporting Initiative guidelines that suggested including social and financial information in environmental reports, making them into "sustainability reports."

The periodic environmental reporting that is becoming commonplace in large corporations is gradually being supplemented with social and economic information and is increasingly referred to as sustainability reporting. Initially, in 1989, environmental reports were usually thought of as a place to publish information on air emissions, effluent discharges, and waste disposal. It then became apparent that they were also good places to publish enthusiastic reports of environmental initiatives and improvements, particularly energy conservation and recycling to reduce waste, both of which were becoming profitable. Safety and health of employees soon followed, primarily because the same corporate staff members responsible for the environment were also responsible for safety and health.

Because environmental and sustainability reporting is voluntary, guidance has been *ad hoc*. As described briefly in this chapter and in more detail in chapter 3, it has come in various forms from a wide range of sources, including industry groups, citizen investor coalitions, accountants, environmental consultancies, and financial analysts. It has also come along with the ISO 14000 family of international environmental management standards and guidelines, which began to emerge in 1996 and continue to be formulated. These standards are promulgated by ISO, the International Organization for Standardization, based in Geneva, Switzerland, which is a coalition of the national standards institutes of countries all over the world. Although the ISO 14001 standard, the only part of the ISO 14000 series against which a company can become certified, does not require external reporting of environmental performance, it does require that a company subscribing to it identify and measure its environmental aspects and impacts. These aspects and impacts, discussed in chapter 10, are the principal basis of most environmental reporting.

As early as 1989, a few particularly environmentally sensitive companies including The Body Shop, Ben & Jerry's, Seventh Generation, and Aveda had endorsed the newly minted CERES principles (see chapter 3). These principles called for annual reporting of not only internal corporate environmental information, but also information on the protection of the biosphere, the sustainable use of natural resources, the reduction of environmental health and safety risks to employees and communities, and the elimination of products that caused environmental damage or health or safety hazards.

With the advent of the ISO 14001 environmental management system (EMS) standard in 1996, all of the topics that were the subjects of an EMS became logical additions to environmental reports. These included a statement of environmental policy, descriptions of the environmental management processes and systems, descriptions of auditing and emergency response programs, and of programs to involve external stakeholders.

In 1999, a partnership between CERES and the United Nations Environmental Program, known as the Global Reporting Initiative (GRI) released the first draft of sustainability reporting guidelines (GRI 1999), followed by a second draft in June 2000 (GRI 2000). These added a plethora of topics including labor productivity, job creation, investments in training, employee retention, labor rights and wages, and working conditions at outsourced operations. They also suggested complicated "integrated" performance indicators including: ". . . an organization's total materials use during a product's life cycle expressed relative to globally sustainable levels measured in terms of resource availability and/or biological or assimilative capacity," and ". . . a composite measure of diversity (economic–social–environmental)."

Clearly GRI's vision of sustainability reporting has moved far beyond a traditional view of environmental reporting.

ENVIRONMENTAL AND SUSTAINABILITY REPORTING ORIGINATED WITH ENVIRONMENTAL DEGRADATION

The idea of sustainable development is a natural extension of the idea of sustainable yield—or maximum sustainable yield (MSY)—long the goal of forestry, fisheries, and wildlife managers. The MSY idea is simple and Malthusian: under good conditions wild populations produce far more offspring than the environment can support. In a state of nature, the excess individuals are crowded out or eaten by predators. Under a state of management, when the predators are people, the manager's goal is to maximize the harvest without excessively depleting the reproducing population. The primary management tools are regulation of the harvest, augmentation of production, and maintenance of habitat.

In the real world—especially when the harvested populations are common property as they are in ocean fisheries and national forests—the manager is usually at odds with forces that would like to harvest more than is prudent and that would prefer not to spend the money required to maintain the habitat and augment the populations. The manager then has the added job of convincing the users and regulators that prudence and investment are necessary for sustainability. They are not usually convinced until there is some clear evidence of degradation, even though the manager has been able to see the problem coming for some time and has kept mentioning it. This is roughly the situation the world finds itself in today with respect to sustainable development.

Sustainable development is the application of the sustainable yield principle to any endeavor; maximize the yield while minimizing the adverse effects, especially adverse effects to the commons of societal well-being and the environment. The natural mode of society for the past several centuries has been to maximize the use of common resources and to minimize the investment to maintain them. This works satisfactorily early on when the common resources are vast and appear limitless. When signs of degradation appear, though, there is a gradual realization that if things go on as they have, the degradation will only get worse.

Sensitivity to global environmental degradation first became broadly evident in the 1960s. Environmental regulations ensued—in the United

States most notably the passing of the National Environmental Policy Act (NEPA) in 1970. NEPA requires that a detailed environmental impact statement (EIS) be included in every recommendation or report on proposals for legislation and other major federal actions significantly affecting the quality of the human environment. EISs and their state equivalents are the precursors of corporate sustainability reporting—they discuss all manner of potential environmental and social impacts—but EISs look forward, not backward, and they deal with specific actions, not with overall organizational behavior. Absurdly, there were (and are) no parallel statutes that require disclosure of significant environmental impacts that occur when actions are taken.

Corporate users of the commons often initially opposed new environmental regulations as unnecessary and overly expensive. Gradually over decades, as the youth of the 1960s replaced their fathers in the seats of corporate power, exercising environmental prudence became an acceptable mode of corporate behavior, with the largest transnational corporations often leading the way. But still, in 1986 when I taught a course entitled "Industry and Ecology" at Stanford University, there were no textbooks on the subject and no corporate environmental reports. The closest things were EISs and a few reports from industrial trade organizations that discussed environmental issues common to particular industrial sectors.

In 1989, Polaroid Corporation produced the first stand-alone corporate environmental report, and was followed by many other large corporations during the next decade. By 1999 almost 25 percent of the top 100 companies in 11 countries (KPMG 1999) had produced an annual environmental, or health, safety, and environment report.

Meanwhile, in 1983 the United Nations had established the World Commission on Environment and Development (WCED), also known as the Brundtland Commission after its chair, Norwegian Prime Minister Gro Brundtland. In 1987 it issued a report, *Our Common Future* (WCED 1987), which famously defined *sustainable development*—perhaps for the first time—as "a form of development that meets the needs of the present without compromising the ability of future generations to meet their own needs." It also called for an international conference on the subject. This conference materialized in 1992 as the United Nations Conference on Environment and Development (UNCED, also known as the Earth Summit and the Rio Conference after its venue in Rio de Janeiro). At UNCED, the delegates forcefully announced their support for the broader agenda of sustainable development in three documents: The Rio Declaration on Environment and Development (United Nations 1992a), Agenda 21 (United Nations 1992b)—a long and detailed action plan and expansion of the principles in the Rio Declaration—and a Statement of Principles . . . on the Management, Conservation, and Sustainable Development of All Types of Forests (United Nations 1992c).

Some of the first commercial efforts at sustainable development preceeded the Rio Conference and were in forestry, so the principles for forestry were well understood, as was the declining status of the world's forests. Thus, the elucidation of sustainable development in forests as a focus of the Rio Conference made sense. The principle idea of sustainable forestry is being able to harvest trees indefinitely into the future with a constant (sustainable) yield; the core sustainability idea in forestry is to make sure there are always trees. The forester's basic sustainability activity is to be sure to plant more trees, and the basic sustainability reporting is on how many trees are in the pipeline and when they will be ready to harvest.

But what of the sustainability of the plants other than harvestable trees that grow in the forest, and of the animals (and, perhaps, indigenous peoples) that visit or make their home there? What of the sustainability of the fish in the newly turbid waters of the rivers that flow out of logged areas of the forest? What of the economic sustainability of the towns around the forest? And what of the sustainability of the towns that depend on a steady stream of tourists who use the forest for recreation? What of the sustainability of the health of the workers who operate the mills, and of the townspeople who breath the airborne emissions from the mills, and who eat the fish that concentrate the toxins that may flow into the rivers in the effluents from the mills? And what if the enzymes and starches the forestry company purchases to make paper come from genetically modified organisms? And to broaden it a bit, what of the sustainability of the Pacific atolls half a world away that may cease to exist due to inundation because of global warming, which might be exacerbated by the harvest and combustion of the forest products, but on the other hand, might be decreased by the vigorous carbon fixation of the vast numbers of young trees resulting from sustainable reforestation?

And finally, to view it from a financial analyst's perspective, what of the sustainability of the company itself? Is it handling all of these other issues in a way that will guarantee its own sustainability?

These are extremely complicated issues. The effects of any company's business operations on most of them are poorly understood and, until recently, most companies did not attempt to analyze them in any detail. Even when they did, they seldom reported the results of the analyses to the public, but times have changed. The growing sensitivity of the public to these kinds of issues has compelled many companies to think hard about them, and to let the public know what they are thinking and doing. The question now is which issues are important to think about and measure, and to report on. The three 1992 United Nations documents turn out to be a good place to start.

THE UN PRINCIPLES FOR SUSTAINABLE DEVELOPMENT OF FORESTS LISTS THE PRODUCTS AND SERVICES NATURE PROVIDES

This report was intended to contribute to the management, conservation, and sustainable development of forests. It identifies the functions and uses of forests as:

- Wood and wood products

- Water

- Food

- Fodder

- Fuel

- Medicine

- Sources of genetic material for biotechnology products

- Shelter

- Employment

- Recreation

- Habitats for wildlife

- Landscape diversity

- Biodiversity

- Carbon sinks and reservoirs

- Photosynthesis

These are the types of products, activities, and ecological services that the UN delegates believed sustainable development should protect, including social and economic considerations along with the environmental ones. Consequently, the measure of their abundance over time is a measure of the sustainability of the forest and a logical component of a sustainability report for a company whose business it is to manage land for the development of natural resources. A similar list would apply to petroleum, mining, agricultural, and renewable energy companies.

THE RIO DECLARATION DESCRIBES WHAT TOPICS SHOULD BE ADDRESSED

The Rio Declaration, a brief document, consists of 25 principles, some of which are useful in determining what should be addressed in an environmental or sustainability report. They include:

- Protection of the environment

- Use of environmental impact assessments if adverse impacts of any activity are likely

- Elimination of unsustainable patterns of production and consumption

- Improvement of scientific understanding of factors influencing sustainability

- Refusal to export harmful activities or substances

- Internalization of the costs of pollution

- Utilization of women, youth, and indigenous peoples in environmental management and development

- Payment of compensation to victims of pollution and other environmental damage

AGENDA 21 EXPANDS THE RANGE OF TOPICS—DOESN'T OFFER SPECIFICS

Agenda 21 is an extremely detailed amplification of the Rio Principles. Chapter 30 of Agenda 21, "Strengthening the Role of Business and Industry," identifies more corporate activities that would be appropriate to discuss in an environmental or sustainability report:

- Encouragement of stewardship and efficient use of natural resources

- Utilization of efficient production processes

- Utilization of clean production technologies and procedures

- Employment of pollution prevention strategies

- Minimization of waste production

- Analysis of the full product lifecycle

- Adoption of product stewardship

- Inclusion of environmental costs of inputs, production, use, recycling, and disposal in the prices of goods

- Use of environmental management systems

- Adoption of worldwide corporate policies on sustainable development

- Use of self-regulation enhanced by environmental audits and compliance assessments

- Minimization of impacts to human health and the environment

- Open dialogs with employees and the public

- Encouragement of inventiveness and competitiveness

- Encouragement of voluntary initiatives

- Research and development of environmentally sound technologies and environmental management strategies

- Transfer of these technologies and management strategies to affiliates and smaller businesses

- Establishment of national councils for sustainable development

The Rio Conference set the stage well. These topics are the essence of virtually all existing corporate environmental and sustainability reporting. The guidelines and scoring systems discussed in chapters 3, 16, and 17, while not explicitly based on them, are effectively interpretations and extensions of the topics laid out in Rio in 1992.

OTHER GUIDANCE—PRIMARILY LISTS OF TOPICS WITHOUT MUCH DETAIL

The United Nations documents do not go into any of the details of what to report and how to report it. It is one thing to suggest that water should continue to be a forest product, or to encourage the stewardship of natural resources. It is quite another to figure out what aspects of water ought to be measured and reported on by, say, a hydroelectric power company, or by what measure a car manufacturer ought to demonstrate stewardship of natural resources. This guidance has fallen, by default, to a variety of volunteer organizations and coalitions. Some of the guidance comes from government agencies and academies, some from industry associations, some from investors and financial analysts, some from environmental and social activists, and some from academics.

So far, however, most of the guidance has been little more than an expansion or a subsetting of the topics in the UN reports; it consists primarily of similar lists without much additional detail. Furthermore, most of it has been generic rather than industry-specific. No one is answering the types of questions posed previously about how a hydroelectric company ought to discuss water, or a car company ought to discuss stewardship of natural resources. Nor, for that matter, does current guidance even suggest what topics a particular industry ought to address.

Two influential sources have been more specific: the National Academy of Engineering has discussed the nature of quantitative sustainability metrics and looked at the relevance of a few specific metrics to several industrial sectors; and the ISO 14031 Environmental Performance Evaluation guidelines have an annex that consists of a long and detailed list of potentially useful metrics that companies could adopt for environmental and sustainability reporting. These are discussed in chapters 3 and 4.

SCORING SYSTEMS FOR SUSTAINABILITY REPORTS CAN ALSO BE VIEWED AS GUIDANCE

The reactive side of guidance is the analysis and scoring of existing reports for completeness, quality, and company environmental and social performance. In essence, these systems constitute guidance as well. Several of them have been applied to groups of corporate environmental and sustainability reports, resulting in published corporate rankings. Some of them are academic in nature and others are business-oriented, especially the SustainAbility/UNEP corporate benchmarking series which are, to some degree, supported by the companies whose reports have been scored. These systems are described in chapter 16.

The scoring systems, like the guidelines, are generic rather than industry-specific, and are relatively non-quantitative. They give credit for topics that are addressed and, to some extent, the depth to which they are addressed, but neither for the intensity with which the company has been pursuing the topic, nor for level of performance. Thus, it is possible for a company to score highly simply because its environmental or sustainability report systematically discusses all of the topics in the scoring system, even if it is just beginning to take its performance in these areas seriously and has little performance to report.

The guidance systems discussed above can also be converted to scoring systems, and I have done just that with the ISO 14031 Environmental Performance Guidelines Annex and the GRI 2000 Sustainability Reporting Guidelines. At Claremont McKenna College's Roberts Environmental Center we have applied these guidelines (converted to scoring systems) to 40 company reports. The results are presented in Appendix B.

SCORING SYSTEMS ARE LIKELY TO BE APPLIED TO YOUR REPORT—BE AWARE OF HOW THEY WORK

In designing an environmental or sustainability report, it is important to be aware that scoring systems are likely to be applied, published, and publicized by third parties without your knowledge or any opportunity for clarification or explanation. It is definitely worthwhile to understand the scoring systems and to make your report responsive to them.

EVERY ENVIRONMENTAL OR SUSTAINABILITY REPORT IS DIRECTED AT ONE OR MORE TARGET AUDIENCES

Your stakeholders are your target audiences. You may choose to address a single target audience, but more likely you will wish to address many, if not most of them.

Employees Want to Feel Good about Their Company

Employees and potential employees are two of the principal potential audiences for an environmental or sustainability report. Volkswagen, for example, printed over 140,000 copies of its impressive 1999 report and offered one to every employee, as well as distributing them widely to potential customers. Why would they do that? Because many of their employees are environmentally and socially conscious and like working for a company that feels the way they do and acts accordingly. Employees who are convinced that their company is serious about environmental and social issues are less likely to change companies, more likely to be proud of their company and to be active recruiters of new employees, and more likely to treat the issues seriously at work, furthering the company's environmental and social goals.

Customers May Discriminate on the Basis of Perceived Sustainability

Nobody is against social justice and a clean environment. The jury may still be out as to how many customers will purchase a product specifically because of the reputation for environmentalism or sustainability of the company that produces it; but other things being equal, it cannot hurt to have a good reputation. Many companies think it definitely helps, and use their environmental or sustainability reports in the showroom and, in abstracted form, in their advertising. Chevron, which has an excellent environmental report, advertises prolifically with drawings of wildlife in unspoiled habitat in the vicinity of their refineries, asking rhetorically "Do people care? People do." This evidently works. In their 1997 "Protecting People and the Environment" report they note:

> *To measure the results of its efforts, Chevron includes questions on environmental reputation in its public opinion survey. In telephone interviews in the company's major U.S. markets respondents are asked to rate Chevron and other major oil companies in their areas by answering questions concerning which one:*
>
> * *Is seriously concerned with protecting the environment?*
> * *Cares about protecting wildlife and endangered species?*
> * *Is a leader in developing fuels to reduce air pollutants?*
> * *Encourages energy conservation?*
> * *Recycles used motor oil?*
>
> *Over the past decade, Chevron has enjoyed significantly higher ratings than other major oil companies on each of these dimensions.*

Financial Analysts, Bankers, and Insurers All Want Assurance That Companies Are Sustainable.

Dow Jones/Sustainability Asset Management, Innovest, and the Investor Responsibility Research Center are three of the most influential of the growing number of financial analysts that use corporate environmental and sustainability reports along with questionnaires, interviews, and financial data to judge the value of companies as investments. Their judgment can have profound effects on stock price, on the generosity of lenders, and on the availability of insurance. Therefore, it can also be worthwhile to be aware of the criteria used by these analysts when designing your corporate report. Some of these criteria are described in chapter 3.

Investors Increasingly Require Evidence of Sustainable Behavior

Investors, particularly large institutional ones such as pension funds and religious organizations, are increasingly expecting evidence of environmentally and socially sustainable behavior. As more information becomes available, both from analysts and from corporate sustainability reports directly, these investors are increasingly likely to direct their funds toward companies with a demonstrably good record. An annual sustainability report is the logical place to create such a record.

Environmental Activists Can Be Your Supporters But They Often Rely on Poor Word-of-Mouth Information

I recently attended a World Environment Center meeting in Santa Barbara, the purpose of which was for corporate environmental executives to help one another do a better job with environmental and sustainability performance. The information the executives were presenting was the sort of thing they put in their environmental and sustainability reports—success stories about environmental and social improvement. We learned, for example, that Anheuser-Busch had just spent $100 million upgrading a brewery in Wuhan, China, $4 million of which was to bring its environmental standards up to those of Budweiser breweries in the U.S. and drastically decrease water use. To the students picketing the meeting in the street (with plenty of press coverage), however, the meeting seemed sinister. The students had no idea what was going on inside—just that it was populated with environmental executives whom they distrusted because of their corporate affiliations.

These students need to get the straight story instead of student-propagated myths. Using academic immunity—a perquisite of professorship—I went out to talk to them during a break and found them interested and receptive. What they needed was believable information. They didn't know anybody at the meeting and they were inherently suspicious of business. But they wanted to know the truth. If they believe you are doing the right thing—as they believe The Body Shop and Ben & Jerry's are—they will support you. If they believe you are doing the wrong thing, as they most assuredly thought Occidental Petroleum (a sponsor of the meeting) was doing with respect to drilling for oil in the proximity of indigenous peoples in the Amazon jungle, they might devote a year after college to trying to shut you down.

They read though; your environmental or sustainability report, if it is believable, will get through to them. More than seeking out reports to read, they surf the Web. They are one constituency that is completely Web-literate, has uniformly fast connections (at least in the U.S.), and expects any information of consequence to be on the Web. It is worth making sure that your Web-based environmental and sustainability materials are easy for them to find on your site, and easy to navigate and print.

CONCLUSIONS

Sustainable development is the concept that development can occur without compromising the possibility of future development; that whatever we as a society—including our corporations—choose to do should not adversely affect the options of future generations. Since development in the form of corporate operations has the possibility of both beneficially and adversely affecting the environment, the economy, and our social systems, it is prudent for corporations and society to pay attention to these issues.

Many companies have chosen to demonstrate that they are paying attention—and taking appropriate actions—by issuing periodic environmental or sustainability reports. And several organizations have sought to influence the contents of these reports by producing guidelines and scoring systems. The guidance and scoring systems produced so far have mostly been generic rather than industry-specific, but they have identified a large number of topics that could be appropriate in a specific situation and that companies ought to consider when designing their reports.

The most effective reports are those that consider a wide range of topics in a transparent way, addressing both company-specific and industrywide issues without defensiveness or too much self-adulation.

2

The Business Case for Environmental and Sustainability Reporting

The business case for environmental and sustainability reporting is closely linked to the business case for improving environmental and social performance. If a firm's performance in these areas is improved from past conditions, or if it is better than that of its competitors, then publicizing the fact has the potential to differentiate the firm's products, to put pressure on its competitors to do likewise at an additional cost of doing business, and to increase positive reactions from stakeholders including employees and investors as well as customers. If performance is improved without communicating it, none of these benefits will be realized. Even if environmental or social performance is lagging, however, a credible commitment to improving it can go a long way toward assuaging concerns among stakeholders, but only if communicated to them.

This chapter must begin with a discussion of why a firm might choose to increase its environmental and social performance. There are two main schools of thought. One, articulated forcefully by Forest L. Reinhardt in his book *Down to Earth: Applying Business Principles to Environmental Management* (Reinhardt 1999) holds that improving environmental performance should be treated as purely a business decision. If such improvement is good for business, measured by the usual business financial tools, in the usual business time frame, then it should be made; otherwise it should not.

The other school, epitomized by Paul Hawken and Amory and Hunter Lovins in *Natural Capitalism* (Hawken et al. 1999) maintains that even though waste of natural resources and ecosystem services may not show up on a business balance sheet, the economy is, after all, embedded in the environment, and companies—and by extension, humanity—will not, in the long term, prosper if these goods and services are depleted. This view is widely held by academic ecologists as well. Stuart L. Pimm makes an extremely clear case in *The World According to Pimm: A Scientist Audits the Earth* (Pimm 2001): If we don't take care of Mother Nature she won't take care of us, and we are not taking very good care of her at the moment. But predictions of pending widespread human starvation and misery made since the 1960s have been strikingly incorrect. As documented in *The Skeptical Environmentalist: Measuring the Real State of the World* by Bjørn Lomborg (Lomborg 2001), the human condition has, in many ways, been improving, and imminent ecological collapse keeps being put off. Lomborg's work, while lauded by *The Economist*, is held in poor regard by much of the scientific community, which does not care for his failure to address the condition of much of the natural environment. The human condition may not be deteriorating, but the quality of our environment is, and many of the published responses to *The Skeptical Environmentalist* point this out bluntly (Bongaarts 2002, Holdren 2002, Lovejoy 2002, Rennie 2002, Schneider 2002). Nevertheless Lomborg, an academic statistician, has made his mark; as I write this, *The Economist* is reporting that he has just been appointed to run Denmark's new Institute for Environmental Assessment.

WHY BOTHER TO IMPROVE ENVIRONMENTAL AND SOCIAL PERFORMANCE?

Even if the human environment is not deteriorating as rapidly as many environmentalists have feared, most parts of the world seem ever more congested, the air in cities—even where it is not getting dirtier—still seems way too dirty and apparently is more toxic than we used to think, and everywhere we look there is less and less nature and more and more development. We tend to think of billowing smokestacks as evidence of problems rather than of progress, and many of us think of environmental regulations as benefiting society rather than interfering with business. And there is reasonably clear evidence that stringent environmental regulations imposed by governments have had little if any negative effect on business competitiveness (Jaffe et al. 1995) and may have enhanced it

(Porter and van der Linde 1995). It is not good for a company to be seen as environmentally insensitive, and even though it may be hard to find customers willing to pay more for environmentally benign goods, there are plenty of people willing to boycott companies that seem to ignore the environment. Thus, at the most fundamental level, improving environmental and social performance is a reasonable defensive action against being "tarred by the same brush" (King and Lenox 2000) as firms that have got themselves into environmental and social trouble. We can all be sure that had Union Carbide properly imagined the consequences of a chemical leak at Bhopal, it would have been more careful, as would have Exxon if it had truly imagined the public relations consequences of running the Valdez aground off Alaska.

A Business Litmus Test for Embracing Environmental Goals

Reinhardt's point in *Down to Earth*, not unexpected coming from a professor at the Harvard Business School, is that while there may be plenty of good business reasons to improve environmental performance and communication, they deserve the same sort of intensive analysis that any other business decision should have. Even if decisions are made only for ethical reasons, the firm should recognize that fact. In the end, though, such improvements may succeed in differentiating less environmentally burdensome products or processes, driving up competitors' costs, managing environmental risks, saving costs of energy or materials, and possibly redefining the industry by doing all these things at once.

In the case of differentiating products or manufacturing and distributing processes, a company can only get a return on environmental investment if it has customers who are willing to pay more for products made more sustainably, or with higher than required environmental and social standards. In order to reap the benefits the firm must be able to communicate the differentiating features to the customers through some form of environmental or sustainability reporting, labeling, advertising, or other means. Finally, the firm must be able to stay ahead of similar improvements by its competitors. If enhanced environmental and social performance succeeds in differentiating products, then continuous improvement is likely to be necessary to stay ahead of imitators.

Better Performance Is Insurance against Risks

Quite apart from product or process differentiation, or raising competitors' costs, improvement of environmental and social behavior can provide a form of insurance against risk. Risks of inadvertent environmental or health and safety damage through accidents, fires, spills, and the like can be greatly decreased through the use of environmental and health and safety management systems. Furthermore, the potential costs of cleaning up spills or recovering from accidents can be greatly decreased by planning responses in advance. The value of such risk reduction may be directly assessable as decreases in ongoing insurance costs, or may be less tangible if the risks were previously ignored or self-insured, but it is real.

Better Performance Can Pay for Itself

Perhaps surprisingly, many improvements in environmental performance can pay for themselves, and may even generate profits. It might seem likely that any simple way to save costs would long since have been adopted by managers attempting to maximize profits, but often this is not the case. There are several reasons. First, while saving costs is important for any business, it is never the central business activity. Therefore cost reduction is likely to get close attention primarily during times of adversity when normal sources of income are waning. Second, in industries for which environmental concerns have been historically unimportant, cost savings potentially associated with better environmental performance may have been completely overlooked. Between periods of financial adversity or environmental sensitivity—sometimes triggered by the appearance of new environmental regulations—new cost-saving technologies and procedures may go unnoticed or seem relatively unimportant. The longer the hiatus between intensive consideration of cost-saving measures, the more likely that effective new technologies will have arisen. Third, new technologies usually require new investment. In times of waning profits, when the technologies are most likely to be noticed, there may be no money or will to make the required investment. Fourth, adoption of new technologies is likely to be disruptive. It may require interrupting production for facility modification or replacement, retraining or replacing employees, and acceptance of new manufacturing paradigms that may be foreign and unappealing to existing managers. Still, as Reinhardt points out, "From a business policy standpoint . . . there is no reason for firms not to look for free lunches—as long as there is a reasonable chance of finding them." According to at least one academic study: " . . . efforts to prevent pollution and reduce emissions drop to the 'bottom line' within one to two years of initiation and . . . those firms with the highest emission levels stand the most to gain." (Hart and Ahuja 1996)

Ethically Motivated Improvements Can Be Funded by the Cost Savings

In *Natural Capitalism*, Hawken, Lovins, and Lovins make a generalized plea for better performance based on an ethical commitment to sustainability and an internalization of environmental costs that might readily be ignored as economic externalities. Nevertheless they spend much of their book identifying ways to save money through environmental initiatives. They are very much of the free-lunch and low-hanging-fruit schools, arguing that there are many opportunities in most companies to get a high and rapid payback from simple environmental initiatives that reduce use of raw and purchased materials and production of waste. They document many approaches including replacing inefficient lights, refrigerators, and air conditioners with more efficient ones; decreasing pumping costs in manufacturing facilities by using fatter pipes; and producing manufactured inputs just-in-time and on-site. A whole host of other materials and waste reduction strategies used successfully by specific companies are also documented.

They advocate four main strategies:

1. *Increase resource productivity.* Do more with less energy, less material, more efficient processes, cleverly-sited facilities and optimal business models. In other words, save money and the environment at the same time.

2. *Copy biology (or as they say, engage in biomimicry).* View industrial processes as analogous to natural ecological processes and eliminate the concept of waste. In nature, organisms must use food and energy as efficiently as possible or they will be outcompeted by other organisms and fail to pass along their genes—the biological equivalent of going out of business. This seems a reasonable analogy for business. In addition, in nature, every organism's waste stream is some other organism's food supply. So, say the authors, if you cannot eliminate waste, you should convert it to a resource by finding something useful (and hopefully economically rewarding) to do with it. This latter analogy is a little forced: Organisms in nature excrete their wastes and are done with it. It is up to the ingenuity of other organisms to find something useful to do with the wastes.

3. *Think closed-loop.* The authors are very enthusiastic about selling services rather than goods, so that the firm is responsible for the full life-cycle of products, and the customer gets the services she needs without ever owning a product. This makes environmental sense, of course, only if the firms selling the services treat the goods they are using in an environmentally responsible manner. Services are not inherently innocuous at all

(Graedel 1998), especially ones that are really manufacturing operations posing as services, as Hawkens, Lovins, and Lovins are proposing. Furthermore, leasing rather than buying products does not necessarily change their impacts, and environmental effects may be more pronounced in their use and consumption than in their manufacture. Also, for consumer goods especially, owning the physical device may be as desirable or more so than having the service provided. A rental Chevrolet may get you there just fine, but not with the style of one's personal Cadillac.

4. *Reinvest in natural capital.* This, I think, is essentially a plea not to trash the commons. If you cut something down, replant it. This makes sense if you own the land and will be coming back to re-cut it someday. It is a lot, though—perhaps too much—to ask individual businesses to be responsible for the commons. This is where industrywide organizations can have a large positive effect, adopting voluntary standards rather than waiting for government regulations.

DOES IT PAY TO BE GREEN?

There are several levels at which this question can be asked. In addition to the somewhat indirect payback of differentiating products, driving up competitors' costs, and managing environmental risks (Reinhardt 1999) are there immediate cost savings from reducing energy and materials use and longer-term cost savings from reducing waste and making other improvements? Is there identifiable improvement in financial performance such as return on sales, return on assets and return on equity? Does the stock price go up? Do external ratings go up?

Immediate Cost Savings Can Almost Always Be Had by Decreasing Energy and Materials Use

Unless a firm has actively been minimizing energy and materials use for some time there is likely to be room for immediate savings. Energy use is most amenable to immediate savings: lights can be turned off when not needed; heat and air conditioning can be turned down. Water use also usually can be decreased significantly with a little effort at conservation—if nothing else, by watering the landscaping a little less. Virtually every corporate environmental report shows substantial decreases in energy and water use from whatever baseline year was selected. With minor investment in low-energy lighting, additional savings are almost always possible because technology keeps producing more-efficient light bulbs and fluorescent ballasts. And new computers are almost always more energy-efficient than the ones they replace, perhaps utilizing energy-efficient flat-panel displays, or automatically putting monitors to sleep and going to standby mode when not in use. Low-water-use toilets are also relatively inexpensive.

Much more aggressive conservation programs are possible as well, but the cost of achieving the savings is usually not reported in much detail, so savings from individual actions are hard for stakeholders to assess. Bristol-Myers Squibb, for example, reports in their 2001 Sustainability Progress Report that since 1997 they have decreased:

- Electricity use per $1000 in sales by 20%

- Water use per $1000 in sales by 35%

- Corrugated packaging use per $1000 in sales by 40%

- Ozone depleting substance use per $1000 in sales by 47%

- Non-hazardous waste disposed per $1000 in sales by 20%

- Hazardous waste disposed per $1000 in sales by 30%

- Air emissions from facility fuel combustion per $1000 in sales by 46%

- SARA 313 U.S. air releases per $1000 in sales by 3%

- SARA 313 U.S. water releases per $1000 in sales by 18%

However, they don't say what these reductions cost.

Many of these decreases in energy and materials use and waste production are relatively short-term: They occur dramatically over a few years, first as the low hanging fruit is harvested and free lunches are eaten, and then by making obvious quick-payback investments. Later it becomes hard to make further reductions until new technology appears.

Overall Financial Performance May Also Be Improved, But Is Less Easy to Evaluate

The problem is determining what caused the change in performance. Was it a direct result of changes in environmental and social performance, or simply of an improvement in management? The only way to tell is to do an experiment, and such experiments are usually accidental and therefore not well designed. One study (Hart and Ahuja 1996) looked at return on sales, return on assets, and return on equity of 127 large firms in the four years following initiation of required toxic release inventory (TRI) reporting in the U.S. when many companies were actively seeking to decrease their toxic effluents. It found that in 1991 and 1992 all three financial variables were significantly correlated with emissions reductions in 1989, and tentatively inferred causality while noting its uncertainty. Another study (Waddock and Graves 1997a) used the same three accounting variables and found a positive correlation between them and one-year-prior and one-year-subsequent social performance, suggesting that prior good financial performance provided the flexibility to improve social performance, which did not adversely affect future performance, and might even have enhanced it. Most recently, King and Lennox (King and Lenox 2001) compared Tobin's q, a measure of "what cash flows the market thinks a firm will provide per dollar invested in assets," to three measures of emissions. They too found that financial performance (as measured by Tobin's q) was better in firms with lower emissions, but, like the other authors, were unable to infer a causal relationship.

Stock Price May Be Enhanced

The Dow Jones Sustainability Group Index (DJSGI) of stocks that are presumably from companies in some way environmentally or socially superior to the more general Dow Jones Global Index (DJGI) did outperform the DJGI from 1993 to 2000 (Cerin and Dobers 2001) but did so with a higher percentage of technology firms, and with firms that averaged two-and-a-half times the market capitalization value of the DJGI firms. Whether it was the market capitalization and technology or the social and environmental qualities that drove this performance is not known (Cerin and Dobers 2001). On the other hand, several studies have found no important differences in stock price performance (Diltz 1995, Hamilton et al. 1993, Waddock and Graves 2000) related to social or ethical screening of investments.

Third-Party Management Quality Ratings Can Also Improve

Another approach to documenting the benefits of improved environmental and social performance is to look for correlations between third-party management quality ratings and aspects of environmental or social management. Waddock and Graves (1997b) discovered that strong performance with respect to stockholders, employee relations, and product–customer relations was correlated with high evaluations in the Fortune magazine management surveys, but performance with respect to environmental stakeholders was not. A similar study (Turban and Greening 1997) used 75 business students to rate the general reputations and attractiveness as employers of 160 companies, then correlated these scores with an independently-derived measure of social performance. They found both reputation and attractiveness as an employer to be correlated with community relations, employee relations, and product quality whereas only reputation was correlated with environmental performance. Good social and environmental performance may just be a byproduct of good management: CEO compensation is positively correlated with firm environmental reputation, but also with size and financial performance (Stanwick and Stanwick 2001); return on assets is weakly correlated with environmental rating but much more strongly correlated with firm and industry growth rates (Russo and Fouts 1997).

THE BUSINESS CASE FOR ENVIRONMENTAL AND SUSTAINABILITY REPORTING

Companies write environmental and sustainability reports to:

- Increase management awareness of environmental and social issues

- Increase employee satisfaction and loyalty

- Influence customers and differentiate products

- Reassure lenders and insurers

- Encourage financial analysts and investors

- Preempt government regulators

- Defuse environmental activists and other critics

They may also write them because they have installed environmental and social management systems, made improvements in performance, and made progress toward their goals, and it seems appropriate to communicate this success. One view has it that ". . . for many companies, external reporting appears to be a bonus spun off from a preexisting internal management exercise" (Ball et al. 2000).

Are Environmental and Sustainability Reports Effective in Reaching These Stakeholders?

Considering the volume of communication going on in the form of reports, material on Web sites, and advertising, there is surprisingly little objective information, though there are plenty of opinions. For example, the consultancy KPMG says, "Companies are not only expected to operate in an environmentally responsible manner, but are increasingly asked to demonstrate this publicly. This is particularly true in the field of environment where public awareness and concern has fuelled the environmental movement" (KPMG 1999). The United Nations Environment Programme, in its preface to a report analyzing corporate environmental reports says "Examining performance allows companies to identify inefficiencies and opportunities for improvement . . . and, as demonstrated by the experience of many companies, this also has economic benefits" (SustainAbility/UNEP 2000). Companies must believe environmental or sustainability reporting is accomplishing something, for they are certainly investing money and time. As the newly merged ChevronTexaco notes in the Social Responsibility section of its 2002 Web pages, "We understand that corporate social responsibility is a cornerstone of future success."

CONCLUSIONS

There are many reasons to improve environmental and social performance. Aside from the obvious ethical ones, and the fact that we all recognize that desecrating the environmental commons will, in the end, harm our children and grandchildren, there are several potential business reasons. It is almost always possible to decrease costs by using less energy, water, and raw materials, and by reducing waste that must be disposed of, all of which will lessen environmental impacts. And it may be possible to differentiate products and services, drive up competitors' costs, and manage environmental and social risks. Several of these possibilities, particularly the differentiation of products and services, will be much enhanced by environmental and sustainability communication, and may not occur at all without it. One way to spread the word is advertising. Another way is by environmental and sustainability reports and Web sites. Whether these succeed in achieving any business function has not yet been examined as well as it should be . . . there are not yet any third-party academic studies that look at this carefully. But many companies are using their reports as part of their general public relations and advertising. Car companies distribute them to employees and put them in their showrooms, and petroleum companies bring them to public hearings. Just how effective they are remains to be seen.

3

Guidelines and Operating Standards for Environmental and Sustainability Reporting

There are several guidelines currently available for writing environmental and sustainability reports. Some have been produced by consumer groups and others by industry. They range from being quite general to being extremely specific, and it is worthwhile obtaining all of them for reference. They do not by themselves, however, guarantee an effective report. As we shall see, effectiveness has a good deal to do with style as well as content.

Although there are many entities and coalitions that have produced guidelines for improving corporate environmental and sustainability performance, relatively few have specifically addressed the topic of reporting the results. The best of them come from:

- Coalition for Environmentally Responsible Economies (CERES)

- Public Environmental Reporting Initiative (PERI)

- European Council Eco-Management Audit Scheme (EMAS)

- The chemical industry Responsible Care Health, Safety and Environmental program

- Global Reporting Initiative (GRI)

In addition to the above reporting standards, there are five excellent sources of suggestions for environmental and social topics that could be included in environmental and sustainability reports, and another under development:

- ISO 14031 Environmental Performance Evaluation Standard, while not about external communication, is about which environmental variables could be measured

- ISO 14063 Environmental Communications Guidelines—presently under development and likely to be a useful adjunct to this book when promulgated

- Social Accountability International (SAI) SA8000 Standard

- World Business Council for Sustainable Development (WBCSD) Guide to Reporting Company Eco-Efficiency Performance

- The Greenhouse Gas Protocol: A Corporate Accounting and Reporting Standard (WBCSD)

- National Academy of Engineering (NAE) Industrial Environmental Performance Metrics

With the exception of the ISO standards, the full text of all of these documents is available without charge on the World Wide Web. The ISO standards are sold—over the Web—and are often included in commercial technical books as well.

CERES REPORTING

The Coalition for Environmentally Responsible Economies was formed in 1989 in response to the Exxon Valdez oil spill. It began as a coalition of America's largest socially responsible institutional investors—state pension funds and religious groups—and 15 major U.S. environmental groups, and has much the same composition today. Initially, it used shareholder resolutions to attempt to force corporations to adopt the ten CERES principles, but with extremely limited success; it wasn't until 1993 that SUNOCO became the first Fortune 500 company to adopt the principles. Success has continued to be slow in coming, with just 50 companies—only twelve of them Fortune 500 companies—endorsing the CERES principles at the end of 2000.

Nine of the 10 CERES principles are not very demanding by today's standards—they involve making a commitment to operate in an environmentally sensitive way and to work at reducing anything that might have an adverse impact on the environment or on people's health. If only from a liability standpoint, few companies today would operate any differently under the first nine principles. The tenth principle, however, requires annual environmental auditing—an expensive and potentially risky business from a legal and regulatory standpoint—and the submission of a highly formalized annual report to CERES, essentially detailing the audit results, which CERES then makes public (CERES 1999a, CERES 1999b, CERES 2000a, CERES 2000b, CERES 2000c). I suspect it has been this auditing and formalized reporting requirement that has prevented CERES from achieving a high level of endorsement. Nevertheless, the required report contents provide one vision of what a comprehensive sustainability report ought to include, as well as clear guidance on environmentally responsible corporate behavior.

A Standard Form CERES Report follows a very specific format consisting of answering 37 pages of questions and filling out 22 tables, adding other relevant information as appropriate. Smaller companies with minimal potential for environmental impact can opt for the Short Form Report with fewer questions and tables, but the same overall topics. There are also specific forms for the electric and gas industries, and for financial services companies. Much of the information required by the forms is general in nature, and some only documents intent, but there are also a number of tables that require standardized quantitative data normalized in a way that would allow clear intercompany comparisons if the reporting became fully standardized.

Perhaps because of its limited success with companies buying into the annual formalized CERES Report and associated audits, CERES, along with the United Nations Environment Programme, launched the Global Reporting Initiative (GRI) in 1998 (see p. 31). For those companies who have endorsed CERES, however, CERES reporting and auditing still continues, although CERES reorganized its 2001 reporting requirements to more closely align with the GRI 2000 guidelines.

PERI GUIDELINES

The Public Environmental Reporting Initiative Guidelines (PERI 1993) were developed during 1992 and 1993 by a small group of manufacturing companies: Amoco, British Petroleum, Dow Chemical, DuPont, IBM, Nortel, Phillips Petroleum, Polaroid, Rockwell, and United Technologies. Thus, unlike the CERES guidelines, they are of industry origin and their *laissez faire* attitude reflects this. Reporting organizations may select any subset of the guidelines, present as much or as little detail as they want, use any format, and report at any frequency—these are guidelines, not requirements.

Nevertheless, they are not short on content. Even though PERI describes the guidelines as simple and nonprescriptive—and they are when compared to the CERES guidelines—they include most of the topics that are found in current corporate environmental reports. They specify ten major topics and about fifty subtopics.

THE EUROPEAN COUNCIL ECO-MANAGEMENT AUDIT SCHEME (EMAS)

The EMAS regulation (EMAS 1993) was adopted by the European Council in 1993 and has been in use at industrial sites since 1995. It consists of 21 Articles and five Annexes, all conditions of which must be met at a particular site for that site to be in compliance. Additionally, registration in the scheme requires a company to adopt an environmental policy that includes commitment to compliance with all relevant environmental legislation, pollution prevention, and achievement of continuous improvements in environmental performance.

EMAS, unlike the ISO 14001 standard, requires a periodic environmental statement. Once a statement is issued, however, periodicity of reissue is supposed to be dictated by significant changes, and may never need occur where conditions are stable. An EMAS environmental statement must include a description of the company's environmental policy, the environmental management system and activities at the site, an assessment of all significant environmental issues, and summary data on pollution emissions, waste and noise production, raw material consumption, and use of energy and water.

Thus it is far narrower than any of the other documents discussed in this chapter except the highly focused SAI standards. But it serves a different purpose—to meet one of the requirements of formal certification.

RESPONSIBLE CARE HEALTH, SAFETY AND ENVIRONMENTAL REPORTING GUIDELINES

The European Chemical Industry Council (CEFIC) in 1998 combined some of its earlier reporting guidance documents based on the international chemical industry Responsible Care program into a new set of Health, Safety and Environmental Reporting Guidelines (CEFIC 1998). These guidelines constitute a set of core "parameters" and it is intended that additional parameters reflecting national or local concerns be added as needed. The 16 core parameters are a small but important subset of the environmental aspects characteristic of chemical industry operations, encompassing three standard safety and occupational health metrics, hazardous and non-hazardous waste disposal, five types of air pollutants, two types of water pollutants (one of which, heavy metals, could also be an air or land contaminant), a catch-all category for other substances that potentially impact human health or the environment, energy consumption and efficiency, and distribution incidents. An important feature of the guidelines is that they specify units (for example, tonnes) but a shortcoming is that in most cases these are not required to be normalized to anything (such as amount of product, numbers of employees, or revenues) so the comparative advantages offered by standardized units are compromised by a failure to require that they be put into context. Still, this is a concrete, industry-sponsored step toward quantitative standardized reporting that ought to be applauded.

GRI SUSTAINABILITY REPORTING GUIDELINES ON ECONOMIC, ENVIRONMENTAL, AND SOCIAL PERFORMANCE

The Global Reporting Initiative is a coalition of companies, business organizations, accounting firms, consulting firms, and nongovernmental organizations established as a project of CERES and the United Nations Environment Programme in 1997. Like CERES, GRI is dedicated to the idea of standardized report content, but with a difference; the GRI reporting guidelines suggest a broad range of topics and an order of presentation, but they do not require anything. The scope can be reduced, the order can be changed, the format can be anything a company wants, the report can be issued at any interval, and the contents of the report can be verified by a third party or not. The result can still be claimed as *a GRI Report*, written in accordance with the guidelines. And, unlike CERES, GRI does not want the reports submitted to it for acceptance.

The GRI Sustainability Reporting Guidelines (GRI 2000) are the most detailed, comprehensive, and prescriptive guidelines to date, with a revision due in the summer of 2002. Following them to the letter would be extremely demanding for any company. Furthermore, they are likely to become even more demanding as sector-specific guidelines are issued to complement the core guidelines. To deal with this hardship, GRI accepts an incremental approach to implementing them; use of any part of them is acceptable with the presumption that future reporting cycles will move toward full adoption, and with the proviso that the reporting organization does not use this flexibility to select only information that reflects favorably on it.

GRI has every intent that its guidelines will become the *de facto* standard for sustainability reporting worldwide, and their consensus approach may eventually be successful in achieving this goal. They make the guidelines freely available on their Web site and actively solicit comments on each draft from anyone interested. They convene open meetings to discuss progress, and frequently make their case at other forums around the world.

Perhaps surprisingly, the broad level of feedback and the search for consensus has not led to lack of specificity; GRI intends that its guidelines have teeth even though, at the moment, there isn't much in the way of jaw muscle. There is very little external pressure so far to adopt the GRI guidelines, but the guidelines themselves are quite substantive. In the end this may be GRI's downfall. Even with its acceptance of any subset of its suggested topics as constituting a GRI report, the underlying presumption of movement toward full adoption of the guidelines may put off some companies.

By GRI's assessment, the greatest degree of consensus has been achieved on the environmental aspects of the guidelines, which by my accounting amount to 27 percent of the total. GRI has been working on these the longest and there is considerable corporate experience in collecting and reporting environmental data. But even so, very few of the companies I have surveyed now report more than about a fifth of the environmental information the GRI guidelines call for (see Figure 4.5 in chapter 4).

From examining corporate sustainability reports it is evident that the general introductory material, particularly a statement of commitment by a senior manager, a company profile, statements of vision and strategy, and descriptions of environmental policies and management systems called for by GRI are more widely accepted (Figure 4.5). But the economic and social topics of the guidelines, which make up 42 percent of the recommended material, are almost entirely disregarded. The notable exceptions are two health and safety topics (reportable health and safety cases; and injury, lost day, and absentee rates) which many companies include.

Thus, although GRI has produced a relatively comprehensive set of reporting guidelines that it represents as consensus-based, the consensus of corporations, based on the empirical evidence of their reports, is far different.

ISO 14031 ENVIRONMENTAL PERFORMANCE EVALUATION GUIDELINES

The ISO 14000 family of voluntary environmental standards is a product of the International Organization for Standardization (ISO), a coalition of the world's national standards institutes. The main business of ISO is to standardize manufacturing specifications, but their global success with total quality management standards (the ISO 9000 family) led to the development of the ISO 14000 standards that have been highly successful as well, being adopted by thousands of companies around the world. There is currently a trend toward integrating the ISO 14001 standard into existing ISO 9001 quality management systems, or implementing both systems simultaneously in an integrated way (Block and Marash 2001).

The ISO 14001 environmental management standard is the only auditable standard in this family—everything else is informational support— and neither it nor any of the informational support in the ISO 14000 series requires external reporting, except that ISO 14001 requires ". . . establishing procedures for . . . responding to relevant communication from external interested parties" (ISO 14001, §4.3.3 Communication). Thus, the ISO 14031 guidelines (ISO 1999) are not intended to specify sustainability report content. Rather, they are intended to help users select performance indicators (topics about which information can be collected) to use in conjunction with an ISO 14001 environmental management system. Nevertheless, Annex A to the guidelines is a very long list of topics, including social and economic ones that are similar to those in the GRI guidelines but more extensive. Whereas the GRI guidelines are intended to be the minimal list of topics that all companies should address in their reports, Annex A is intended as a list from which companies can choose—or get ideas for—topics to collect data about. Even though the ISO 14000 standards do not address annual environmental or sustainability reporting, the ISO 14031 standard is a good place to get ideas about what to include in a report.

There are three main categories, and two subcategories of topics:

- General management characteristics
- Environmental Performance Indicators
  - Management Performance Indicators
  - Operational Performance Indicators
- Environmental Condition Indicators

The general topics that appear on the first six pages of Annex A are roughly comparable to the introductory material in the GRI guidelines.

Like these GRI topics, they are the most widely addressed in existing reports and almost all of them seem to be applicable to any company.

The Environmental Performance Indicators (EPIs) are subdivided into Management Performance Indicators (MPIs) and Operational Performance Indicators (OPIs). MPIs include topics associated with implementation of policies and programs, environmental compliance and associated activities, financial performance, and community relations. OPIs deal with a company's use of inputs such as energy, water, and materials; with physical facilities and transportation; and with products, services, wastes, and emissions. These are the minimal topics that one would expect in a good environmental report and Annex A lists over 40 MPIs and over 60 OPIs.

You might expect that only a few of these would be applicable to any particular operation, but in fact they are very well chosen and almost any manufacturing company could use almost all of them. That makes the number a little daunting, and the ISO standards do not seem to contemplate collecting data on over a hundred environmental performance indicators. Still, the list is by no means complete and the reality is that ordinary companies do influence the environment in a good many ways. It is not out of the question that most of these indicators could reasonably be addressed in a complete environmental or sustainability report. Most companies presently address far fewer topics, however. One of 10 large petroleum companies whose reports I analyzed (Appendix B) addressed 18 of them but the average for all 10 companies was only four.

The 34 Environmental Condition Indicators (ECIs) are things that can be measured in the environment rather than in a facility or in or about a product. Some of these relate specifically to the concentration of pollutants and other measures of environmental quality—not necessarily related to company operations—in the vicinity of a facility. Others relate to contamination, diseases, and population dynamics of nearby plant and animal (including human) populations. The GRI guidelines include just a few of these topics, and very few environmental or sustainability reports address any of them.

ISO 14063 ENVIRONMENTAL COMMUNICATIONS GUIDELINES

At this writing there is an ISO TC 207 committee (Working Group 4), of which I am a member, writing ISO 14063, a new environmental communications standard tentatively entitled "Environmental management— Environmental communication—Guidelines and examples." It is not likely to be intended as a specification standard or for certification purposes, but rather as general guidance on environmental communication, much like this book. When promulgated it should be a useful adjunct to the other guidelines described in this chapter, and to this book.

SAI SA8000 STANDARD

Social Accountability International was founded in 1997 as the Council of Economic Priorities Accreditation Agency and is affiliated with the Council on Economic Priorities. The SA8000 Standard (Social Accountability International 1997) is a statement of appropriate social accountability in the workplace covering child labor, forced labor, health and safety, compensation, working hours, discrimination, discipline, free association and collective bargaining, and social aspects of management systems. This is a subset of the social aspects potentially included in a sustainability report, but it sets a normative standard and is useful to check company operations against.

WBCSD: MEASURING ECO-EFFICIENCY—A GUIDE TO REPORTING COMPANY PERFORMANCE

The World Business Council for Sustainable Development (WBCSD) was formed in 1995 through a merger between the Business Council for Sustainable Development and the World Industry Council for the Environment. According to WBCSD, "Eco-efficiency is at the heart of [its] philosophy."

Its guide to measuring and reporting company eco-efficiency performance (Vervaillie and Bidwell 2000) is an excellent source of ideas for what things a company ought to be measuring. Not only what things, but the units in which they should be measured, the measurement methods, and where the data might come from—topics discussed in this book in chapter 4.

THE GREENHOUSE GAS PROTOCOL: A CORPORATE ACCOUNTING AND REPORTING STANDARD (WBSCD AND WORLD RESOURCES INSTITUTE)

This is another WBSCD reporting guide (WBSCD undated) intended to "... develop and promote internationally accepted greenhouse gas (GHG) accounting and reporting standards. ..." It explains how to calculate

GHG emissions, how to account for them, and how to report them. The reporting section is quite explicit and if followed, would constitute a very high-quality section of an environmental or sustainability report.

NAE INDUSTRIAL ENVIRONMENTAL PERFORMANCE METRICS: CHALLENGES AND OPPORTUNITIES

The U.S. National Academy of Engineering has been active in promoting the idea of industrial ecology—likening industrial processes to ecological ones in order to harmonize the two—and in developing realistic measures of environmentally important industrial variables. Its book on industrial environmental performance metrics (National Academy of Engineering 1999) presents both an argument for better industrial environmental performance and reporting, and a close look at the environmentally important aspects of the automotive, chemical, electronics, and pulp and paper industries with an eye toward defining what they should measure and report.

By concentrating on specific industries rather than on industry in general—as have all of the other reports discussed in this chapter—it provides a much clearer analysis of the difficulties and potential value of establishing quantitative metrics for realistic intercompany (or even interfacility) comparison. As it turns out, this is far more difficult than most reporting guidelines would lead you to believe.

It is obvious that environmental reporting would be most valuable to its users if it allowed quantitative comparison among companies. Any careful reading of a series of environmental reports from the same industry, however, makes the problem self-evident: it is very difficult from reading the reports to determine environmental superiority. The NAE book goes a long way toward explaining why. Even if companies were trying their level best to provide environmental data suitable for benchmarking themselves against other companies, they would be hard pressed to do so. It's almost always apples and oranges.

In the end, the best the authors of the National Academy of Engineering book could come up with was a list of 10 generic metrics so nonspecific that no two companies would be likely to use most of them in the same way. The list consists of:

- Materials use (normalized in some appropriate way)

- Water use (normalized in some appropriate way)

- Energy use (normalized in some appropriate way)

- Percent of recycled materials in products

- Percent of products that are leased

- Resource consumption and/or emissions during product use

- Average use of packaging

- Emissions from manufacturing (normalized in some appropriate way)

- Recordable health and safety incident rates

- A sustainability metric of some type

The lesson to take from this serious and distinguished committee seems to be that it is going to be difficult—maybe even impossible—to come up with standardized quantitative metrics that allow direct comparison of companies. If so, then highly standardized reporting guidelines like those of CERES and GRI are not going to achieve their desired ends and companies might just as well continue to use environmental and sustainability reports as they presently do: to attempt to influence customers, analysts, employees, and other target audiences without worrying too much about standardization.

CONCLUSIONS

The documents discussed in this chapter provide a rich source of ideas for the content of environmental and sustainability reports. They also reflect a tug-of-war between people who would like to set up an absolute, totally formulaic standard—a fill-in-the-blanks approach—and people who would like a cafeteria approach. As long as the resulting report is not being judged against an absolute standard, there is little reason to feel too constrained by guidelines, especially if following guidelines fails to increase the quality of intercompany comparison.

Accordingly, most companies writing environmental and sustainability reports today are probably correct in being more interested in reaching and influencing selected target audiences than they are in conforming to a set of guidelines. As discussed in the next chapter, however, that may change. There is a rapidly developing industry involving financial analysts, accounting firms, and environmental/sustainability activists that is judging the environmental performance and sustainability of individual corporations, and is using, to various degrees, environmental and sustainability reports as the basis for that judgment.

Be sure to look at all of the guidelines addressed in this chapter—most are freely available over the World Wide Web though you may have to purchase a commercial book on the ISO 14031 guidelines (or the guidelines themselves) to see them. Together, the guidelines provide a wealth of detailed suggestions and ideas for things you might include in a sustainability report. Depending on how well established your company environmental management system is and how much data it is feasible for you to collect, you may already meet the standards of many or all of these guidelines. If you do, there is no reason not to proclaim it. As noted, you almost cannot avoid meeting the GRI standard in any case, however GRI would like you to be committed to addressing every single one of its points at some time in the future if you are going to claim GRI compatibility now.

On the other hand, meeting the letter of these standards will not necessarily get your report high grades from third-party scoring systems, nor will it guarantee your report will be effective with your target audiences. At this stage in the evolution of environmental and sustainability reporting, there is more to be said for reaching your target audiences than for satisfying third-party guidelines.

Furthermore, the best environmental and sustainability reports provide information that allows comparison with other companies in the same industrial sector. For that reason, you should be sure to obtain the environmental or sustainability reports of your peer companies. You may be able to take a leadership role in developing a standard set of metrics that will allow intercompany comparison, and at the very least, you will be able to compare your company's performance to that of your peers. That will help you decide what makes the most sense for you to emphasize.

4

What Should Go
into a Report?

This chapter analyzes the principal environmental and sustainability report writing guidelines and scoring systems to determine the emphasis placed on different topics in each, and then looks at the results of one study of 106 reports and another study of 40 reports to see how well existing reports match that emphasis. The guidelines and scoring systems are by no means identical in their emphasis, and there is substantial variability in emphasis among the reports of large corporations, even within the same industrial sector. Although most companies touch on most of the topics, few rigorously follow any of the guidelines.

The purpose of an environmental or sustainability report is to transmit information to stakeholders—people who have some sort of an interest in your company. Different classes of stakeholders expect different kinds of information and may respond best to different kinds of presentation. Corporate management would like an attractive multipurpose report with a positive spin and an optimistic outlook—ideally one that successfully differentiates the company's products and services—if it doesn't cost too much. Employees are likely to value credible assurance that the company is serious about its commitment and is approaching its environmental and social responsibilities in a systematic and competent way. They also like to read about themselves and their own initiatives. Customers want assurance that the company is acting responsibly, and many value a strong pro-environment stance. Lenders and insurers want to know that risk is being addressed realistically and are likely to want specifics of risk management activities. Analysts and investors also want to know that risks are minimized and would prefer that environmental and social investments not only reduce risk, but increase profitability as well. Government regulators and environmental activists want quantitative numerical information on environmental, social, and economic performance that they can use to compare a firm's performance with regulations and with the performance of its peers.

Is it desirable and possible to meet the needs of all of these stakeholders with a single report? Absolutely, but it requires careful attention to selecting the appropriate level of detail and to presenting it in an attractive and efficient manner. This chapter presents an overview of content selection based on existing guidelines, scoring systems, and analysis of reports. Chapter 5 illustrates techniques of effective communication and presentation, with discussions of specific reports and Web sites.

WHAT INFORMATION SHOULD BE INCLUDED IN YOUR REPORT?

How do you decide what topics to include and how much emphasis and space to devote to each of them? The 10 rules that make up part 2 of this book give specific guidance and include examples from reports of a variety of companies. They were derived by analyzing the existing guidelines (chapter 3), report scoring systems (chapter 16), and reports of some of the largest companies (chapter 18). Each guideline, scoring system, and corporate report includes its own set of topics and organizes them into different categories. The only way to compare them and look for commonality is to impose the same organization on all of them. Thus, I have subdivided each of them into 10 categories that have become the topics of the 10 rules for effective reporting (part 2) and underlie the Pacific Sustainability Index report writing checklist and scoring system (chapter 17, appendix A). The 10 topic categories are described following and their relative importance illustrated by how much weight is given to each of them in the two most comprehensive guidelines (GRI 2000 and ISO 14031 Annex A) and four report scoring systems (Davis-Walling & Batterman, SustainAbility/UNEP, Deloitte Touche Tohmatsu, and the Pacific Sustainability Index). There is also data from a study that summarized the content of 106 reports from U.S. companies, and an introduction to the 40-company analysis presented in appendix B.

TOPICS FOR EFFECTIVE ENVIRONMENTAL AND SUSTAINABILITY REPORTING

Company Profile

This category includes a description of the products, services, brands, facilities, production processes, locations, numbers of employees, income, markets, and customers. It is intended to give an overview of those characteristics of the company that are important to its potential environmental and social impacts. It may also include the name and contact information for a technically knowledgeable person willing to answer questions and provide additional information.

Environmental and Social Vision and Commitment

This category includes characterization of the firm's environmental and social vision and commitment, usually signed by a corporate executive. Many firms have statements from different levels of managers; often the CEO and the environmental manager make separate statements. Statements often include commitments to minimize consumption and environmental impacts, and to better serve employees and other stakeholders. They also often address why such commitments are being made and what the impediments and challenges to fulfilling them are.

Environmental and Social Stakeholders

This category includes information about the identification of and consultation with interested parties including management, employees, investors, customers, suppliers, contractors, lending institutions, insurers, regulatory and legislative bodies, neighboring and regional communities, media, academic institutions, environmental groups, and nongovernmental organizations.

Environmental and Social Policy and Management

This category includes a statement of environmental and social policy, a description of the internal organization charged with carrying out this policy, and its strategy and management systems for doing so. It also includes an explanation of any voluntary regulations or standards of conduct subscribed to, and any voluntary certifications such as a certified ISO 14001 environmental management system.

Environmental and Social Aspects and Impacts

Environmental and social aspects are those characteristics of the firm and its industry that are likely to have an impact, either beneficial or adverse. The way in which they are systematically identified and addressed, even though significant impacts have not resulted, contributes to a sense of openness and honesty. All significant impacts, of course, should be discussed.

Environmental and Social Performance Indicators

This category comprises descriptive material about the things that actually get measured (such as the amount of electricity and water used), including the rationale for measuring them, and the ways in which the measurements were made. This category includes what indicators (environmental, social, and financial metrics) were measured, how and why they were chosen, how they were measured and aggregated, and why the units they are presented in were chosen. It does not, however, include the performance data itself.

Environmental and Social Initiatives and Mitigations

These are the usually voluntary activities undertaken by the firm and its employees to improve environmental and social performance and to mitigate any significant adverse impacts. Initiatives range from helping to clean up neighborhoods around a manufacturing facility to monetary contributions to wilderness preservation foundations. Mitigations include restoring old manufacturing plant sites (brownfields) and cleaning up contaminated sites.

Environmental and Social Performance

This category comprises the quantitative results of monitoring the performance indicators. On the environmental side it includes how much material of various types was used, how much energy was used and its source, how much water was used and how much was recycled, how many and what types of emissions were released to air and water; how much waste was produced and how much of it was landfilled, how many incidents and violations there were, how much impact is being caused by the use of products, and how much the company is doing to protect and enhance the natural environment. On the social side, it includes the treatment and compensation of employees, the social performance of suppliers and contractors, and geographic differences in social performance. The data in this category should include anything that has a potential environmental or social impact.

Environmental and Social Costs and Investments

This category includes how much money was spent improving social and environmental performance, repairing damage, and paying penalties and fines for nonperformance.

Environmental and Social Goals and Targets

This category includes the goals and targets that have been established, and why.

WHAT DO THE GUIDELINES AND SCORING SYSTEMS SAY ABOUT THESE CATEGORIES?

How much of your environmental or sustainability report ought to be devoted to each of these topics, and how much relative emphasis should be put on environmental and social issues? One set of answers comes from inspecting the various report-writing guidelines and scoring systems. This is not a particularly straightforward process inasmuch as they categorize their topics in quite different ways. To simplify the process, I have used the 10 categories above to classify all of the environmental topics under direct company control in the GRI 2000 and ISO 14031 guidelines (see chapter 3), the existing scoring systems from SustainAbility/UNEP, Deloitte Touche Tohmatsu, and Davis-Walling & Batterman (see chapter 16), and the new Pacific Sustainability Index (see chapter 17). Topics not under direct company control (social and other topics) differ among these systems and include provisions for verification and feedback on the report, discussion of details about the report and its contents, characteristics of the external environment that are not under direct company control but which it may influence (ranging from water quality in a river from which a company draws and to which it discharges water, to CO_2 concentration of the global atmosphere), health and safety considerations, financial aspects of the company, human resources consideration, and some other minor topics. These are all presented in a comparative way in the following three graphs.

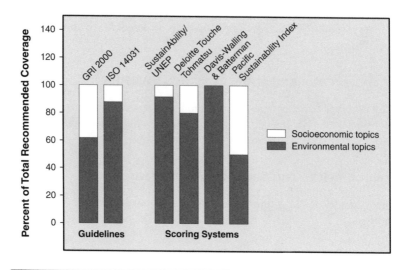

Figure 4.1   Percentages of environmental and social and other topics covered by two guidelines and four scoring systems.

Figure 4.1 illustrates how the different guidelines and scoring systems apportion their content between environmental and the social and other topics. The GRI 2000 guidelines, the leading sustainability reporting guidelines, have 62% of the topics dedicated to environmental issues and the remainder to social and fincial considerations. Of the topics in ISO 14031 Annex A, 88% concern environmental aspects and potential impacts of the company, but 12% have to do with the natural environment external to the company's facilities and direct control.

For the SustainAbility/UNEP scoring system I classify all but 8% of the topics as environmental, whereas for the closely related Deloitte Touche Tohmatsu system nonenvironmental topics make up 20% of the total. The Davis-Walling & Batterman system is 100% environmental. The Pacific Sustainability Index treats environmental and social topics equally and, as described in chapter 17, scores them separately.

Figure 4.2 shows a breakdown of the environmental topics in each of the guidelines and scoring systems into 10 environmental categories. The GRI 2000 guidelines include all 10 topics, with environmental performance the largest single category (32%), followed by company profile (18%) and environmental policy (15%). In the GRI scheme, the remaining topics are each worth less than half of any of these, and the skimpiest coverage (1.5%) is given to environmental goals and targets.

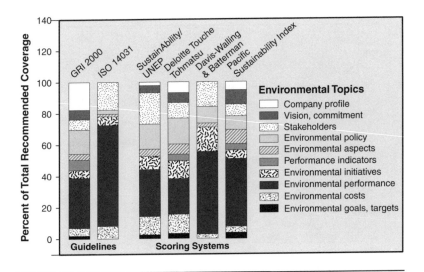

Figure 4.2 Distribution of environmental topics in two guidelines and four scoring systems.

The ISO 14031 guidelines are heavily weighted toward environmental topics (56%), followed by information about stakeholders (15%) and costs and investments (7%). There is no suggestion that there be a corporate profile, any visionary statements or commitments to goals, nor that the company discuss the rationale for the performance indicators chosen. The four scoring systems are generally more comprehensive than the ISO 14031 topic list, with differences in emphasis. Neither SustainAbility/UNEP nor Davis-Walling & Batterman give credit for discussing the rationale for the indicators chosen. Deloitte Touche Tohmatsu and the Pacific Sustainability Index address all of the topics.

The distribution of social and other topics is quite different among the guidelines and scoring systems (Figure 4.3). Of the 38% of the GRI 2000 guidelines devoted to nonenvironmental topics, over 60% consists of human resources and social topics and most of the remainder is company financials. The "other" topics of the ISO 14034 Annex A list comprise primarily external environmental issues that cannot be directly managed by the company. SustainAbility/UNEP has one topic on third-party verification, one on a description of the content of the report itself, one on the global environment, and one on health and safety. Davis-Walling & Batterman do not address anything except environmental issues. Almost all of the Pacific Sustainability Index treatment of nonenvironmental issues is related to human resources and other social issues.

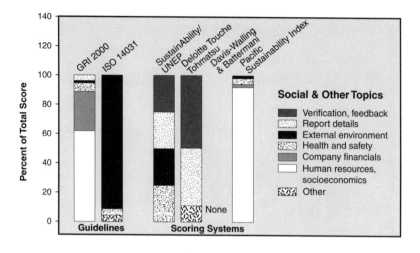

Figure 4.3 Distribution of social and other topics in two guidelines and four scoring systems.

WHAT CAN BE LEARNED ABOUT CONTENT FROM INSPECTING CORPORATE ENVIRONMENTAL AND SUSTAINABILITY REPORTS?

One way to analyze the content of a corporate environmental or sustainability report is to measure the percentage of the report devoted to specific topics. The results of one such study of the 1996 reports of 106 American companies are summarized in Figure 4.4.

The 16 topics used in the study (Lober et al. 1997) to calculate average percentage of space occupied in the reports fit into five of my categories: vision/commitment, stakeholders, environmental policy, environmental initiatives, and environmental performance. Environmental performance alone made up over 68% of the content, higher than any of the guidelines or scoring systems except the ISO 14031 Annex A list.

My students and I (Morhardt et al. submitted for publication) scored 40 environmental and sustainability reports from the world's largest corporations in four industrial sectors: electronics, motor vehicles and parts, petroleum refining, and gas and electric utilities. We used the two sets of guidelines and the three existing scoring systems (prior to development of

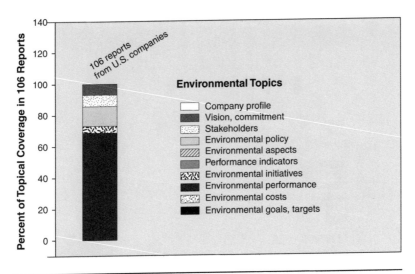

Figure 4.4 Distribution of topics from 1996 environmental reports of 106 American corporations, estimated from data in Lober et al. (1997).

the Pacific Sustainability Index) and found that the comprehensiveness of coverage (the score) was particularly low for the GRI 2000 and ISO 14031 guidelines. Figure 4.5 shows the total scores from the GRI 2000 scoring system for the 40 companies.

The total scores were low, with an average score for all companies of only 17% of the total possible score. The score bars are partitioned into the 10 topics, but because the scores are low and the bars are short, the relative distribution of the topics is hard to see. To rectify this problem, each bar has been expanded to 100% in Figure 4.6 to show more clearly the distribution of topics addressed.

The GRI 2000 guidelines include all 10 environmental topics (Figure 4.2) as well as other topics (Figure 4.3), but, as can be seen in Figure 4.6, not all reports address all of them. At one extreme, the very low score for Tosco reflects the fact that only two of the topics were covered. Some of the higher-scoring companies addressed all 10 topics plus the "other" category (BMW, Phillips Petroleum), but others did not (ENEL, Tokyo Electric). The lower-scoring companies usually did not address all 10 categories. As the average scores increase, there is increasing likelihood that all topics are covered. In the extreme case—a perfect score—all topics in the scoring system are necessarily addressed, but when the scores for all companies are low, as in Figure 4.6, relatively good performance can be achieved without

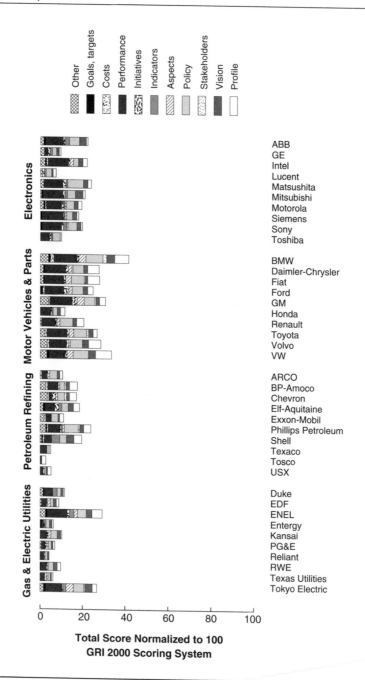

Figure 4.5 Scores of environmental or sustainability reports of 40 corporations from a scoring system based on the GRI 2000 reporting guidelines.

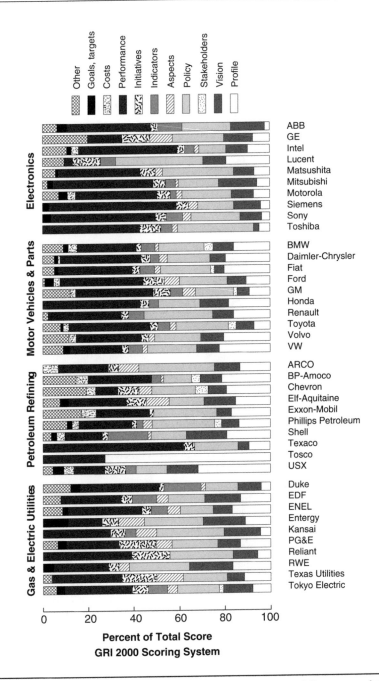

Figure 4.6 Distribution of topics in the environmental or sustainability reports of 40 corporations from a scoring system based on the GRI 2000 reporting guidelines.

addressing all of the topics. Appendix B has similar diagrams of this 40-company analysis for the other scoring systems.

LOW-HANGING FRUIT

It should be obvious from Figures 4.5 and 4.6, as well as from the comparable figures in appendix B, that most companies could easily improve their comprehensiveness of reporting, and therefore their scores, by paying more attention to reporting guidelines and scoring systems. Most companies have far more information about their environmental and social performance than presently finds its way into reports. I would bet that this under-reporting is primarily unintentional, and that as companies become more familiar with the various guidelines and what their peers are reporting, comprehensiveness scores will increase rapidly.

CONCLUSIONS

There are a great many topics that companies address in their environmental and sustainability reports—the most extensive of the guidelines, ISO 14031, has almost 200 topics. Yet there are many specific topics included in existing corporate environmental and sustainability reports that are not mentioned in ISO 14031 Annex A or in the next most comprehensive system, the GRI 2000 guidelines. This chapter showed that four of the six guidelines and scoring systems are overwhelmingly focused on environmental rather than social and other topics. In all systems, the largest environmental category is performance metrics—the amount of material, energy, and water used, the emissions and waste produced, and a variety of other metrics including recycling and product stewardship. But the scoring systems and guidelines are not at all uniform in the weight they attach to the different topics. Performance metrics, for example, range from 23 to 64% of the recommended environmental coverage. One study of 106 reports from U. S. companies in 1996 showed that environmental performance metrics constituted 68% of the report contents then, suggesting that companies were even more biased toward reporting environmental performance than they are now. When viewed through the scoring systems, however, the results from a sample of 40 reports from the world's largest companies shows that the highest scorers tend to discuss a wide range of topics, including those characteristic of sustainability reports.

5

Effective Presentations in Print and on the Web

There are many different approaches used by corporations when writing environmental and sustainability reports. Some reports are extremely short, with a broad overview and some summary data; others are extremely long, verging on 200 pages, with four-color photographs, fancy graphics, and long data tables. Some are loose collections of Web pages, and others are carefully designed interactive Web sites. Long and fancy does not necessarily mean better though. This chapter discusses the relative effectiveness of a variety of approaches, using real examples.

What makes an effective presentation? What makes an attractive report? How do you get in all the information needed for credibility without making the report too long and unreadable? Should a Web site duplicate the printed materials? Is a printable Web version equivalent to a printed report? Should data details be consigned to a Web site? How interactive should Web sites be? Is it just as good to have only a Web site and no printed report?

There is no commonly accepted way to write an environmental or sustainability report. The wide range of approaches, styles, and content—even within reports from the largest companies in a single industrial sector—is confusing and has led to the many writing guidelines and scoring systems described in chapters 3, 4, 16, and 17. Few reports follow any of these guidelines, and those that attempt to do so usually follow them loosely at best. To give a sense of the range of possibilities, I have selected reports that use different approaches and described them individually in this chapter, noting their good and bad points.

Most of the reports described here are called "environmental reports" by their companies. Many of them are just that, with few of the extra social, economic, political, cultural, and ethical components that full-bore sustainability reporting implies. But some are beginning to include these other components, and a few are labeled "sustainability reports."

HOW EFFECTIVE IS FOLLOWING REPORT-WRITING GUIDELINES?

Following guidelines and scoring systems may assure comprehensiveness, but not necessarily persuasiveness. Careful following of the more detailed reporting guidelines, particularly the GRI guidelines (GRI 2000 at the time of this writing) and the CERES guidelines (CERES 1999a, CERES 1999b, CERES 2000a, CERES 2000b) will result in quite comprehensive coverage, but only an accountant could love the CERES reporting format, and the GRI 2000 guidelines leave the format up to the writer, so quality of presentation is independent of the guidelines. There are no formal guidelines for Web sites although I make some suggestions toward the end of this chapter. The remainder of the guidelines discussed in chapter 3 are either intentionally vague to allow maximum flexibility in reporting, or, like the ISO 14031 Environmental Performance Evaluation standard, not so much reporting guidelines as lists of environmental and social topics that should be managed actively. In any event, most stakeholders are unlikely to even have any idea that there are guidelines unless the report mentions them. An announcement that specific guidelines are being followed may carry weight with naïve readers, but most knowledgeable readers will judge the content for themselves. Consequently, the main reason to follow guidelines is to be sure that your coverage is reasonably comprehensive. Nevertheless, many environmental and sustainability reports prominently advertise that guidelines are being followed.

CRITICAL REVIEWS OF REPORTS

Baxter: 2000 Sustainability Report and Executive Summary—*Informative But Not Very Attractive*

Baxter International is a $6 billion manufacturer of medical therapies for people with life-threatening conditions, and one of the first companies (along with Procter & Gamble [P&G]) to issue a sustainability report under the GRI 2000 guidelines. The full report is printed in stark black and white on glossy paper, and the summary is printed with garishly colored headings and a few murky photographs. They both use sans serif typefaces throughout and this, combined with the strange choice of color gives them an amateurish quality. Neither of these documents is visually inviting.

Substantively, on the other hand, both documents address the economic, social, and environmental aspects of the business in a clear manner. The economic and social components, in particular, are presented in the context of sustainability much more clearly than in most other reports. For example, the financial section gives a highly detailed breakdown of worldwide environmental costs and the savings and cost avoidance achieved from making the expenditures. The business case for environmental investments at Baxter is that they would have spent $98 million more in 1999 (and even more in previous years) for raw materials, production processes, energy, disposal costs, and packaging if no environmentally beneficial actions had been implemented since 1992.

On the social front, Baxter reports increased women's representation at various executive levels since 1996—not something commonly reported or requested by the GRI guidelines—but also notes that there is room for improvement; women represent only four percent (one woman) among the company's 25 most highly paid people. Most companies simply fail to address this problem and Baxter should receive kudos for acknowledging it. Perhaps they will correct it as well. Baxter also frontally addresses topics that get activists excited; the report explains and defends the use of polyvinyl chloride (PVC) in their devices, xenotransplantation (in this case organ transplants from pigs to humans), and animal testing—all hot-button issues.

BMW's 1999/2000 Group Environmental Report—*Very Long and Very Convincing*

BMW is a German automobile and aircraft engine manufacturer. Its 177-page report is all business and very nearly a textbook on the environmental issues facing the world's automobile and aircraft engine manufacturers. It leaves the reader who is willing to plow through it with a sense that BMW is as thoughtfully and thoroughly committed to long-term environmental protection as it is possible for a company to be. A big part of the source of this feeling is that the main rationale for BMW's environmental commitment is completely transparent and completely business-related—"The social and ecological acceptance of a make of automobile and its manufacturer have been a competitive factor for some years now." How does BMW hope to achieve this acceptance? By ". . . reconciling the conflict between people's justified demands for mobility and ecological requirements" through, it appears, creative and elegant engineering, driven by a strong social conscience and a desire to be at the forefront of environmentally-sensitive product innovation with little, if any, performance penalty or decrease in comfort.

BMW is operating on the concept articulated by the Berlin Federal Environment Agency that "it is better to technically improve a large number of cars with internal combustion engines than to spend the same amount of money on equipping a very few cars with exotic technology." The words of importance here are "technically improve"; quite a different thing from just improving gasoline mileage or recyclability. One gets the strong impression that BMWs are not merely environmentally better year by year—they are better in all respects and come from a company that instead of complaining about environmental regulations is proud to be years ahead of them in many instances. The report makes me feel that driving a BMW is not only likely to be a technologically satisfying experience, but will go a long way to help saving the environment as well.

This is an extremely powerful message and one that most writers of corporate environmental and sustainability reports would surely like to convey. No one in his right mind really believes that driving any car will have a positive effect on the environment. But as long as one is going to drive anyway, wouldn't it be better to get a car from a company that is enthusiastically doing something to minimize the adverse effects of its products on the environment? This environmental sensitivity makes it possible for me to justify, in theory at least, buying a car far more luxurious and with higher performance than I need.

So why is this report so convincing? Primarily, it seems to be a totally straightforward and honest characterization of the company's long-standing interest in environmental issues and a thoughtful exposition of what will work and what won't. Many corporate environmental and sustainability reports are mainly a litany of the voluntary or minimally subsidized nonbusiness environmental activities of their employees—teaching school children about the environment in their spare time, cleaning up the local wetland, starting a community recycling center. Despite its length, there is none of this in BMW's report.

Not that I doubt for an instant that BMW employees are engaged in these kinds of activities, maybe even with considerable BMW financial assistance, but the company doesn't regard these as corporate activities, and doesn't feel it needs to get credit for them. Instead the report tells you how BMW thinks automobile companies ought to approach environmental protection and then supports the position in an articulate and convincing way. BMW doesn't give the impression of trying to subvert the issues; it doesn't, for example, take on the plausibility of CO_2 causing global warming, something that is undeniable from a scientific standpoint but hotly contested by many companies. It just gets on with exploring systems for reducing CO_2 production.

Bristol-Myers Squibb Company: On the Path Toward Sustainability, 2001 Sustainability Progress Report—*Elegant, Restrained, Extra Informative*

Bristol-Myers Squibb Company is the world's fifth largest pharmaceutical company and can afford to put out any kind of report it wants. It chose to follow the GRI 2000 sustainability reporting guidelines, which it does with style, illustrating clearly that covering a lot of ground does not require either a very long report—this one is 40 pages—or a mechanical format. The report is done in full color, but with a flat rather than glossy finish, and with small photographs, boxes, or graphs on every page that leaven it while maintaining a serious appearance.

The report includes four years of data on some 16 environmental performance metrics all normalized to worldwide sales figures. It presents them first in a single table toward the beginning, then subsequently in graphic form with explanation. The same graphs are available at the company Web site along with the raw (non-normalized) data.

It also includes considerably more information on social issues than do most reports, and for that reason can legitimately be called a sustainability report. In addition to the usual health and safety information, it discusses wages and benefits, nondiscrimination, flexible work arrangements, compliance with labor laws and standard practices, employee grievance procedures, human rights, and more.

All in all, this is a very attractive and informative report that conveys a strong sense of environmental and social commitment and performance.

Canon 1999 Environmental Report—*Lots of Data, Minimal Hype, Low Cost*

Canon is a large Japanese company that produces computer peripherals, copying machines, cameras, video camcorders, and related equipment. Although it has produced two even better reports since this one, this remains an example of a very effective low-cost approach that smaller companies might choose to emulate. The 28-page report is printed in black and white with a green spot color for graphs and highlights on 100 percent recycled paper. It has no photographs or graphics other than tables and figures with data in them, but it is attractive and accessible nonetheless. This was Canon's first effort at gathering all of its statistical information in one publication, and Canon has continued the practice annually since 1999.

This is purely an environmental report. It discusses environmental policy, environmental management systems (ISO 14001 at 23 manufacturing sites, with more coming at R&D and sales sites), environmental expenditures, and goals and performance in:

- Energy consumption

- Water consumption and recycling

- Chemical substance control

- Emissions to air and water

- Waste recycling

- Product recycling

- Packaging reduction

The results are presented briefly—a paragraph or two of text and a data figure for each subtopic—stating philosophy, goals, and performance. Where goals were not met there is no effort to disguise it. Additional data on water, air quality, noise, vibration, and odors at each site are posted on Canon's Web site.

The statement of corporate environmental philosophy and summary of goals is exceptionally clear. The crisp, parallel presentation of all topics is excellent, as is the candor about where Canon stands with respect to its goals and performance. This format makes it extremely easy to add sustainability topics—just a matter of adding some more pages in the same format. For a low-budget, high-impact report, this one is hard to beat.

Matsushita 1999 Environmental Report—*Strong Message, Superb Graphics, Soy Ink*

Matsushita Electric Industrial Co., a Japanese maker of electronics and industrial electrical equipment, is the 24th largest company in the world, with annual revenues of $65 billion and nearly 300,000 employees. Its brands include National, Panasonic, Technics, and Quasar.

Its environmental report is a brief 36 pages long, printed on recycled paper (that has a matte finish and looks like it has been recycled) with soy ink. In fact, as the report documents, Matsushita's packaging, product explanations, and product catalogs for air conditioners and audio equipment are all printed with soy inks, which are environmentally superior to conventional inks. This is a report with very few photographs and little marketing hype, but with extensive and highly effective graphics—schematic drawings of energy-saving technologies, manufacturing process diagrams, flowcharts, data graphs, and tables. The graphics all make good use of color, and explain the company's systematic approach to environmental protection as clearly as any good textbook would.

The large number of self-contained examples of environmental responsibility, each taking just a few column inches and crisply explained with a minimum of text, is very effective. A reader browsing through the diagrams and reading only occasional snippets of text still gets the message of environmental innovation and implementation. The presence of so many examples gives the overwhelming impression of a company that is not just thinking or talking about environmental protection, but is doing a good deal about it and has been for quite some time.

Nippon Steel Environmental Report 2001— *Highly Concentrated with Great Graphics and Lots of Information*

Many environmental reports from the metals sector are not very ambitious. This report from Nippon Steel is a notable exception, as are reports from NKK, another Japanese steel manufacturer, and POSCO, a Korean one.

The Nippon Steel report is 41 pages long, available both in hard copy and on the Web as portable document format (PDF) files, two facing pages at a time. The Web version prints out half size, two pages on a single 8.5 × 11 inch sheet so it is a little hard to read, but if you have the printed copy, or if your eyes are up to the half-size version, the report gives a detailed view of the steel industry, including the environmental aspects of its processes and the way steel makers minimize their environmental impacts. It is designed similarly to the Matsushita Electrical Industrial Company report described previously, with lots of small flowcharts, photographs, schematic views of processes, and data tables and graphs. The information is transferred to the reader crisply, informatively, and accessibly. It takes no more than a glance to ascertain the topic and its importance, and the combination of photos, diagrams, and flowcharts is quite effective.

Procter & Gamble: 2000 Sustainability Report Executive Summary—*A Disappointing Eight-Page Foldout*

Procter & Gamble (P&G) put their full report on the Web and distributed this summary, maybe on the theory that not many people want to read the full report and can get anything they really need from this; I'm not so sure.

Two pages are devoted to statements by the CEO, chairman, and director of corporate sustainable development. The CEO and chairman note, justifiably, that three of their new products contribute to sustainable development (by implication, in the developing world): a micronutrient supplement, a water purification system, and a fruit and vegetable rinse (to reduce contamination). It is perhaps a stretch to make a similar claim, as they do, for a drug marketed in the U.S. and Europe for the treatment and prevention of postmenopausal osteoporosis. And even though these are worthy causes, the company's main product lines are items like Pringles Potato Crisps, Old Spice aftershave, and Charmin toilet paper which do not seem, on their own, to have much to do with sustainable development. More to the point might be how these are manufactured, packaged, and distributed in a sustainable way, but these topics are hardly mentioned. The director of corporate sustainable development reiterates the thoughts of the chairman and CEO without offering much additional in the way of substance other than that waste reduction saved P&G $505 million in the past six years.

The main body of the summary devotes one page to a few statistics (headquarters location, number of employees, number of common stock shareholders, P&G's brands and business units), half of the next page to a restatement of some of the chairman, CEO, and director's observations and the other half to business unit totals of tons of product shipped, recycled raw materials, packaging used and amount from recycled sources, waste and percent recycled, and energy and water consumption. This latter information is not put into any kind of perspective and it is difficult to see how anyone might use it. Are these good results or not?

The next page presents some financial trends, notes that 59 percent of employees are male and that in the U.S., 16 percent of management employees and 19 percent of other employees are minorities. It also notes that in North America, philanthropic contributions were up this year by 2.6 percent to $28,292,768, and gives occupational health and safety incident and lost workday rates, and number and dollar value of environmental and health and safety fines. Like information on the previous page, none of this is put into perspective.

The final page highlights Open Minds, an unexplained $265,000 educational charitable project in Asia, and DASH, a project to improve Italian pediatric hospitals. It also includes what appears to be an advertisement for the new osteoporosis medicine, Actonel.

All in all, from the information in this summary there is very little I could say about P&G's overall environmental and sustainability programs. I came away with the feeling that they are trying to get a lot of credit for a few isolated programs, while ignoring the issues associated with the bulk of their operations.

Swisscom Systematic Environmental Protection—*One Big Sheet of Paper*

Swisscom, a large Swiss telecommunications company, is managed from an ultramodern highly energy-efficient building in Warblaufen. Visiting it— with its natural lighting, no air conditioning, district heating, rainwater for the WCs and plants, and a 30-second walk to the commuter train—gives the clear impression of an extremely environmentally sensitive company. And as its environmental report is quick to point out, telecommunications save paper ("An e-mail has 1/200th the environmental consequences of an international letter").

But this is a printed report—on one large sheet of paper, 23 × 30 inches, folded like a map. You have to go find a table to unfold it on. I doubt that this format saved much money; it's an expensive-looking graphic design printed in four colors on both sides, but the format definitely keeps it short. This short, though, is not necessarily so sweet. The business end of the report is a giant circular graphic filled with fairly uninformative sound bites:

> *Inherited problems create a need for action. Like many other companies, Swisscom must also tackle the problems of polluted or even contaminated ground.*

I'm not sure whether polluted or contaminated is worse, but I don't think I learned much from that statement.

Here's another one:

> *Classification of electricity consumption. The main proportion of electricity consumption arises from the operation and air-conditioning of the telephone exchanges. Exchanges 32%, cordless transmission 13%, air-conditioning/ventilation 31%, lighting 11%, work tools/EDP 8%, miscellaneous 5%. Eco-fact. Reduction of air-conditioning: increase of the operating temperature in 20 installations from 20° C to 25° C.*

Is that clear?

The environmental manager told me that they decided to test the telephone switch manufacturer's temperature specification and let the temperature keep rising until there was a problem. But there wasn't one. Modern electronics turn out not to need to be cooled as much as their predecessors did, so Swisscom was able to save a lot of electricity by not cooling the computer rooms so much. I don't think I would have figured that out from the sound bite.

The giant-sheet format and graphic presentation are not necessarily bad, but this version does not seem to be very effective in getting Swisscom's environmental message across. The problem seems to be that the public relations sound-bite experts usurped the technical experts and style superseded substance—it is not easy to understand what the point of the sound bites is. The take-home message might be that too much innovation in reporting format is not necessarily good, and can be distracting.

Pacific Gas and Electric Corporation 2000 Environmental Report—*Different, But Distracting*

Another example of perhaps too much innovation is Pacific Gas and Electric (PG&E) Company's odd-sized (6.5 × 8–inch) 62-page booklet. It has a good deal of environmental information, but its quirky use of type-as-graphics, strange mix of typefaces, and lack of illustrations save highly stylized data graphs, makes it seem highly inaccessible to me. It is not posted on the PG&E Web site, but the much more conventional PG&E 1996 Environmental Report is. The 1996 report is, by contrast, clearly written, nicely formatted, and a generally exemplary product. Most companies gradually improve their reports over time. PG&E opted to change theirs radically, but in a peculiar direction.

Volkswagen 1999/2000 Environmental Report—*A Handsome, Readable Magazine*

Volkswagen's sustainability performance was judged at the top of the automobile industry by Sustainability Asset Management (SAM) in 1998, according to Volkswagen's 1999/2000 Environmental Report; and its 1999/2000 Environmental Report received the highest score of any automobile manufacturer in SustainAbility/UNEP's 2000 Benchmark Survey (SustainAbility/UNEP 2000), 16 percent higher than its closest rival, Ford Motor Company. Its average report score in the five scoring systems used in appendix B put it at the top as well, essentially even with BMW. Thus, in addition to having superior environmental performance, there is a general agreement that Volkswagen knows how to write an excellent sustainability report.

Some of this success may be related to the length of the report. The current round of scoring systems favors long reports; the longer a report is, the more likely that all of the topics in the system will be addressed, and addressed in enough detail to get a high score. Current scoring systems (other than the Pacific Sustainability Index, see chapter 17) are not concerned with performance, so that good performance reported concisely may not score as highly as ordinary performance reported at length.

But the real power of this report is that it conveys the feeling that not only is Volkswagen paying close attention to all the important environmental and sustainability issues, it is successfully dealing with them. As Rudolf Stobbe, Volkswagen's chief environmental officer says in Volkswagen's 1999/2000 Environmental Report, "We have reached our environmental goals virtually across the board." The centerpiece of this report is Volkswagen's "3-litre car," the Lupo 3L TDI, the first production vehicle that can cover 100 kilometers on less than three liters of fuel. Although BMW eschews this concept in its report—indeed almost ridicules it as an exercise in producing the sort of car almost no one would want— Volkswagen glorifies it as a test bed for new technology already finding its way into its other vehicles. Besides, the car must be attractive to at least some consumers; one article in the press (*VDI-Nachrichten* 7/20/1999) about the Lupo 3L TDI was titled "Saving fuel can be fun," and *Fortune* magazine said "More green, less clatter—at last a diesel you might want to own" (*Fortune* 1/21/2002). Volkswagen has managed to equate its investment in a 3-liter car with an overall corporate philosophy that is reminiscent of advertising for the 1960 VW Beetle: "Think small."

A visit to the Volkswagen environmental department in Wolfsburg reinforces a feeling of concern for the environment and dedication to quality: it is six o'clock on a summer Friday afternoon before a four-day holiday; the lights are off, the air conditioning is off, the windows are open, and the environmental staff is all there, working like crazy.

Still, there is considerably more to an effective report than the range of topics covered or to the quality of the performance and the dedication of the staff. What makes Volkswagen's report truly excellent is its accessibility. Although it is long, it looks and reads like a magazine. It is broken up into bite-sized pieces with most pages beginning with a new topic and heading—it can be read equally well back to front. There is a nice mix of small photographs of people, of cars, and of manufacturing facilities. There is plenty of white space. The headings in each chapter are a different color, and the colors are subtle. The data are there, but they are spread throughout the report. High quality design in reports, as well as in cars, sells.

Volvo: 1999 Environmental Report—*Glossy, Concise, and Packed with Information*

Volvo is a Swedish maker of cars, trucks, buses, construction equipment, and engines. Its 1998 and 1999 environmental reports are models of elegance and conciseness, but differ because between these two years the

Volvo Car Corporation was sold to Ford Motor Company. This reduced the remaining company's sales by almost half, but shortened the environmental report by only 4 pages, from 23 to 19. Those 19 pages are very informative, highly approachable, and easy to read.

The overall effect is one of a short but very high quality newsmagazine. There are articles, sidebars, small color photos of people and products, and easily grasped tables and graphs of data on environmental performance. Nothing about it seems like hype. Rather, it is a clear-headed assessment of the environmental issues facing commercial transportation vehicles and a road map for Volvo's solutions to these issues. Volvo's expressed philosophy is pragmatic and environmentally sensitive. After the divestiture of Volvo Car Corporation overall group goals had not been formulated, but those of the individual businesses are stated and progress toward them openly assessed.

The previous group goals included one that stated, "75 percent of all Volvo employees shall be satisfied with the manner in which Volvo is managing its environmental responsibilities." But despite its strong external environmental reputation, Volvo had only achieved 61 percent employee satisfaction with its environmental management in 1998. I know of no other company that has suggested this as a goal, and it is certainly an ambitious one—you cannot fool the employees. It remains to be seen if the new company will adopt it. The business-specific goals, mostly already met, have primarily to do with achieving known regulatory requirements ahead of schedule.

Volvo Car Corporation: Environmental Product Declarations—*Focus on the Product Rather Than on the Company*

After Volvo sold its car corporation to Ford in early 1999, it suddenly made little sense for the car operations to prepare a corporate environmental statement. Instead Volvo decided to produce environmental product declarations (EPDs) for specific car models, full of customer-oriented information about the environmental impacts of cars throughout their lifecycles, from cradle to grave. Volvo's intent is to develop and report information that will allow direct comparison of the environmental impacts of all their car models, and, if other manufacturers follow suit, with all car models everywhere.

The EPD for the Volvo S40/V40 1.9T North American models is packed with data summarized in a single spider web plot that Volvo hopes will become a standardized way of comparing the environmental impacts of different cars in a single glance. Confining the information to a single plot stringently limits the number of variables that can be displayed, and the ones chosen are strictly environmental:

- Percent of Volvo manufacturing facilities involved in the production of the car with a certified environmental management system

- Percent of supplier companies with a certified environmental management system

- Percent of dealerships with a certified environmental management system

- Energy used to manufacture one car (100 minus the percent of 18,000 MJ used)

- Materials used to manufacture one car (percent of raw materials, by weight, not becoming waste)

- Solvent emissions occurring during manufacture of one car (100 minus the percent of 30 kg emitted)

- Percent of legally allowed emissions released from the tailpipe during driving (California Code of Regulations, Title 13 Motor Vehicle, 50,000 miles)

- Percent of legally allowed gasoline evaporation from the car (California Code of Regulations, Title 13 Motor Vehicle, 2-day diurnal test)

- Percent of CO_2 emissions of the least-efficient 1997 Volvo variant (283 g/km)

- Percent of maximum potential use of recycled plastics

- Percent of plastic components labeled with chemical composition (to facilitate recycling)

- Completeness of dismantling handbook and hazardous materials phaseout plan

This is a small percentage of the topics suggested in any of the sustainability guidance documents, and to display them on the same graph, they had to be converted to percentages—so Volvo had to pick rather arbitrary best and worst case limits for many of them. I suspect that both the limited number of topics and the arbitrariness of the scales will decrease the chances of other manufacturers using identical standards, and therefore decrease the possibility of direct comparison of cars from different companies. It seems to me a better decision would have been to use Canon's approach, leaving the number of variables open-ended and using absolute or ratio values rather than percentages wherever it made sense.

Whatever shortcomings this report has, the idea of focusing on the environmental attributes of individual products remains appealing because it may be the most rational way to use environmental data to ascertain corporate intent and to encourage corporate responsibility. The newest facilities and the most recent initiatives are those that will speak for the current leadership's commitment to sustainability. Corporate environmental initiatives usually begin at individual facilities, often associated with a particular product line. If these initiatives are rewarded, either by kudos—internal or external—or by financial success, then they are likely to spread. If they are not, and they begin to look like unjustified costs, then they are likely to be terminated.

WEB-BASED REPORTS

It has become commonplace to put Adobe Acrobat PDF files of printed environmental or sustainability reports on the Web. Sometimes this works well, but often not. It works well if the printed documents have been designed both with online viewing and printing in mind. Usually, however, the graphics used in printed reports are not very amenable to printing on a standard computer printer, and page layouts often require two side-by-side pages to be decipherable. Some companies solve this by having separate versions of the same information, one in PDF format (since they have the electronic files of the printed documents anyway), and one in the HTML format of Web pages. This is usually an improvement, but often still kludgey.

Other companies have never had printed reports or have switched from printed ones to Web-based ones. This saves money, allows instant updating, and generally makes life easier for the company.

Lucent, for example, produced what appear to have been printed reports in 1996, 1997, 1998, and 1999 (although I have only the downloaded PDFs from their Web site). In 2000 they switched to a strictly Web-based HTML format. Their previous PDF format documents were designed to print well from a computer printer and once printed were good standalone documents. Their 2000 Annual Report, although the content is similar, is more a collection of Web pages with frames which, although they look good on a large high-resolution screen, print out as narrow columns of text surrounded by white space and strike me as significantly less accessible than the previous PDF documents.

Apple Computer's strictly HTML Web-based environmental site is also a full environmental report that takes some doing to navigate through, but prints out significantly better than the Lucent site.

DaimlerChrysler produces a printed report, but the Web-based PDF is formatted perfectly for American 8.5 × 11 inch printing and so is almost as easy to use in computer-printed format as their printed report.

ExxonMobil's 2001 Safety, Health, and Environment Progress Report on the Web is in HTML format, loads and navigates effortlessly, and looks like a facsimile of a printed report, but it is not obvious that a printed report exists. This Web site makes almost no use of hyperlinks to drill down deeper, and is therefore simple and straightforward: unlike many Web-based reports it does not leave you with the feeling that there is material hidden somewhere that you have yet to discover.

Almost all of the reports cited in this book are available both in printed form and on the Web. Although the information is the same, or even more detailed on the Web, and trees, printing costs, postage, and transportation impacts have been saved, the effects are just not comparable. Well-designed reports printed and bound on high-quality paper—ideally non-glossy, recycled, and printed with soy inks—carry the message much more strongly, at least for me, than do Web sites.

CONCLUSIONS

The reports reviewed here are quite different from one another, ranging from a few pages to nearly 200 pages. Some draw you in and make you want to read (and believe) them; others take a fair bit of commitment even to open the cover, much less read with any attention. Some are full of data; others are full of anecdotes. Some are quite formal; others read like magazines and sound bites. Some do a much better job than others at explaining their company's environmental or sustainability performance, but few make a serious attempt to compare their performance to that of the competition; they leave that to the analysts. And though it may seem that style should take a distant second place to substance in matters as weighty as these, no one is required to read these reports, and if they are not attractive, no one will.

After reading hundreds of these reports, both on the Web and in printed form, I advise that you do a printed version and get it into the hands of as many stakeholders as you can for it to be maximally effective. But you still have to put it on the Web because that is where most stakeholders will see it first. Make the Web version easily navigable and printer-friendly.

Ironically, the most easily navigable reports on the Web seem to me to be PDFs of the printed reports. Extensive use of hyperlinks works extremely well for browsing catalogs and placing orders, but for a report it leaves the reader with a fragmented vision of what is being offered and very little sense of the completeness of the coverage.

The remainder of this book addresses issues of both style and substance with the intent of giving you all the information you need to produce a highly effective environmental or sustainability report. Nonetheless, it is important to examine as many existing reports as you can, both in print and on the Web. This art form is evolving rapidly and every new report seems to reflect new—and often better—ideas about what an environmental or sustainability report should be.

II

Ten Rules for Writing Highly Effective Environmental and Sustainability Reports

Part 2 comprises 10 rules for effective report writing. Each rule corresponds to one of the ten topics that should be included in every environmental and sustainability report. A description of each rule is followed by excellent (or sometimes not-so-excellent) examples from the reports of large corporations.

6

Company Profile

This is your opportunity to let the reader know what your company is all about and to set the stage for a real understanding of the issues you face, the amount of effort you are expending to resolve them, and your success at doing so. You should describe products, services, brands, and markets, as well as your divisions and facilities. Whether you are writing an environmental or sustainability report, you should also summarize your company's financial condition, and your health and safety record. Finally, you should provide a knowledgeable contact person.

RULE 1—DESCRIBE YOUR COMPANY IN A WAY THAT SETS THE STAGE FOR A DISCUSSION OF ENVIRONMENTAL AND SOCIAL CONSIDERATIONS

Companies, particularly manufacturing companies, are complex operations and very few people have an inkling of how most industry works. Every time I tour a factory or a refinery or a research laboratory or a waste treatment facility or a power plant I'm amazed at how much I didn't know about how that particular operation really functions, and what environmental and social issues are taking most of the management's time. I would guess that most people, including many with strong environmental and social opinions about how industry operates, have visited very few industrial operations. Things that seem completely obvious to anyone on the inside are completely mysterious to people on the outside, and this ignorance more often leads to suspicions of corporate misbehavior than to a sanguine belief that all is well. Your environmental or sustainability report is directed at people who want to know what your company does and how it operates. This is an opportunity to tell them.

Describe Your Products, Services, Brands, and Markets

The first thing most people don't know about your company is all the products and services you offer. Why not? Because most companies never advertise their entire range of products, and most consumers are interested in specific products, not the entire range of corporate activities. Stakeholders reading this report are likely to be different. They want to know what you produce and the environmental and social consequences of producing it. One approach, nicely done by a few companies in the pharmaceutical sector, is to devote a page or so to listing products or kinds of products.

The Abbott Laboratories 1999 Environmental Health and Safety Report does a very nice job of displaying its products in a two-page spread with some small photographs of the best-known products in several of its divisions. Only a small selection is displayed, but you get a sense of the range of products Abbott offers.

The Bristol-Myers Squibb 2001 Sustainability Progress Report does the same thing by product category in about half a page: medicines, nutritionals, medical devices, and beauty care products, and its consumer brands along with a postage stamp–sized picture of over-the-counter (and maybe prescription—the picture is too small to tell) pharmaceuticals.

Pfizer, another pharmaceutical giant, in its 1999 Environmental Health and Safety Report lists its major products on a single page illustrated with a pie graph of 1998 revenue mix. I think a better illustration would have been some little pictures of Viagra, Barbasol shave cream, and Visine eye drops.

Three Japanese consumer electronics companies are even more impressive in illustrating their products, but instead of putting the information up front in a separate section, they spread product information throughout their reports, and use it to illustrate all of their different environmental initiatives.

Mitsubishi Electric, in their 2001 Environmental Sustainability Report has little diagrams and photographs of products and processes on nearly every page. This approach transmits a very high density of information in an extremely painless way: just idly browsing through the report almost automatically makes one an expert on Mitsubishi's product mix, and even if you don't go to the trouble of deciphering the diagrams, they clearly contain real information that you automatically assume reflects Mitsubishi's environmental excellence.

Toshiba's and Sony's 2001 environmental reports are based on the same model. They are crammed to the gills with little pictures of products and diagrams of processes, and you cannot leaf through them without coming away with the sense that not only do these companies talk the talk, they walk the walk. The reports seem to be permeated with a sense that even the tiniest changes in products and processes that might help the environment are worth making and have been promptly implemented as soon as they were conceived. The effect on me is to favor these products in the marketplace.

The focus on environmental characteristics of products is not restricted to consumer products. Bosch devotes more than a third of its 1998 environmental report to a sector-by-sector product rundown, some of which are parts that go into other companies' cars or industrial machines and electro-hydraulic adjustment drives for wind turbines. Even though no consumer is likely to purchase a car because it has Bosch parts, or electricity specifically because it came from a Bosch-hydraulically-adjusted wind turbine, the manufacturers of these products might be influenced by Bosch's attention to detail, as might a range of other stakeholders.

It is certainly helpful to the reader to make your products known, and a very effective way to do this is to use the products and their manufacturing processes to illustrate environmental and social initiatives throughout a report.

Describe Your Divisions, Facilities, and Activities

A fundamental aspect of understanding a company is knowing where it operates. The simplest, and I think best, approach is a map, but maps are underutilized.

The electric utilities sector is among the most facility-intensive of industries, and most facilities have substantial potential environmental impacts that the companies spend millions of dollars minimizing and mitigating. Many of these impacts are site-specific: the specific location of the facilities is what determines what fish populations, recreational opportunities, and local air qualities are impacted. Among the 19 largest utilities with environmental reports, however, only 5 provide any sort of facilities map. These include RWE in Germany, TXU in Texas, Kansai in Japan, FPL in Florida, and AEP in the American Midwest. The environmental reports of

Centrica, Chubu, DTE Energy, Dominion, Duke, EDF, Entergy, First Energy, Kyushu, Northeast Utilities, PG&E, Reliant, Tepco, and Tohoku have no maps at all, or in one case, just a simple one showing the location of the headquarters.

Industrial forests are even more land-intensive, and have immense consequences for the preexisting ecology. Any realistic environmental assessment of the industrial forestry practiced by the forest and paper products industries must be map-based. Nevertheless, none of the largest forestry products corporations provides a map of their forests in their environmental literature. Not Boise Cascade, Georgia-Pacific, International Paper, Kimberly-Clark, Louisiana Pacific, Mead, Oji Paper, Stora Enso, or Weyerhauser, although Kimberly-Clark Europe and Oji Paper do have maps of the locations of their paper mills.

The same thing is true for the chemical industry, although the Asahi Kasei Group has a nice map of its offices and plants and Henkel has maps of the continents accompanied by a list of the cities in those continents where it has plants. BASF has a postage stamp–sized map of the world with large dots showing the locations of only its emergency response facilities. The other large chemical manufacturers including Akzo Nobel, Bayer, Dow, DuPont, ICI, Norsk Hydro, PPG, and Rohm & Hass have no maps at all.

Why so few maps? Maybe creating maps is beyond the capabilities of the graphic designers doing the reports, but that seems unlikely. Many more companies list the locations of their facilities than map them, so it is not entirely a matter of trying to keep readers in the dark. My advice is use a map. Everyone can read them, they transmit the extent of your operations in a single glance, and they can be attractive graphically. While you are at it, be sure that the different corporate divisions are marked on the map. There are some good examples of reports utilizing maps, but not many.

The Toyota North American Manufacturing 2000 Environmental Report has a nice map of North America showing where its manufacturing facilities are, the number of employees at each site, the kinds and volume of products (cast aluminum parts, catalytic converters, steering columns, engines, and the like) and numbers of cars by brand (Avalon, Camry, Corolla, Sequoia, and so on) produced at each site.

The RWE One Group Multi Utilities 2000 Environmental Report's map of power plant sites in Germany identifies the type of plant (fossil-fired, nuclear, hydroelectric, wind, and photovoltaic), and gives their net capacities in megawatts. Kansai goes even further, showing the type of fossil fuel (LNG, oil, blast gas), two capacities of transmission lines, switching stations, and major substations.

Texas Utilities (TXU) shows the locations of types of power plants, but not their capacity.

The Novartis 2000 Health, Safety, Environment Report has a series of five world maps that show the locations of its major sites by division (Pharmaceuticals, Generics, Consumer Health, CIBA Vision, Animal Health), the percent of each division's sales by region, and a list of the major products and brands each division produces.

The Bristol-Myers Squibb 2001 Sustainability Progress Report has a world map that labels countries (without showing the country boundaries) and lists the cities in which it has operations, but puts specific information about the operating facilities on a Web site noted beside the map. This has the distinct advantage for the company that facility information can be updated, but the disadvantage for the reader, at least in this Web site, that the information is not uniform across all facilities.

Matsushita Electric Works 2001 Environmental Report has a really nice drawing (shown in Figure 6.1) illustrating their business activities, as well as summarizing their environmental aspects. Plus they also have a series of maps showing the locations of all of their facilities and domestic (Japan) manufacturing plants.

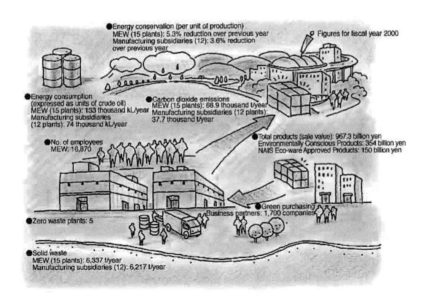

Figure 6.1   Drawing of the environmental aspects of Matsushita Electric Works.
Reproduced with permission from Matsushita Electric Works 2001 Environmental Report.

Of course, all of this information could be put into tables instead—most companies do it that way—but it does not seem to me to be as compelling in tabular form.

Describe Your Company's Financial Condition

This section should give enough information about the financial condition of the company to clarify its size and profitability and the way this is distributed geographically. For publicly held companies just a small subset of the annual financial report will do.

The Bristol-Myers Squibb 2001 Sustainability Progress Report summarizes its scale of activity nicely in a short paragraph:

> *Bristol-Myers Squibb is a publicly traded company, listed on the New York Stock Exchange (BMY). Our primary customers include governments, wholesale distributors, and major retail establishments. Total company revenue, including discontinued operations, was $21.3 billion in 2000, with about 34 percent of our sales outside the U.S. Our medicines Pravachol (pravastatin sodium), Glucophage (metformin) and Taxol (paclitaxel) lead the list of 31 product lines in our key businesses with annual global sales of more than $100 million each. In 2000, net earnings increased 13 percent over 1999. Companywide spending on research and development exceeded $2 billion in 2000.*

Another excellent approach, exemplified by the paper and forest products company, Mead in its 2000 Sustainable Development Report, is to have a full page devoted to key financial actions such as acquisitions, divestitures, and expansions, as well as summarized results from the financial report, perhaps with a few tables and graphs.

This is enough. If people want more they can look in the annual report.

What Is the Demographic Nature of Your Workforce?

It is not a bad idea to tell us something about your mix of employees. BMW in its 2001/2002 Sustainable Value Report says that:

> *BMW employees come from over 100 different nations. Around 12.4 percent of BMW AG workers are from countries outside of Germany. Consequently, the guidelines of the long-term BMW Group personnel policy focus on transcending national and cultural borders. For over 30 years, this principle has been a mainstay of BMW campaigns to prevent discrimination both inside*

and outside of the company. The main emphasis of this work is on cross-cultural learning designed to bring different nationalities and ethnic groups together.

Professor Joachim Milberg, BMW Group chairman of the board says "If we, as a company, are made to 'feel at home' everywhere in the world, then it must be important for us to ensure that everyone who comes to work for BMW is treated equally and respected as an individual." This kind of sentiment seems worthy of any company in search of excellence.

Ford Motor Company in its 2000 Corporate Citizenship Report says, "During 2000, we made important strides in creating a workforce at all levels that is broadly inclusive, and draws on the talents of all elements of the communities in which we do business."

BP, noting that only 9 percent of its senior management was female and only 11 percent non-Anglo-American, held a Global Women's Summit in November 2000 that ". . . served as a strategic planning forum focusing on diversity issues. Senior management, both male and female, high-potential female employees, and a wide range of women in their early careers from BP's global operations in 18 countries attended the conference." I think that revealing the problem of low diversity—which is endemic in most American and European corporations and is not likely to come as a surprise to any of the readership—and demonstrating a serious intent to do something about it says good things about BP. After reading this I suggested to my daughter that she should consider applying for a job at BP.

Anything you can say to make it clear that you are thinking about diversity and using it to your company's advantage is appropriate here.

How Is Your Health and Safety Record?

The responsibility for writing corporate environmental and sustainability reports has traditionally fallen to the same employees who were already in charge of health and safety. Consequently, most reports contain health and safety information, and "Health and Safety" is often part of the report title. Thus, health and safety information is the most widely reported of the nonenvironmental sustainability topics. You should include a statement of commitment to minimize exposure of employees to anything that might endanger them.

The Phelps Dodge Mining Company states in its environmental inventory "At Phelps Dodge, we believe that all injuries and occupational illnesses can be prevented, and that safety is a fundamental responsibility of each employee of the company." It then goes on to specify the responsibilities of management, facility managers, and all employees.

DuPont, in its 2000 Sustainable Growth Progress Report, says, "We believe that all injuries and occupational illnesses, as well as safety and environmental incidents, are preventable, and our goal for all of them is zero. We will promote off-the-job safety for our employees." It backs this up with an impressive graph comparing itself favorably to the rest of the chemical industry and to the manufacturing industry average. I believe that companies should make such comparisons whenever they have the data. The Pacific Sustainability Index (chapter 17) specifically gives credit for such comparisons.

You should also provide evidence of health and safety training if appropriate to your industry. Emergency response planning and strategies could be included here as well. In particular, you need to include information on numbers of accidents, lost workdays, and deaths, but also anything particularly relevant to your industry.

In its undated brochure entitled "Health, Environment, and Safety at Bayer," the U.S. division of this Swiss company observes that:

Bayer spends millions of dollars annually training, equipping, and qualifying our six HAZMAT teams. They respond to an average of 40 incidents each year on railways, highways, and waterways around the country. Some may involve Bayer products, but many do not. It's all part of Bayer's commitment to keeping our communities safe.

The chemical manufacturer ICI reports on work-related allergies and noise induced hearing loss on its web site.

Weyerhaeuser, in its 2001–2002 Citizenship Report talks about its:

. . . prevention-focused approach to help lower the risk of preventable diseases, such as hypertension, heart disease, substance abuse, and diabetes. For example, thanks to a concerted companywide effort, from 1998 through 2000, over 2,500 employees and family members enrolled in our Tobacco Cessation Program at 183 locations.

Have You Identified Someone Stakeholders Can Contact?

Bosch glued a removable postcard inside the back page of its 1998 environmental report that would get you annual reports or environmental reports in German or English, or information about a specific subject (if it would fit on a 2.5-inch line). They also provide the names and phone numbers of environmental specialists in each department and the phone and fax numbers and e-mail address of a single contact in Stuttgart. How could anything be simpler? If you want to know more about Bosch's environmental protection activities they certainly tell you who to contact.

A few companies are similarly accommodating—in the pharmaceutical sector, for example, Bristol-Myers Squibb gives the mailing and e-mail addresses of their senior director of EHS who will personally answer your questions, and AstraZeneca gives you the name and e-mail address of its reporting and communications (SHE) manager—but a more typical approach, used by Abott Laboratories, American Home Products Corporation, Eli Lilly, Johnson & Johnson, and Novartis is to provide only a postcard, although Novartis provides a fax number and generic health and safety division e-mail address and American Home Products gives you the name (but not the phone number or e-mail address) of the vice president for environmental affairs. Merck offers a phone and fax number for its Manufacturing Division public affairs group but no contact person; Aventis gives only a mailing address.

Why not provide the name of a knowledgeable contact person and an easy way to reach her? It is very aggravating to wander through a hierarchy of corporate assistants trying to reach someone who knows something. Anyone intent on making a suitable contact will probably eventually succeed, but why make it difficult? If companies the size of AstraZeneca, Bosch, and Bristol-Myers Squibb can make their senior environmental managers easily accessible, answering environmental queries cannot be that onerous or time-consuming. Easy access certainly enhances the appearance of corporate transparency and willingness to engage stakeholders.

RECOMMENDATIONS

Describe your company in enough detail that everyone comes away with a real understanding of what it does, where it operates, how many people it employs, and what your health and safety record is. Then identify one or more knowledgeable people whom the reader can contact. Make contact easy—provide telephone and fax numbers and a personal e-mail address. Sending an e-mail to info@company.com does not inspire confidence that the return will contain anything useful. In fact, I often get automated responses saying someone will get back to me, but often no one does.

7

Vision and Commitment

This section presents an opportunity for the highest corporate management to make it clear that the company takes environmental and social matters seriously and is committed to excellence in them as well as in other aspects of the business. The executive statement should be visionary, should commit to minimizing consumption of natural resources and environmental impacts, and should establish both a business and an ethical case for such behavior. It should also be clear about the impediments and challenges facing the company in this regard. This openness and vision should permeate the report.

RULE 2—PROJECT A SUSTAINED, VISIONARY, AND REALISTIC CONCERN FOR THE ENVIRONMENT AND FOR SOCIETY

Having a positive, progressive attitude is free, and is prerequisite to credibility. The more history of this attitude you can demonstrate, the greater your credibility. Most environmental and sustainability reports begin with statements by one or more high corporate executives; the Global Reporting Initiative (GRI) guidelines, for example, specify a statement by the CEO. These statements set the tone of the report, and convey a well-established and continuing commitment to improvement. And they often reference the corporate environmental policy. The body of the report then often takes up the executive's theme. Done well, the theme resonates throughout the report, being frequently reinforced and gaining credibility as it is developed.

This chapter first considers the differing effectiveness of opening statements of several corporate executives. Second, it takes a look at the wording of corporate environmental policies. Third, it turns to environmental and sustainability themes that are carried throughout reports.

The Best Executive Statements Are Visionary Rather Than Mechanistic

It is possible merely to tick off the points in the company's environmental policy, but the effect is wooden. The GRI 2000 guidelines, while claiming not to specify the content of the statement, suggest that it should include:

- Highlights of report content and commitment to targets

- Declaration of commitment to economic, environmental, and social goals by the organization's leadership

- Acknowledgment of successes and failures

- Performance against benchmarks, previous year's performance, targets, and industry sector norms

- Major challenges for the organization and its business sector in integrating responsibilities for financial performance with those for economic, environmental, and social performance, along with the implications of this on future business strategy

This list seems reasonable to me, but in execution it is capable of resulting in formulaic and uninspiring prose. There is not much point in having a detailed executive statement if it is impossible to get through—an all too common situation. I favor a briefer, more visionary approach, consigning the details to the body of the report.

Canon has a nice take on it—people everywhere should be prosperous and happy:

> *In the years to come, we will continue fostering environmental protection activities with the aim of contributing to world prosperity and the happiness of people everywhere.* (Fujio Mitarai, President and CEO, Canon 1999 Environmental Report)

P&G says something similar but it is not as convincing because it seems to be considering only the consumers of its products whereas Canon seems to be considering everyone:

> *We see sustainable development, or sustainability, as closely aligned with our Company's Statement of Purpose, to "... provide products and services of superior quality and value that improve the lives of the world's consumers."* (A. G. Lafley, President and Chief Executive and John E. Pepper, Chairman of the Board, P&G, 2000 Sustainability Report)

Volkswagen's environmental manager exudes enthusiasm toward environmental protection that is palpable when you visit the Wolfsburg headquarters:

> *At present, we are witnessing in many issues an exciting process on the environmental stage—the transition from a general environmental debate to practical activities designed to protect the environment.* (Horst Minte, Head of Environmental Affairs, Strategy and Business Processes, Volkswagen 1999/2000 Environmental Report)

Matsushita's president articulates his policy in an understated way, but when you come right down to it, true coexistence with the environment is what all companies should be striving for:

> *We have always believed that company management must recognize the importance of coexistence with the global environment.* (Yoichi Morishita, President, Matsushita Electric Group [National/Panasonic] 1999 Report)

Be Sure to Make a Business Case for Following Your Vision

Visionary statements are more believable if they openly discuss the business advantages of adopting them, but not many firms do. This is strange, because most companies are quite aggressive in cost cutting, and many cost-cutting measures such as using less energy, water, and materials, and producing less waste are also clearly good for the environment.

The Sony 2001 Environmental Report uses highly detailed environmental accounting to estimate that its environmental and social investments and expenses cost ¥28 million, but were offset by a savings of ¥19 million. Sony may not yet have made a profit on these investments, but they certainly achieved a large offset.

DuPont's 2000 Sustainable Growth Progress Report observes that:

During this period of substantial reduction of our environmental footprint, annual environmental costs, on a pre-tax basis, dropped from a high of $1 billion in 1993 to $560 million in 1999. And in an era of increasing oversight by regulatory agencies, environmental fines and penalties were at a 10-year low of $170,000 in 1999.

BMW has optimistic observations about its role in globalization:

The debate on globalization usually overlooks the positive role played by the European and North American companies with their stringent environmental protection standards. These companies exert enormous pressure to modernize on the production plants in those countries which have recently assumed a greater involvement in the global trading of cultural, scientific, and economic goods . . . [E]very company operating on the world market is, to a certain extent, an ambassador of its home country, its culture, and in this sense it also exports values such as democracy, history, education, and its understanding of environmental protection. (Carl-Peter Forster, Member of the Board of Management of BMWAG, BMW Group 1999/2000 Environmental Report)

Volkswagen's vision is that leadership in business also requires being a leader in sustainability issues:

Being a leading player in the global automotive industry is today inextricably linked with being a leading player in terms of environmental protection, sustainability, and the conservation of the natural foundations of life. (Klaus Volkert, Chairman of the General and Group Works Council of Volkswagen AG, Volkswagen 1999/2000 Environmental Report)

Toyota's president and its environmental officer, in Toyota's 2001 North America Environmental Report, express similar sentiments less poetically but with the same sensibility:

Toyota believes that if a corporation is to advance in step with society, three things are necessary: first, it must steadily reduce the environmental impact resulting from its corporate activities; second, it must provide wide disclosure to reveal the environmental impact of its activities and the status of measures it is taking to reduce that impact; and third, it must form alliances and cooperate with other industries and with groups involved in environmental preservation. (Hiroshi Okuda, President, Toyota Motor

Corporation, and Shinichi Kato, Senior Managing Director in Charge of Environmental Issues)

The giant Scandinavian forest products company Stora Enso, in its 1999 Environmental Report, relates its philosophy to the demands of consumers and other stakeholders and their ability to communicate with one another:

> *More and more stakeholders want to ascertain that market acceptance of the company's products is based on sustainable codes of conduct. Credibility is a precious asset in today's society, characterized as it is by the rapid flow of information.* (Björn Hägglund, Chairman of the Stora Enso Environment Committee)

The Volvo 1999 Environmental Report pragmatically notes that higher gas mileage sells trucks:

> *The products and services which we offer must help to reinforce our customers' competitiveness and profitability. . . . In many instances, environmental care and the commercial interests of our customers go hand in hand, fuel consumption being one example. As a result, the development of vehicles and engines affording lower fuel consumption and lower greenhouse gas emissions is a high Volvo priority.* (Leif Johansson, President of AB Volvo and CEO)

I recommend making it clear that some of your firm's environmental and social initiatives have a clear business purpose in addition to any ethical considerations. It makes you seem astute to be doing well by doing good.

Include a Commitment to Minimize Consumption

Along the same lines, it makes sense to make a commitment to reduce consumption of energy, water, materials, packaging, and anything else that costs money and harms the environment. Any reduction is good for the environment—you do not have to set aggressive goals because of the commitment—and any improvement is better than nothing. At least you are moving in the right direction.

The Sony 2001 Environmental Report puts it concisely:

> *The Earth has limited resources, including raw materials, energy, and water, that must be used and reused efficiently. Sony is pursuing a continuous increase of resource productivity in its business processes and the reduced use of virgin materials, energy, and water whenever possible. Sony is consequently promoting the reuse and recycling of resources.*

Canon, in its 2001 Environmental Report puts forward the motto "maximizing resource efficiency through complete elimination of wasteful practices" which is precisely what we want them to do, but the explicit approach spelled out by Sony seems more concrete.

Include a Commitment to Minimize Environmental and Social Impacts

DuPont, in its compact, 8-page Sustainable Growth 2000 Progress Report, makes a very strong statement of commitment that could serve as a model for any company. The one-page statement has many parts; here are two, one on environmental impacts of new facilities, and a second on waste generation and emissions.

On new facilities:

We will assess the environmental impact of each facility we propose to construct and will design, build, operate and maintain all our facilities and transportation equipment so they are safe and acceptable to local communities and protect the environment.

On the goal of zero waste and emissions:

We will drive toward zero waste generation at the source. Materials will be reused and recycled to minimize the need for treatment or disposal and to conserve resources. Where waste is generated, it will be handled and disposed of safely and responsibly. We will drive toward zero emissions, giving priority to those that may present the greatest potential risk to health or the environment.

These are not numerical goals; they are simply statements of how DuPont would like to be operating if it could. If your company holds values such as these, it ought to make similarly strong statements even if the numerical results that are likely to occur in the short term are far from the ultimate commitment.

Be Open about Impediments and Challenges

At one time, not so long ago, companies were loath to admit to having any negative environmental or social impacts at all. These days leading companies are more likely to assume they have environmental and social impacts, be willing to discuss them, and to make a commitment to minimizing them. Most statements of commitment by executives, however, fail to discuss any difficulties they expect to encounter. Owning up to the problems associated with achieving one's commitments is not a sign of weakness. Rather it increases the perception that you may actually plan to live up to the commitments, even though they may seem optimistic.

Dow Chemical Company's Public Report—2000 Results articulates a " 'Vision of Zero'—no harm to the environment, to our people or to any of the people that we 'touch' in the value chain" which it openly admits to being an ". . . ambitious and extremely difficult objective . . . " It goes on to admit that "Candor and full disclosure in a Public Report require that we present commentary not only on positive developments but also on the more troubling aspects of social responsibility that confront the company," in this case a workforce reduction and improper use of the company's e-mail by employees. This is a new degree of corporate openness from previous business as usual and strengthens, I think, Dow's credibility.

Continue the Broad Sustainability Themes Throughout the Report

The best way to convey corporate environmental and sustainability ethics is to make sure they permeate the report. This argues for a report that is long enough to allow revisiting the theme in different settings. In fact, the reports that do it best are very long ones—those of the German automobile manufacturers BMW (175 pages) and Volkswagen (105 pages) that are described in chapter 5.

RECOMMENDATIONS

The best corporate environmental and sustainability reports strike a tone of genuine long-standing commitment and responsibility, and illustrate it with plenty of examples. If your company has such a history, your environmental or sustainability report is the place to showcase it and the longer and deeper the history, the better. The best statements of corporate responsibility have a visionary quality to them. The lesser ones seem to carry a subtext of being dragged into the process when all the company wanted to do was keep its eye on the ball and make money. It is important not to project the latter viewpoint, even if some employees can't help feeling that way and don't care who knows.

If, on the other hand, your company has just become aware of the importance of environmental and sustainability values and activities, it can be quite effective to own up to that fact as long as you can honestly and convincingly show that you are now committed. Most small and medium-size businesses have felt little need to embrace these issues—the large transnational companies are leading the way and are only now beginning to impose their standards on the supply chain. But for small and medium-size companies, now is certainly the right time to jump on board. There is a window of opportunity to distinguish yourself from other suppliers, and large companies would prefer to deal with suppliers who hold their own values and espouse them publicly.

8

Stakeholders

The purpose of an environmental or sustainability report is to inform—and hopefully communicate with—stakeholders. Reports are likely to be better focused if the stakeholders for whom the report is intended are identified in the report and are kept in mind during the writing of it. The report also offers an opportunity to describe feedback from stakeholders, and to let them know what you are doing about that feedback.

RULE 3—IDENTIFY AND DESCRIBE THE ENVIRONMENTAL AND SOCIAL STAKEHOLDERS THAT ARE IMPORTANT TO YOUR COMPANY

Stakeholders are the people and institutions that have a stake in your company. Some or all of them are the intended readers of your environmental or sustainability report. They include:

- Customers

- Internal company management

- Nonmanagement employees

- Contractors and suppliers

- Competitors and trade organizations

- Shareholders and institutional investors

- Financial analysts and mutual fund specialists

- Lending institutions

- Insurers

- Legislators and regulators

- Environmental groups and nongovernmental organizations with social and environmental agendas

- Local communities in the vicinity of your facilities

And the list could go on.

To a large extent the same document can meet most of their needs, but it makes sense to decide if the good will of some of these groups merits special treatment. Furthermore, since your company is probably already interacting with organizations in most of these categories, your environmental or sustainability report is a good place to report on these interactions and how they influence your operations. These sections need not be long. It is, or certainly should be, a normal part of corporate management to identify significant stakeholders, communicate with them, and make use of the resulting information. It is good to have a plan for stakeholder communication and to implement it. The act of planning to report on these interactions is likely to encourage more communication and interaction, and will increase corporate transparency. That seems to me a good thing as long as it does not waste the company's time. Hence, not all the potential stakeholders should be singled out for special interaction. Those that may have a significant effect on company success, however, belong here.

Identifying, Describing, and Consulting Stakeholders, Some Examples from Corporate Reports

There are various ways that companies identify and consult with stakeholders. To some extent they are dependent on the type of facilities the company has. If the manufacturing processes are interesting and safe, one way is to invite interested parties inside the company.

Mead, in its 2000 Sustainable Development Report says it engages many interested people through public tours of its paper mills, in its community advisory panels, and in its annual Paper Knowledge Seminar. That is to say, it makes its facilities and some of its knowledge available to the public and to specifically interested parties and attracts input that way. My own experience is that being invited inside a company, particularly to view its manufacturing operations, creates a positive feeling toward the company that is hard to achieve any other way.

The ABB Group in its 2000 Annual Sustainability Report notes, "With 97 percent of all ABB manufacturing and service sites having implemented ISO 14001, our own house is in good order. We will now focus more on our suppliers' environmental performance . . . [p]reference will be given to suppliers that have implemented environmental management programs and, in particular, to those that are ISO 14001 certified."

BASF, the largest chemical company in the world, says in its 2000 Environment, Safety, Health report "What goes on inside BASF? Many people who live and work near our sites ask themselves this question. We have established Community Advisory Panels at many sites with the aim of providing satisfactory answers and increasing our neighbors' trust and confidence in us." BASF representatives, in a type of business that is less than ideal for public tours, regularly meet with stakeholders including schools, environmental associations, and others.

The Danone Group (1999 Social Responsibility Report) engaged a sociologist from the French National Center for Scientific Research to interview employees in its Mexican fresh products subsidiary to develop "A social development model . . . whose roots had become firmly embedded in Mexican culture."

NKK, the Japanese steelmaker produced its 2001 Environmental Report after receiving the highest rating of AAA from the environmental-leaning stock analysis firm Innovest. This high rating made NKK want to ". . . promote a wider understanding of NKK's efforts to be an environmentally responsible citizen." Sometimes stakeholders unexpectedly approach you with good news.

Volkswagen also was singled out by external analysts, and devotes a page in its 1999/2000 Environmental Report to its high ratings from Zurich-based Sustainability Asset Management (allied with Dow Jones as Dow Jones/SAM), and the independent Munich ratings agency "ökom."

The Korean steel company POSCO, in its 2001 Environmental Progress Report notes that ". . . the company is involved in activities with research centers, environment-related academic societies and nongovernment organizations at home and abroad" as well as making technological exchanges with competing steelmakers worldwide and as a member of the environmental subcommittees of the International Iron and Steel Institute, International Stainless Steel Forum, and Southeast Asia Steel Association. It identifies its stakeholders through a broad variety of contacts.

Phillips Petroleum, in its 1998 Health, Environmental, and Safety Report discusses its Citizen Advisory Panels, which it has at its largest operating facilities as a part of its Community Awareness and Emergency Response initiative.

Total Fina Elf, in its 2000 Environment and Safety Report observes that "The financial community now scrutinizes the environmental performance of listed firms closely, and our task is to supply the desired information in response to that demand."

Information Obtained from Consultation with Stakeholders and Its Use by the Company

Interaction with stakeholders should be a two-way street, and probably generally is. The public learns more about the company and the company finds out how to be a better neighbor, interaction with trade organizations and technical exchanges with colleagues result in better products, listening to customers improves service, listening to environmental groups changes company practices, meeting with regulators results in better performance and less subsequent regulation.

On one of its EHS Focus Web pages, GE credits a partnership between GE employees, managers, and federal regulators for the company's success in the U.S. OSHA voluntary protection program.

Mostly, however, in their environmental and sustainability reports companies dwell on what they are doing for their communities rather than on how they are responding to community input. Illustrating responsiveness would be valuable.

RECOMMENDATIONS

Your environmental or sustainability report is the appropriate place to document and discuss interactions with any of your stakeholders concerning environmental and social matters. It is valuable to report your initiatives in setting up meetings, giving tours, and the like, but it is even more valuable if you describe what information you are getting back, and how you are using and responding to it. After all, a major purpose of engaging stakeholders is to find out how to meet their needs. Most stakeholders think far more highly of a company that listens and modifies its behavior appropriately than of one that only promulgates its own positions.

9

Policies and Management Systems

You should have and include in your report a formal corporate environmental, or environmental/health/safety (EHS) policy, which, as sustainability issues take hold, should begin to include social policy elements as well. You should also describe enough of your EHS management organization so that its importance in the company is evident, and you should identify—and if necessary, describe—your environmental management system. It is also valuable to identify and describe any voluntary regulations and standards of conduct to which you subscribe, any trade or professional organizations to which the company belongs, and any voluntary certifications.

RULE 4—DESCRIBE THE POLICIES, SYSTEMS, AND ORGANIZATIONAL STRUCTURE YOU USE TO MANAGE ENVIRONMENTAL AND SOCIAL ISSUES

Environmental Policy Statement

Corporate environmental policies are generally simple and brief—as policies should be—leaving the details to concrete statements of goals.

Hewlett-Packard's environmental policy from their Web site dated March 7, 2000, is a 128-word model of brevity and clarity:

Design our products and services to be safe to use, to minimize use of hazardous materials, energy and other resources, and to enable recycling or reuse.

Conduct our operations in a manner that prevents pollution, conserves resources, and proactively addresses past environmental contamination.

Integrate environmental management into our business and decision-making processes, regularly measure our performance, and practice continual improvement.

Ensure our products and operations comply with applicable environmental regulations and requirements.

Provide clear and candid environmental information about our products, services, and operations to customers, shareholders, employees, government agencies, and the public.

Inform suppliers of our environmental requirements and encourage them to adopt sound environmental management practices.

Foster environmental responsibility among our employees.

Contribute constructively to environmental public policy.

Apple Computer's policy,* from its Web site on 12/11/2001, is a little longer at 173 words, but still a model of simplicity:

Meet or exceed all applicable environmental, health, and safety requirements and verify our performance through audits.

Where laws and regulations do not reflect best management practices, we will adopt our own environmental, health, and safety standards to protect human health and the environment.

Support and promote sound scientific principles and fiscally responsible public policy that enhance environmental quality and health and safety.

Advocate the adoption of prudent environmental, health, and safety principles and practices by our contractors, vendors, and suppliers.

---

*From Apple Computer's Environmental, Health and Safety Policy, as posted on the World Wide Web at http://www.apple.com/about/environment/corporate/corporate.html , ©2002. Reprinted with permission of Apple Computer, Inc.

Communicate environmental, health, and safety policies and programs to Apple employees and stakeholders.

Design, manage, and operate our facilities to maximize safety, promote energy efficiency, and protect the environment.

Strive to create products that are safe in their intended use, conserve energy and materials, promote safety, and prevent pollution throughout the product lifecycle including design, manufacture, use, and end-of-life management.

Ensure that all employees are aware of their role and responsibility to fulfill and sustain Apple's environmental, health, and safety management systems and policy.

Apple does not produce an annual environmental report but has an excellent Web site that, as it points out, contains all the information that would be in a report if they produced one. In effect, it does produce one—it just doesn't print it. For computer companies, in particular, this seems appropriate. Most of Apple's stakeholders have no trouble visiting the site on the Web.

Matsushita's 1999 Environmental Report has a more detailed environmental policy than Apple's, but prefaces it with a persuasive environmental statement:

Fully aware that humankind has a responsibility to respect and preserve the delicate balance of nature, we at Matsushita acknowledge our obligation to maintain and nurture the ecology of this planet. Accordingly, we pledge ourselves to the prudent, sustainable use of the earth's resources and the protection of the natural environment, while we strive to fulfill our corporate mission of contributing to enhanced prosperity for all.

Most environmental policies are much longer than any of these and get bogged down in details. Short and crisp with a clear sense of vision is best. Guidelines for implementing the policy can be as long as needed, but do not need to find their way into the environmental report.

Social Policy Statement

Some companies producing formal sustainability reports have also adopted social policies. ABB was one of the first companies to publish a formal social policy, which it did in its ABB Group 2000 Annual Sustainability Report:

1. ABB in society. *To contribute within the scope of our capabilities to improving economic, environmental, and social conditions through open dialogue with stakeholders and through active participation in common efforts.*

2. Human rights. *To support and respect the protection of internationally proclaimed human rights.*

3. Children and young workers. *To ensure that minors are properly protected; and as a fundamental principle, not to employ children or support the use of child labor, except as part of government-approved youth training schemes (such as work-experience programs).*

4. Freedom of engagement. *To require that all employees enter into employment with the company of their own free will; and not to apply any coercion when engaging employees or support any form of forced or compulsory labor.*

5. Health and safety. *To provide a safe and healthy working environment at all sites and facilities and to take adequate steps to prevent accidents and injury to health arising out of the course of work by minimizing, so far as is reasonably practicable, the causes of hazards inherent in the working environment.*

6. Employee consultation and communication. *To facilitate regular consultation with all employees to address areas of concern. To respect the right of all personnel to form and join trade unions of their choice and to bargain collectively.*

   To ensure that representatives of personnel are not the subject of discrimination and that such representatives have access to their members in the workplace.

   To make sure, in any case of major layoffs, that a social benefits and guidance plan is in place, and already known to employees or their official representatives.

7. Equality of opportunity. *To offer equality of opportunity to all employees and not to engage in or support discrimination in hiring, compensation, access to training, promotion, termination, or retirement based on ethnic and national origin, caste, religion, disability, sex, age, sexual orientation, union membership, or political affiliation.*

8. Mobbing and disciplinary practices. *To counteract the use of mental or physical coercion, verbal abuse, or corporal/hard-labor punishment; and not to allow behavior, including gestures, language, and physical contact, that is sexual, coercive, threatening, abusive, or exploitative.*

> *To develop and maintain equitable procedures to deal with employee grievances, and disciplinary practices.*

9. Working hours. *To comply with applicable laws and industry standards on working hours, including overtime.*

10. Compensation. *To ensure that wages paid meet or exceed the legal or industry minimum standards and are always sufficient to meet basic needs of personnel and to provide some discretionary income.*

    To ensure that wage and benefits composition are detailed clearly and regularly for workers, and that compensation is rendered in full compliance with all applicable laws and in a manner convenient to workers.

    To ensure that labor-only contracting arrangements and false apprenticeship schemes are not used to avoid fulfilling ABB's obligations under applicable laws pertaining to labor and social security legislation and regulations.

11. Suppliers. *To establish and maintain appropriate procedures to evaluate and select major suppliers and subcontractors on their ability to meet the requirements of ABB's social policy and principles and to maintain reasonable evidence that these requirements are continuing to be met.*

12. Community involvement. *To promote and participate in community engagement activities that actively foster economic, environmental, social, and educational development, as part of ABB's commitment to the communities where it operates.*

13. Business ethics. *To uphold the highest standards in business ethics and integrity and to support efforts of national and international authorities to establish and enforce high ethical standards for all businesses.*

Environmental and Social Organization

There are many possible approaches to describing a company's environmental management organization. Many companies say almost nothing about it except to identify the person in charge.

Duke Energy, in its 2000 Progress Review: Environment, Health and Safety in Action report, for example, contents itself with a large picture of one of its senior resource managers holding a topographic map.

BASF, in its 2000 Environment, Safety, Health report, gives you a picture of its five top environmental managers plus an organization chart showing that they report to the board member responsible for the Responsible Care program.

Sony, in its 2001 Environmental Report, provides an organization chart indicating the four business units that have environmental offices, and the regional environmental conservation committees, which report to the corporate conservation committee, but mentions nothing about the makeup of these organizations or their day-to-day activities. It does, however indicate that the regional committees convene two to four times a year.

DaimlerChrysler, in its 2001 Environmental Report provides something more concrete, allowing you to infer its organization at the managerial level by listing the names, titles, divisions, addresses, telephone and fax numbers of 45 environmental managers spread throughout the company.

Matsushita's 2001 Environment Report has a nice organization chart that lists types of functional units in the company (such as special subcommittees, divisional companies, plants, sales offices) and describes what each of them does to promote environmental activities. This chart gives a much more concrete view of the locations of environmental activities than found in most reports.

Organization charts are potentially quite useful to the reader who wants to understand internal company processes, but most of the ones presented in corporate environmental and sustainability reports are too general or at too high a management level to convey much information. DaimlerChrysler provides information that would be highly useful to anyone wanting to make direct contact, but could have enhanced it with an organization chart showing the relationships between the 45 managers. If you don't mind having your environmental and health and safety managers talking to the public, and you should encourage them to do so, then an organization chart that clearly identifies functional responsibilities and facility locations will quickly get the public to the correct person to answer questions.

Environmental and Social Management Systems

The promulgation of the ISO 14001 environmental management system standard in 1996 and its rapid adoption by the largest transnational companies has led many other companies to adopt it or to initiate the process of doing so. Many of those not seeking ISO 14001 certification *per se* have gotten their proprietary environmental management systems certified by a third-party auditor as being substantially equivalent to an ISO 14001 system.

One of the most aggressive companies with respect to sustainability reporting, Bristol-Myers Squibb, was one of the first companies to self-declare that their proprietary environmental management system meets or exceeds the requirements of ISO 14001. They contracted with an outside consultant to assess the corporate environment, health, and safety evaluation program, and the consultant concluded that the program was generally consistent with and in several cases exceeded expectations of established ISO 14001 criteria.

ExxonMobil also has its own proprietary management system; the Operations Integrity Management System (OIMS) that Lloyd's Register Quality Assurance audited using its ISO 14001 lead auditors. Lloyd's concluded it met the requirements of an ISO 14001 environmental management system, and in the ExxonMobil report, Meeting Environmental Expectations, 2001, a full page is devoted to describing the Lloyd's auditing process, another full page to a facsimile of the certificate Lloyd's issued, four more pages describing the 11 elements of the OIMS, and a full page table comparing the 11 elements to statements in ISO 14001. ExxonMobil wants to be sure that it convinces not only Lloyd's, but the reader, of OIMS's equivalence to ISO 14001.

Companies adopting the ISO 14001 standard itself, because it is so well known, need say little about it other than to document the facilities that are in compliance with it and to provide a schedule for achieving compliance in the remaining facilities.

It is worthwhile to relate your experience with ISO 14001. The ABB Group 2000 Annual Sustainability Report observes that, after six years of experience implementing ISO 14001 in over 500 facilities, implementation really does improve the company's environmental performance, usually due to a number of relatively small projects, and often results in cost savings. ABB also notes that implementation of ISO 14001 is also applicable to sales companies, installation companies, and full-service contracts at a customer's site.

There is no standardized social management system. Most companies seem to put the health and safety management into the environmental management system and the social management into the human relations department.

Voluntary Regulations and Standards of Conduct

There is a plethora of voluntary regulations and standards of conduct, many of which are developed by industrial trade organizations and are sector-specific. The most highly developed of these is the chemical manufacturing industry's Responsible Care program, and few chemical manufacturing companies fail to mention this program in their environmental or sustainability reports.

Similarly, many members of the American Forest and Paper Association have adopted the industry-initiated Sustainable Forestry Initiative whereas a variety of large retailers and wood products manufacturers, such as Home Depot, Lowe's Home Improvement Warehouse, and Andersen Windows support the NGO-derived Forest Stewardship Council.

At many of its U.S. facilities, ExxonMobil subscribes to the Occupational Safety and Health Administration (OSHA) Star program, a component of the agency's Voluntary Protection Program (VPP) to emphasize site safety.

International Paper has the greatest number (61) of business sites of any company in the U.S. certified by the federal and state OSHA VPP and all but one of them reaches VPP Star status.

Any voluntary regulations or standards of conduct subscribed to should certainly be included.

Voluntary Certifications

Some standards allow voluntary or third-party certification. The most obvious are the ISO 14001 standard and the SA8000 social accountability standard.

The U.S. Environmental Protection Agency (EPA) Green Lights and Energy Star programs are also widely subscribed to, but some programs are entirely internal like Matsushita's NAIS Eco-Ware Approved Products program. There are many industry-specific certifications as well—for example the ECO-OK or the Better Banana Project—subscribed to by Chiquita and other banana growers.

RECOMMENDATIONS

Your environmental policy should be prominent at the beginning of your report, and should be followed shortly thereafter by a description of your environmental and social management systems. An advantage of adopting ISO 14001 is that it requires little explanation—companies adopting proprietary environmental management systems often feel obligated to spend pages explaining how their systems are comparable to ISO 14001 and offering third-party testimonials. How much of your health, safety, and environmental organization you should reveal is primarily a function of how you want it to interact with readers of the report. You should certainly identify at least one knowledgeable contact person and provide several avenues of contact including telephone, fax, and e-mail, but you may also describe the overall organization and include an organization chart, either with names, or just with functional positions. Finally, any voluntary standards of conduct, membership in trade organizations, and voluntary certifications should be identified and described.

10

Aspects and Impacts

Nothing is more credible than openness and transparency, but most companies find it difficult to discuss problems and miss this opportunity. Secrecy is often foolish, especially with respect to industry-wide issues; your industry's critics know what the issues are and know what you could be doing about them, so you might as well be open. This is probably true for most of your company-specific issues as well.

RULE 5—DESCRIBE THE ENVIRONMENTAL AND SOCIAL ASPECTS AND IMPACTS FACED BY YOUR INDUSTRY AND YOUR COMPANY

The more open and forthcoming an environmental or sustainability report is about adverse environmental and social effects, the more believable it is. Reports loaded with news of environmental awards and community service but with little about potential and actual adverse effects read like public relations brochures and do little to establish credibility. On the other hand, reports that lay out the environmental and social issues facing a company and its industry, make a serious effort to assess the significance of the actual impacts, and demonstrate progress, however minimal, towards improvement, conjure a sense of high quality and involved management. It is clearly difficult for some companies to admit anything adverse—there are many environmental reports that avoid the real issues. But what these reports imply about their companies is the opposite of what is intended. They reveal a management unwilling to admit deficiencies in public, and imply an unwillingness to recognize and deal with environmental and social issues internally as well.

Ideally, a report should identify the potentially significant environmental and social issues characteristic of the industry and the company, explain how these were identified and how their significance is being assessed, and provide quantitative data that either shows improvement over time, or is accompanied by a commitment to improvement buttressed by a plan of action.

This chapter first defines environmental and social aspects and impacts, then discusses the meaning of significance as applied to them, and finally offers some examples of environmental and sustainability reports that do a good job of addressing aspects and impacts.

Aspects and Impacts

Environmental aspect is a term first brought to prominence, and perhaps first used, in the ISO 14000 family of environmental standards. It is intended to be a neutral term, inclusive of all ways in which a company and its operations could reasonably be expected to interact with the environment, including beneficial ways. It can be inferred that every company also has economic and social aspects—both adverse and beneficial ways in which it can influence the well-being of its financial stakeholders (investors, lenders, insurers) and the economy, and ways it can influence its social stakeholders (employees, customers, local communities) and society as a whole.

ISO 14001 defines an environmental impact as "Any change to the environment, whether adverse or beneficial wholly or partially resulting from an organization's activities, products, or services." Social impacts, like environmental impacts, are simply the social aspects that are realized—like environmental impacts, significant ones can be beneficial or adverse.

Identifying Environmental and Social Aspects

The Pacific Sustainability Index scoring sheet (appendix A) includes many possible aspects. State and federal environmental statutes, regulations, and guidelines are also good sources of information on how to identify environmental and social aspects and on how to assess their significance. The ISO 14000 standards and guidelines, particularly the ISO 14031 guidelines, address possible environmental aspects. The Social Accountability International SA8000 standard (Social Accountability International 1997) lists social aspects. Potential aspects can also be derived from environmental report scoring systems (Davis-Walling & Batterman 1997, Deloitte Touche Tohmatsu 1999, SustainAbility/UNEP 1996, SustainAbility/UNEP 1997, SustainAbility/UNEP 2000), sustainability reporting guidelines (GRI 2000), and a book by Marilyn Block (Block 1999).

Table 10.1 is a list of environmental aspects that might be associated with new projects, but relevant to existing facilities and operations as well. It is a condensation of appendix G of the Guidelines for Implementation of the California Environmental Quality Act (CEQA), the noncondensed form

Table 10.1 Potential environmental impacts condensed from appendix G of the Guidelines for Implementation of the California Environmental Quality Act* (California 2001). (Environmental aspects are potential environmental impacts.)

Aesthetics	Have a substantial adverse effect on a scenic vista
	Substantially damage scenic resources
	Substantially degrade the existing visual character or quality
	Be a source of substantial light or glare
Agriculture	Potentially convert prime or unique farmland to nonagricultural use
	Conflict with existing agricultural zoning
	Potentially influence conversion of farmland to nonagricultural use
Air Quality	Conflict with or obstruct implementation of an air quality plan
	Violate any air quality standard
	Contribute substantially to an existing or projected air quality violation
	Result in a cumulatively considerable net increase of any criteria pollutant for which the region is in non-attainment
	Expose sensitive receptors to substantial pollutant concentrations
	Create objectionable odors affecting a substantial number of people
Biological Resources	Have a substantial adverse effect on a sensitive or special status species
	Have a substantial adverse effect on any riparian habitat, wetlands, or other sensitive natural community
	Interfere substantially with the movement, corridors, or nursery sites of any native resident or migratory fish or wildlife species,
	Conflict with any local policies or ordinances protecting biological resources

*Modified to simplify and to generalize beyond new projects in California.

continued

Cultural Resources	Cause a substantial adverse change in the significance of a historical resource
	Cause a substantial adverse change in the significance of an archaeological resource
	Destroy a unique paleontological resource or site or unique geologic feature
	Disturb any human remains
Geology and Soils	Expose people or structures to substantial rupture of a known earthquake fault
	Expose people or structures to substantial strong seismic ground shaking
	Expose people or structures to substantial seismic-related ground failure
	Expose people or structures to substantial landslides
	Result in soil erosion or the loss of topsoil
	Be located on a geologic unit or soil that is unstable
	Be located on expansive soil creating substantial risks to life or property
Hazards and Hazardous Materials	Create a significant hazard to the public or environment through routine transport, use, or disposal of hazardous materials
	Create a significant hazard to the public or environment through reasonably foreseeable upset and accident conditions involving the release of hazardous materials into the environment
	Emit hazardous emissions or handle hazardous or acutely hazardous materials, substances, or waste within one-quarter mile of an existing or proposed school
	Be located on a hazardous materials site which would create a significant hazard to the public or the environment
	Be a safety hazard for people residing or working near an airport or airstrip
	Impair implementation of or physically interfere with an adopted emergency response or evacuation plan
	Expose people or structures to a significant risk of loss, injury or death involving wildland fires
Hydrology and Water Quality	Violate any water quality standards or waste discharge requirements
	Substantially deplete groundwater supplies or interfere with groundwater recharge
	Alter existing drainage pattern in a manner which would result in substantial erosion or siltation
	Alter existing drainage pattern in a manner which would result in substantial flooding
	Create or contribute runoff water which would exceed the capacity of existing or planned stormwater drainage systems or provide substantial additional sources of polluted runoff

continued

continued

Hydrology and Water Quality *(continued)*	Substantially degrade water quality
	Expose people or structures to significant risk of loss, injury, or death involving flooding
	Expose people or structures to significant risk of loss, injury, or death from inundation by seiche, tsunami, or mudflow
Land Use and Planning	Physically divide an established community
	Conflict with any applicable land use plan, policy, or regulation including habitat conservation and natural community conservation plans
Mineral Resources	Result in loss of availability of valuable or locally important known mineral resource
Noise	Exposure of persons to or generation of noise levels in excess of standards
	Exposure of persons to or generation of excessive groundborne vibration or noise levels
	Result in a substantial temporary, periodic, or permanent increase in ambient noise levels
	Result in a substantial temporary, periodic, or permanent increase in ambient noise levels in the vicinity of an airport or private airstrip
Population and Housing	Induce substantial population growth
	Displace substantial numbers of existing housing [units]
	Displace substantial numbers of people
Public Services	Interfere with or require new facilities for fire protection, police protection, schools, parks, and other public facilities
Recreation	Increase the use of parks and other recreational facilities such that substantial physical deterioration of the facility would occur or be accelerated
	Require new or expanded recreational facilities which might have an adverse physical effect on the environment
Transportation and Traffic	Result in a substantial increase in traffic
	Exceed an existing traffic service standard
	Result in change in air traffic patterns
	Substantially increase hazards due to a design feature or incompatible uses
	Result in inadequate emergency access
	Result in inadequate parking capacity
	Conflict with alternative transportation
Utilities and Services Systems	Require new or expanded water supplies or treatment facilities
	Require new or expanded wastewater treatment facilities
	Require new or expanded storm water drainage facilities
	Require new or expanded solid waste disposal facilities

of which is available on the Web (California 2001). It represents the list of environmental issues that California agencies felt should be considered when creating, modifying, or expanding any sort of activity. Most of the aspects must be "substantial" in some way to be worthy of consideration but the threshold for substantialness is undefined. The list is by no means complete—perhaps no list could be—and it omits some of the more obvious aspects routinely included in corporate environmental reports, such as energy consumption and CO_2 emission. Still, it is a good place to start examining potential environmental aspects because it represents an official viewpoint about what sorts of issues may be considered important.

Environmental aspects are likely to vary among facilities and companies, because the physical and biological environment varies geographically, and the type of operation greatly influences the nature of the environmental aspects. An electrical utility's hydroelectric generating units will have entirely different environmental aspects from wind turbines or nuclear steam generation units and are often in entirely different ecosystems. Southern California Edison's hydroelectric units are mostly in mountain canyons, while its nuclear power plant is on the Pacific coast. Air quality aspects from a gas-fired power plant in the Los Angeles Basin will be completely different from air quality aspects of a nuclear power plant just down the coast.

Social aspects occur because wherever people work there is a demographic profile of the workforce, a possibility of accidents and illness, some level of compensation, and the possibility of discrimination and unfair labor practices. There is also a community in the vicinity of many facilities that may in some way be affected by the company's operations. For many companies, particularly the large transnational ones that are the leaders in writing environmental and sustainability reports, very few of the possible adverse social aspects are realized. Thus if the topics of child and forced labor, intentional discrimination, corporal punishment, illegal compensation, unfair labor practices, and illegal work hours come up at all (as GRI requires for full compliance with its GRI 2000 standard), they come up in the form of a one-sentence denial of their existence. It may be deemed important to mention these topics, but companies intentionally engaging in such practices are not likely to admit it voluntarily.

Significance of Impacts

What constitutes a significant impact? This is a very difficult question. I offer here the definitions presented by the President's Council on Environmental Quality (CEQ) for The National Environmental Policy Act (NEPA) and the California Governor's Office of Planning and Research guidelines for implementing the California Environmental Quality Act

(CEQA). These guidelines reflect a quarter century of often litigious struggles to come up with a straightforward threshold of significance, but as you will see, they fall short of the mark. It is agreed that the magnitude of the impact must be taken into consideration along with the sensitivity of the environmental feature being impacted, but just how to do that remains an *ad hoc* process. Consequently, when making the determination for use in an ISO 14001 environmental management system, or for inclusion in an environmental or sustainability report, it is well to realize that there are no absolute standards, or even well established rules of thumb. Many organizations have adopted algorithms to facilitate the determination (see Block 1999, for some examples), but at the end of the day these are inherently subjective. I point this out to save you the trouble of agonizing over significance. You might as well set your own criteria.

According to the President's Council on Environmental Quality (CEQ 1983): 'Significantly' as used in NEPA requires considerations of both context and intensity:

> a. *Context. This means that the significance of an action must be analyzed in several contexts such as society as a whole (human, national), the affected region, the affected interests, and the locality. Significance varies with the setting of the proposed action. For instance, in the case of a site-specific action, significance would usually depend upon the effects in the locale rather than in the world as a whole. Both short- and long-term effects are relevant.*

> b. *Intensity. This refers to the severity of impact. Responsible officials must bear in mind that more than one agency may make decisions about partial aspects of a major action. The following should be considered in evaluating intensity:*

>> 1. *Impacts that may be both beneficial and adverse. A significant effect may exist even if the federal agency believes that on balance the effect will be beneficial.*

>> 2. *The degree to which the proposed action affects public health or safety.*

>> 3. *Unique characteristics of the geographic area such as proximity to historic or cultural resources, park lands, prime farmlands, wetlands, wild and scenic rivers, or ecologically critical areas.*

>> 4. *The degree to which the effects on the quality of the human environment are likely to be highly controversial.*

5. *The degree to which the possible effects on the human environment is highly uncertain or involves unique or unknown risks.*

6. *The degree to which the action may establish a precedent for future actions with significant effects or represents a decision in principle about a future consideration.*

7. *Whether the action is related to other actions with individually insignificant but cumulatively significant impacts. Significance exists if it is reasonable to anticipate a cumulatively significant impact on the environment. Significance cannot be avoided by terming an action temporary or by breaking it down into small component parts.*

8 *The degree to which the action may adversely affect districts, sites, highways, structures, or objects listed in or eligible for listing in the National Register of Historic Places or may cause loss or destruction of significant scientific, cultural, or historical resources.*

9. *The degree to which the action may adversely affect an endangered or threatened species or its habitat that has been determined to be critical under the Endangered Species Act of 1973.*

10. *Whether the action threatens a violation of federal, state, or local law or requirements imposed for the protection of the environment.*

The California Environmental Quality Act requires a mandatory finding of significance for projects which:

> . . . *have potential to degrade the quality of the environment, substantially reduce the habitat of a fish or wildlife species, cause a fish or wildlife population to drop below self-sustaining levels, threaten to eliminate a plant or animal community, reduce the number or restrict the range of a rare or endangered plant or animal or eliminate important examples of the major periods of California history or prehistory*

> . . . *have impacts that are individually limited, but cumulatively considerable . . .* (that is, *". . . the incremental effects of a project are considerable when viewed in connection with the effects of*

past projects, the effects of other current projects, and the effects of probable future projects)

. . . have environmental effects which will cause substantial adverse effects on human beings, either directly or indirectly

Notice that the qualifiers "substantial" and "considerable" are often important in determing significance but are not defined. The guidelines request that "the significance criteria or threshold, if any, used to evaluate each question" should be described, leaving this determination up to the person determining significance. In fact, neither CEQA nor the CEQA guidelines describes specific thresholds of significance or how they may be used (Governor's Office of Planning and Research 1994).

Marilyn Block, in her book *Identifying Environmental Aspects and Impacts* (Block 1999), suggests the use of two or more of nine five-point scales for:

1. Severity

2. Likelihood

3. Frequency

4. Boundaries

5. Controllability

6. Regulatory status

7. Reportability

8. Stakeholder concerns

9. Duration

For each impact, a score of one to five is assigned for each of the scales used, and then the points are added or multiplied together to get a final score. The most highly scoring impacts are then selected as the significant ones, but does a high score really mean that they are significant?

It is evidently very difficult to come up with a universal formula for determining environmental significance. Agencies have been making determinations of significance under NEPA since 1970 and such determinations continue to be routinely litigated in the courts. Writers of environmental impact statements struggle with this issue daily without any good resolution. The most a reader of an environmental or sustainability report can expect is an explanation of the threshold of significance the writer used to decide what to include in the report.

Explaining Aspects and Impacts Faced by Your Company and Industry

All companies have specific environmental and social aspects and impacts, many of which are also shared by competitors. Your company's performance in dealing with these issues is most meaningful if put in context with the issues common to your industry.

Roche, in its 1999 Safety and Environmental Protection at Roche: Group Report, provides an excellent five-page introduction to the issues associated with the production of pharmaceuticals. It abandons its segregation of issues into air, water, waste, and energy as in previous years' reports, and discusses the overall issues associated with pharmaceutical production processes. First it distinguishes between physical processes (grinding, mixing, dissolving, coating), chemical processes (changing molecular structure chemically), and biological processes (using organisms to do the chemistry), then goes on to describe its approaches to optimizing process development.

We learn that for a pharmaceutical manufacturer, the main activity having an influence on environmental impact is process design. There are often many ways to make a product, each with its own advantages and disadvantages, including economic and environmental ones.

> . . . *[I]mprovements integrated directly into the process produce better results than measures which only take effect after the process has been completed. Particular emphasis is placed on the principles of ecoefficiency—the optimal use of energy in the manufacture of a product—and sustainability—the greatest possible use of renewable raw materials. The degree of environmental compatibility of a process can also be shown by using a mass balance approach, systematically identifying and describing all the inputs and the outputs of a process: large quantities of waste, emissions or heat generated during the process can harm the environment. . . . The manufacture of a product can be improved either by modifying individual process parameters or by introducing a completely new process. In the case of ganciclovir, a pharmaceutical active substance used for treating specific viral infections, process development has resulted in a manufacturing procedure that now involves two synthesis steps rather than the previous six, requires reduced quantities of starting materials, and generates less chemical waste. Moreover, the yield of the desired end product is around 25 percent higher in this new process. Positive reasons for adopting this process include not*

only the environmental improvements achieved, but also the finan-
cial savings resulting partly from the reduced requirement for raw
materials and partly from the reduced disposal costs. Similar con-
siderations in connection with the production of vitamin B2
(riboflavin) resulted in the replacement of the chemical manufac-
turing process by a microbiological process. Since the new fer-
mentation process does not require any organic solvents, it does
not produce any emissions of this type into the environment.

It also becomes clear that recycling, rather than disposing, of solvents
constitutes a major opportunity both to save costs and to decrease environmental impacts.

Roche purifies a large proportion of the various solvents by distil-
lation and then reuses them in the same processes. To obtain both
environmental and economic benefits from this approach, several
requirements must be met: where possible, the solvents should not
be mixed with other substances; they must occur in sufficiently
large quantities; the infrastructure must be in place for the trans-
port and storage of the solvents.

Roche introduces the important environmental aspects of its business,
and then provides examples of how it is working to minimize them, all the
while reducing costs. The reader comes away with an understanding that
the company is open to discussing the issues and is systematically working
to reduce adverse impacts in a way that makes economic sense.

Bristol-Myers Squibb, another pharmaceutical giant, following the GRI
2000 reporting guidelines in its 2001 Sustainability Progress Report, goes
beyond the Roche report in discussing economic, social, and "integrated"
performance. The economic content is minimal, referencing the company's
annual report, but the social performance section addresses wages and benefits, percentages of women and minorities in U.S. operations, flexible work
arrangements, child labor, and other social issues. This is clearly a first
attempt, devoid of much in the way of meaningful data other than on U.S.
women and minorities, but it is a start, and reflects an effort few other companies are yet making. Bristol-Myers Squibb evidently finds the "integrated
performance" category proposed by GRI as undefined as I do. They devote
a page to it, but the page is essentially free of any information.

In the automotive sector, the Ford 2000 Corporate Citizenship Report
has a 17-page section on environmental performance that discusses each of
the major issues facing Ford, and by extension, most of the automotive
industry. Not only does it provide numerical data on Ford's performance,

but it also gives a good sense of the range of issues the automotive sector is facing and what Ford is doing about each of them. Ford is making good progress at reducing CO_2 and other emissions from new vehicles, incorporating recycled materials, decreasing water use, and decreasing the use of "materials of concern" such as mercury, cadmium, and lead. Having certified all of its manufacturing facilities to the ISO 14001 environmental management standard, Ford is now asking its suppliers to become certified as well. It is making less progress in improving vehicle fuel economy and energy used in manufacturing and elsewhere such as transportation of vehicles to end users, and in nonregulated emissions to air and water.

Total Fina Elf's 2000 Environment and Safety Report provides a clear overview of the health, safety, and environmental issues in its complex operations, typical of a large multinational petrochemical corporation. Its activities include oil and gas exploration and production, and refining, marketing, and transportation of petrochemicals, chlorochemicals, fertilizers, and polymers, as well as a variety of specialty chemicals. These activities take place within 26 country subsidiaries, 16 refineries, and 183 chemical plants and, as the report observes, "It is hard to compare health and safety hazards or the environmental impact of an oil exploration and production subsidiary in Libya, for example, with those at a paint factory in the Netherlands." It therefore refers readers to the specific environmental reports of each of the group's business segments for more detail.

Nonetheless, Total Fina Elf's 44-page overview is a candid introduction to and tutorial on the issues. For example, on the subject of improving air quality the report observes that:

> *Gases produced by human activities fall roughly into two broad categories: those liable to impair air quality, such as sulfur dioxide, nitrogen oxides, hydrocarbons, and so on, and those whose action may have a planetary impact by modifying the earth's climate, that is mainly greenhouse gases, such as carbon dioxide (CO_2), methane, nitrous oxide, etc. . . . The chief culprits responsible for the emission of compounds affecting air quality are combustion processes, evaporation associated with production processes or during transfer or handling of certain products, for example, motor and heating fuels, chemicals, and so on. In tandem with naturally-occurring emissions, these man-made emissions can also significantly affect air quality in large urban areas.*

After reading this we know what petrochemical companies ought to be reporting about combustion products and evaporation during refining and processing.

In the metals sector, Nippon Steel's 2001 Environmental Report does a good job of explaining why it reports on nonobvious environmental aspects. One such aspect is the fact that molten blast furnace (BF) slag when quenched with water becomes water-granulated slag which can be made into BF cement with much less energy than producing Portland cement from scratch. Thus an environmental variable reported by Nippon Steel is trends in BF cement usage and relative energy consumption and CO_2 production relative to Portland cement. Nippon Steel also recycles waste tires as a partial substitute for scrap iron and coal in the scrap-melting furnace in which the steel cords in the tires are melted by the heat generated by burning the tires. They use this process to recycle 6 percent of the tires recycled in Japan and report a rapidly growing tire recycling program. Innovative conservation and recycling programs are much better appreciated if explained like this in enough detail that anyone can understand them.

Canon's 2001 Environmental Report provides one of the best examples of explaining industry environmental aspects and impacts and its solution to them. It identifies each of its environmentally-friendly technologies, explains the problem that technology was designed to solve, followed by quantitative environmental results. For example, in laser printers the toner is melted (fixed) with heat, which normally requires maintaining the fixing roller at 200°C. Canon's on-demand fixing technology uses only a quarter of the electricity of roller fixing by using an instantly heating ceramic heater. The technology is illustrated in a small schematic diagram followed by a graph showing the growing trend of substantial energy savings to users. In 2000 the accumulated energy savings since the technology was introduced in 1995 were more than 4.5 million MWh. The report discusses many more environmental innovations and provides quantitative data wherever it is available.

RECOMMENDATIONS

An environmental or sustainability report makes much more sense to the reader if the performance data it presents are put into context. The context, which should include prior performance, is made much clearer if it is couched in terms of industrywide issues that are adequately explained. Most reports simply present some data with little or no indication of why the specific metrics were selected. The best reports, however, show why the problem exists by reference to manufacturing processes or product operation, explain what the range of alternatives are, then discuss how the company is planning and proceeding to solve the problem. This information doesn't need to go into a separate section of the report. It is best presented as a preamble to each of the data graphs or tables documenting performance.

Any report would be much clearer if the procedures were explained for identifying environmental and social aspects, and determining which of these were significant enough to merit inclusion in the report. Any company having an ISO 14001 environmental management system in place has already done this for environmental aspects and impacts and the same procedures could be rapidly employed for social aspects and impacts as well. This information is seldom included in environmental and sustainability reports, but it should be. It would increase transparency and credibility, and for many companies, the data already exist.

11

Performance Indicators

The selection of environmental and social performance indicators determines the transparency of your reporting. Performance indicators should reflect the kinds of impacts your industry is generally thought to have, as well as impacts unique to your company. You should also include any indicators that you are required to collect for regulatory reasons.

RULE 6—SELECT NUMERICAL PERFORMANCE INDICATORS THAT CAN BE COMPARED WITHIN YOUR INDUSTRY

How do you decide what environmental and social performance data to present in your report? Should it primarily be data you have on hand from required monitoring programs, such as toxic emissions, spills, and injuries? Should it include energy and materials consumption that you are monitoring primarily to reduce costs? Should it include voluntary recycling programs and voluntary materials substitutions? Should it include community program participation by employee volunteers? How about awards you have made to employees, or have been made by third parties to the company? All of these and more are included by some companies and omitted by others. The purpose of this chapter is to help you decide what data to present.

The best metrics are those that have real environmental and social consequences, that can be measured accurately, and for which you can improve performance. It is also valuable if companies in the same industry use the same metrics and report them in the same units.

The heart of a credible environmental or sustainability report is a suite of quantitative performance metrics, but how do you decide what metrics to use? Start by looking at the published guidelines and scoring systems and at the reports of your peer companies and of those from related industries. To give you a sense of the range of possible metrics, I have included in appendix C a list of metrics taken from 74 corporate environmental and sustainability reports from eight industrial sectors. There are about 2000 different metrics on this list. Inspection of appendix C will show that much of this variation is minor—different titles for similar or identical variables—but there is much real variation in this choice of performance indicators as well. At present, they are anything but standardized. For example, CO_2 is reported in over 40 different ways, ranging from total emissions and emissions segregated by fuel source to emissions prevented and amount of CO_2 sequestered. What appendix C does not show are the numerical units in which each of these metrics is reported. CO_2 is reported in over 20 different units including percent of some previous years' levels, percent less than would have been emitted had gasoline been burned or a conventional diesel engine used, tons, metric tons (tonnes), kg/kWh, lbs/kWh, g/km, kg/tonne fuel, kton/employee, tons C/ha per year, and more. Some of these are interconvertible—changing lbs to kg, or tons to tonnes—but many are not: they are simply different metrics.

It is the intent of this chapter to encourage thoughtful selection of metrics that reflect the real issues your company and industry face, report them in the most transparent way, and in a way that allows intercompany comparison. You should describe how they were selected, how they are measured, and why they are appropriate. Often the relative importance of the data is unexplained. The reader is left to guess how much the results benefit the environment, how they compare to results achieved by other companies, how difficult they were to achieve, and how much additional improvement can be expected. You should take pains not to let this happen in your report.

Some Examples of Unexplained Metrics

What does it mean when Eli Lilly and Company mention in their 1999 Environmental Health and Safety Report that the Tippecanoe Laboratories in Lafayette, Indiana reduced the use of methanol by 126,636 kg? Is this one percent or 99 percent of their prior usage? Is it bad to use methanol or is this just a cost-saving measure? Is the recovery of 64,306 kg of hexamethyldisilazane mentioned in the same sentence more significant or less? And why is it that the Korea plant reduced its isobutanol usage by 5,554 kg, with no mention of methanol or hexamethyldisilazane? Perhaps Korea does not use these latter chemicals, or perhaps it did not succeed in reducing their use. The report offers no perspective whatever, so the reader can make little sense of the results.

Slightly more informative is that a new production line in the Lilly Technology Center eliminated a second carton and display tray for sample products, reducing paperboard packaging by more than 500,000 pounds per year. But is 500,000 pounds a drop in a very large bucket, or a major percentage decrease companywide? Or maybe it doesn't matter. Perhaps in absolute terms 500,000 pounds of paperboard is significant any way you look at it. Why not let the reader know? And how much additional packaging could be eliminated elsewhere in the company? We are left to guess.

The most informative reports systematically identify the environmental and social issues that face the company and its industry and use performance indicators that address them in the most transparent manner. Transparency is enhanced by explaining why particular indicators were chosen, by making clear their benefits and shortcomings, and by expressing them in units that allow comparison with competitors and with other industries.

Include Performance Indicators for Areas of Significant Impact

In the previous chapter I argued that transparency was best served by a candid overview of the environmental, social, and economic issues facing your company and your industry. Clarification of these issues should include a description of your environmental and social impacts, their significance, and what you are doing about them. If you are certified against ISO 14001 you will already have information on environmental impacts documented and ready to go in your environmental report. You should be sure to include it. You should document social and economic impacts (or lack thereof) not required by ISO 14001. By including a discussion of these in your environmental or sustainability report, both you and your readers will have a good idea of what performance metrics you ought to be reporting, at a minimum. In this chapter I argue that first of all you should close the loop by selecting and describing performance indicators that address the areas in which you are having significant impacts.

Include All Regulatory Performance Indicators

Another set of performance indicators you already are likely to have is data required by EPA, OSHA, and other federal, state, and municipal agencies. In the United States, large companies collect information on toxic releases under EPA's Toxic Release Inventory (TRI) program. This should be included. If the amount of information is too much for the format of your report, the full data set should be made available on a Web site referenced in your report. All companies have injury and accident data and should include it. Any other environmental or social data you report to the government should be synthesized into relevant performance indicators and included as well.

Include Data on Industry Issues

Be sure to include performance indicators for any issues that are associated with your industry, whether or not they apply to your company or are significant. If they are the source of significant impacts for your competitors, then you can benefit by documenting that they are not significant for you. It is an error to fail to mention your success at avoiding problems common to your peers. If your industry has a history of leaking underground storage tanks, but you removed your last one three years ago, be sure to mention it. If you have eliminated solid waste be sure to report it. If you are no longer using mercury in switches, capitalize on it by describing how you achieved it.

You can identify industry issues by examining the environmental and sustainability reports of the largest companies in your industry, by reviewing publications and Web sites of your industry's trade organizations, by reviewing critical reviews of your industry's performance from nongovernmental organizations (NGOs), and by viewing government documents summarizing issues in your industrial sector. The U.S. EPA Sector Notebook Project, for example, publishes descriptions of the industrial processes and their environmental aspects for 32 different industries (Table 11.1). EPA also produces many additional industry-specific guidance documents on pollution prevention, design for environment, environmental accounting, and case studies of environmental management, all available free on its Web site. These provide a rich source of industry-specific environmental aspects that you should consider addressing.

Include Relevant General Topics

One way to be sure that you are discussing all relevant topics is to assemble a checklist from other more-general sources including the GRI 2000

Table 11.1   U.S. Environmental Protection Agency Sector Notebook Project reports.

Document Number	Industry
EPA/310-R-98-001	Aerospace Industry
EPA/310-R-98-002	Agricultural Chemical, Pesticide, and Fertilizer Industry
EPA/310-R-98-003	Agricultural Crop Production Industry
EPA/310-R-98-004	Agricultural Livestock Production Industry
EPA/310-R-97-001	Air Transportation Industry
EPA/310-R-95-001	Dry Cleaning Industry
EPA/310-R-95-002	Electronics and Computer Industry*
EPA/310-R-95-007	Fabricated Metal Products Industry*
EPA/310-R-97-007	Fossil Fuel Electric Power Generation Industry
EPA/310-R-97-002	Ground Transportation Industry
EPA/310-R-95-004	Inorganic Chemical Industry*
EPA/310-R-95-005	Iron and Steel Industry
EPA/310-R-95-006	Lumber and Wood Products Industry
EPA/310-R-97-004	Metal Casting Industry
EPA/310-R-95-008	Metal Mining Industry
EPA/310-R-95-009	Motor Vehicle Assembly Industry
EPA/310-R-95-010	Nonferrous Metals Industry
EPA/310-R-95-011	Non-Fuel, Non-Metal Mining Industry
EPA/310-R-98-005	Oil and Gas Exploration and Production Industry
EPA/310-R-95-012	Organic Chemical Industry*
EPA/310-R-95-013	Petroleum Refining Industry
EPA/310-R-97-005	Pharmaceuticals Industry
EPA/310-R-97-006	Plastic Resin and Man-Made Fiber Industry
EPA/310-R-95-014	Printing Industry
EPA/310-R-95-015	Pulp and Paper Industry
EPA/310-R-95-016	Rubber and Plastic Industry
EPA/310-R-97-008	Shipbuilding and Repair Industry
EPA/310-R-95-017	Stone, Clay, Glass, and Concrete Industry
EPA/310-R-97-009	Textile Industry
EPA/310-R-95-018	Transportation Equipment Cleaning Industry
EPA/310-R-97-003	Water Transportation Industry
EPA/310-R-95-003	Wood Furniture and Fixtures Industry

*Spanish translation available

Source: http://www.epa.gov/ebtpages/ireporting.html

guidelines, the ISO 14031 Annex A list, and the Pacific Sustainability Index scoring sheet (appendix A in this book). Most of the topics listed in these documents apply to any manufacturing company, and the ones dealing with social issues apply both to manufacturing and service-sector companies. These lists may seem daunting—the Pacific Sustainability Index, for example, covers 140 different topics—but viewed closely, few of them are irrelevant to most manufacturing companies' operations.

Some Examples from Corporate Reports

Dow Public Report—2000 Results makes what appears to be a trial run of presenting 21, perhaps hypothetical, sustainable development measures in a spider web graph (see Figure 13.8, pg. 142). These 21 economic, social, and environmental goals that characterize sustainable development for a Dow business include corporate economic profit, business economic profit, business net present value changes, non–Organization for Economic Cooperation and Development (OECD) production, non-OECD sales, energy use, water, emissions, greenhouse gases, waste generated, loss of primary containment, natural resource use, revalorization, lifecycle assessment, needs assessment, public perception, community involvement, non-OECD jobs/employee, diversity, empowered employees, and employee health. Dow proposes to compare business unit performance in each of these areas with ideal performance, although the report does not indicate how ideal performance might be calculated. Volvo Car Corporation, in its Environmental Product Declarations, uses a similar type of graphic but with a very clear explanation of how the results were obtained (see chapter 5 for a description).

DuPont, in its brief eight-page Sustainable Growth 2000 Progress Report, includes total recordable injuries and illnesses, incidents (environmental, process, and transportation), global air toxics, global carcinogenic emissions, global greenhouse gases, global energy consumption, global hazardous waste (broken down by continent, but separately reporting data from the United States and Mexico), and the U.S. Toxics Release Inventory data reported to the U.S. EPA subdivided into waste generated, deepwell disposal of hazardous waste, and total releases to air, water, and land. The report also includes data on earnings per share, dividends per share, net sales by geographic region, and Six Sigma annualized benefits, which reflects increases in productivity in terms of dollars.

Henkel's 2000 Sustainability Report reports energy consumption (purchased energy—electricity, steam and district heating generated outside the sites—coal, fuel oil, gas), CO_2 emissions (including those from the purchased energy), NO_x emissions, SO_2 emissions, dust emissions, volatile organic carbon (VOC) emissions, water consumption and volume of wastewater, chemical oxygen demand (COD) emissions into surface waters, heavy metals emissions into surface waters, waste (for recycling, hazardous and nonhazardous waste for disposal), and consumption of chlorinated hydrocarbons. Rather than normalizing these to production, the data are plotted on graphs showing percent changes both in production and the performance indicator in question. Henkel also reports sales by business sector and region, occupational accidents by region, and complaints from neighbors.

Coors 1999 Environmental, Health and Safety Progress Report includes TRI data for its Golden Colorado brewery, hazardous waste from its Valley Metal Container can and lid plant and Rocky Mountain bottle manufacturing facilities, number of reportable air releases of ammonia at the Golden brewery, energy consumed at all facilities (both total and normalized to barrels of beer sold), and nonhazardous solid waste to landfills from all facilities.

Diageo (comprising UDV, Pillsbury, Guinness, and Burger King), in its 2000 Environmental Report, supplies total annual data and data normalized to output, segregated by each of its four divisions, for CO_2 emissions, energy use, solid waste, liquid effluent, and water use. UDV data are normalized to cases of product, Pillsbury's to tonnes of food produced, Guinness's to hectoliters of beer made (allowing, after conversion to barrels, a comparison with Coors assuming that beer made = beer sold), and Burger King to sales volume. It also reports its performance in the Business in the Environment Index of Corporate Environmental Engagement, shown relative to the FTSE 100 average performance, and performance for companies within the noncyclical consumer goods sector.

PepsiCo's 1999 Environmental Commitment report begins with an overview of the grocery industry's performance in packaging recovery (going up impressively), percent of soft drink containers in municipal solid waste (going down impressively), and a 36 percent reduction in amount of packaging per pound of snack foods (between 1972 and 1987—time for some new data it seems) owing to thinner bags. Lightweighting of containers has reduced PepsiCo's use of aluminum by 35 percent since 1972, polyethylene terephthalate (PET) in plastic bottles by 28 percent since 1979, and glass in bottles by 25 percent since 1984. Tropicana Products, a division of PepsiCo, has had similar reductions, as has Frito-Lay. There is lots more anecdotal information in the report, such as the fact that all tree removals are chipped and then reused in the gardens, but no data tables or graphics showing corporate use of energy and water, or amounts of emissions.

Georgia-Pacific Corporation's 2000 Environmental and Safety Report identifies and briefly discusses 11 corporate environmental measures for which it subsequently provides time-series data. These include environmental capital spending, environmental training hours, on-time completion of audit items, Toxics Release Inventory emissions and discharges, citizen complaints, notices of violation resulting in fines, wastewater incidents, hazardous waste generated at chemical plants, gypsum wallboard/rock reclaimed, recovered paper consumption, pulp and paper mill water use, and pulp and paper mill biological oxygen demand (BOD) and total suspended solids (TSS) in discharges. It also promises to report on five additional metrics in the next report: process wastewater reused by packaging plants, wood waste reused by building products manufacturing facilities, total reduced sulfur emissions from pulp and paper mills, SO_2 emissions from pulp and paper mills, and NO_X emitted from pulp and paper and building products facilities. The company also provides data on safety measures including Georgia-Pacific's Voluntary Protection Program, number of annual safety inspections, a comparison of the company's safety performance versus the OSHA industry rate, the percentage of work hours in the industry top quartile, time operating injury-free, and the OSHA incidence rate.

Weyerhaeuser's 1999 Annual Environment, Health, and Safety Report begins with the number of acres harvested and planted within one year in the United States and Canada, the number of acres commercially thinned, the number of seedlings produced (some of which are sold), the number of acres subjected to watershed analysis, and the numbers of seedlings planted and acres involved in Australia, New Zealand, and Uruguay converting agricultural land to plantation forests. (These data mostly measure Weyerhaeuser's business activities rather than its environmental performance, I would think.) It then details U.S. TRI and Canadian National Pollutant Release Inventory (NPRI) data by compound, emissions to air of CO, VOCs, particulate matter, NO_X, SO_X, and total reduced sulfur. It also documents the disposition of wood products facility and pulp and paper mill residuals (the stuff left over) as landfilled, incinerated, burned for energy (by far the largest category), applied to land for soil amendment, reused/recycled for beneficial use, and disposed of as hazardous waste. Weyerhauser also subdivides its energy use by fossil fuels, biomass fuels, purchased electricity, and purchased steam, which it reports normalized to ton of production. Strangely, the apparent successor to this report, Weyerhaeuser's 2001–2002 Citizenship Report, "A report on environmental performance, business practices, community activities, and employee relations," omits most of these performance indicators.

BMW's 2001/2002 Sustainable Value Report begins with a single page showing a five-year time series of revenues, numbers of vehicles built and delivered, investments, profits, number of employees and trainees, average employee seniority, and five environmental variables: energy consumption, production process water input, production process wastewater, CO_2, and waste, all reported both as total amounts, and normalized to unit produced. These data are supplemented in the body of the report with fleet fuel consumption, characterization of amounts of industrial materials and renewable raw materials used in some BMW cars, and a two-page table with details on waste, energy consumption, expenditures, the paint process, emissions, and wastewater. There are also extensive additional data on employees and health and safety.

Fiat's 1999 Environmental Report uses 12 metrics: energy produced with methane, energy produced with fuel oil, internally produced electricity, total energy consumption, total water requirements, actual water consumption, water recirculation index (percent recycled), total waste generation, waste to landfills, waste recycling index (percent recycled), solvent emissions generated from paint shops, and use of halogenated solvents.

Burlington Northern Santa Fe's 1999 (apparently, the report itself is undated but the latest data are from 1998) Providing Environmentally Sound Transportation report shows a time series of hazardous waste tonnage at each of eight of its major facilities (all showing a reduction over time), documents the company's removal of underground storage tanks and PCB transformers, and provides data on release incidents per 10,000 shipments and accidents per million-ton-miles. Not much data, but the report gives a sense of the issues facing the railroad industry, discussing care of wetlands, past soil contamination from cleaning railroad cars and the potential for more from fueling spills, air emissions from locomotives, and ecological problems caused by spills from trains—in 1998 27 cars full of grain derailed near Glacier National Park in Montana, attracting grizzly bears; the company cleaned it up promptly.

East Japan Railway Company's 2001 Annual Environmental Report begins with a two-page drawing (in the manner of the Matsushita Electric Works drawing reproduced in Figure 6.1), giving a very nice sense of the complexity of the railroad business and the associated environmental issues. This it supplements with more detailed drawings throughout the report, and all sorts of data on sources of energy, emissions, efficiency, and strategies for improving performance (including impediments). This report is one of the best I have seen in providing extensive numerical performance data in a format that is easy—almost enjoyable—to assimilate. If you want to understand the environmental and social issues of the rail transportation business in a quantitative way, this report makes them crystal clear.

Chubu Electric Power's 2001 Environment Report compares its thermal efficiency (41.52 percent) and transmission/distribution losses (4.9 percent) to the rest of the Japanese electric industry, and has a nice graph (from the Central Research Institute) illustrating the relationships between CO_2 emissions and fuel types. Fossil fuels produce the most in this order: coal > petroleum > liquefied natural gas > liquefied natural gas combined cycle. When the whole lifecycle is taken into account, nonfossil fuels produce CO_2/kWh, in this order: solar > wind > geothermal > nuclear > hydroelectric.

Entergy's 2000 Focus on the Environment report uses data from a Natural Resources Defense Council report to compare Entergy's and about 50 other utilities' CO_2, SO_2, and NO_x emissions per megawatt-hour to each other, to U.S. industry averages, and to Kyoto goals for CO_2 (how well U.S. generating plants would have to do on average), EPA standards for coal for SO_2, and EPA new source limits for NO_x.

RECOMMENDATIONS

Transparency should be your goal. For your performance to be fully transparent, it is up to you to select and present the data that fully reflect your company's performance and put it into perspective. To be sure you are using all of the appropriate metrics, you should consult checklists and scoring systems such as GRI 2000, ISO 14031, and the Pacific Sustainability Index scoring sheet. You should also examine the environmental reports of other companies in your industry. Ultimately, though, it is up to you to examine your company's operations to determine for yourself its environmental and social aspects and impacts. If you are using an environmental management system such as ISO 14001, you will have gone through this exercise already for environmental aspects and impacts. The data you are collecting for ISO 14001 should form the core of the environmental parts of your reporting, but for a sustainability report you will have to go *beyond* ISO 14001 to collect social data as well. For full transparency, you should address a wide range of your environmental and social aspects—all the ways in which your company might credibly interact with the environment and society as a whole—whether or not they result in impacts. This is, admittedly, a large order, and one that may take several generations of environmental or sustainability reports to begin to fill. Nevertheless, it should be your ultimate goal.

12

Initiatives and Mitigations

Anything a company does that has beneficial environmental and social effects should be included in its environmental or sustainability report, but the amount of space allocated ought to be related to significance, and the motivation ought not to be hidden. Many routine and required business activities have environmentally and socially beneficial outcomes, and these should be showcased, but the business benefits should also be clear, and incidental benefits should not eclipse good systematic environmental and social management.

RULE 7—DESCRIBE INTERESTING ENVIRONMENTAL AND SOCIAL INITIATIVES AND MITIGATIONS, BUT DON'T OVERDO IT

Mitigations are, in the context of National Environmental Policy Act Environmental Impact Statements, actions that are required to offset unacceptable environmental impacts. If you provide enough mitigation, you can take the action, build the project, and expand the refinery. In other words, they are activities that must be undertaken if you want to proceed. Site remediation might be thought of as mitigating prior unacceptable environmental impacts—often required by new statutes and regulations such as the Superfund law, but sometimes undertaken voluntarily.

Initiatives are voluntary activities, undertaken for ethical reasons, because of stakeholder—not regulatory or legal—pressure, for public relations benefits, or for all three reasons and others as well. Many initiatives reported in environmental and sustainability reports are taken by employees on their own time to help their local communities. The line between mitigations and initiatives is not necessarily clear, however. It may be ethically appropriate and beneficial from a public relations standpoint for an oil company to convert a former refinery site to a wildlife refuge, or to create an emergency care facility for wildlife that could be damaged by an oil spill, but it may also head off incipient litigation and decrease the risk of large settlements should wildlife be damaged by a spill. Nevertheless, for whatever reason they are undertaken, initiatives and mitigations are intended to be beneficial to the environment and society and they should be an integral part of any environmental or sustainability report.

The trick is to present initiatives and mitigations factually without making them the focus of the report, or making them out to be more than what they are. After all, environmental and social initiatives and mitigations are not your core business, and even though this is the environmental report, which by its very nature should be addressing your impacts and what you are doing about them, most of what you are doing in this regard is likely to be better characterized as routine good management than as an initiative.

To report initiatives, you have to be taking some. This chapter lists some of the initiatives being reported by large companies. Your company may have similar examples to report, or these examples may offer some suitable suggestions. You may suspect that some of the initiatives below, although presented in the reports as purely voluntary measures to enhance society and the environment, are closer to mitigations. Something about the company's operations may have essentially required the company to undertake them: for example, hydroelectric projects in the United States are licensed by the Federal Energy Regulatory Commission, which routinely requires the development and maintenance of recreational facilities such as boat ramps, campgrounds, and trails as part of the license conditions. These can certainly be claimed and reported as environmental initiatives—they can be regarded as enhancing the environment and society—but I would think it generally appropriate to come clean and say what the activities are really all about if there is more to them than meets the eye.

Examples of Initiatives and Mitigations in Environmental and Sustainability Reports

The Asahi Kasei 2001 Edition Environmental Preservation, Product Safety, Operational Safety and Health Responsible Care Report identifies four initiatives to alleviate the environmental effects of product distribution. Asahi Kasei is working with its customers to increase the volumes of individual purchases, replacing disposable 25-kg bags with returnable one-ton flexible containers, changing over from shipment by road to shipment by rail and coastal sea lanes, and most interestingly, shortening shipping distances by arranging product swaps with other producers—Asahi Kasei ships its products to a nearby competitor who has a production facility nearer Asahi Kasei's customer. The competitor then delivers to the customer. Asahi Kasei also has a product line that can increase the average lifetime of Japanese homes from 26 years—after which they are normally demolished and landfilled [!]—to 60 years.

The Clorox Company and the Environment 1999 report pronounces that Clorox is saving 15 million pounds of corrugated packaging annually simply by redesigning a shipping container without internal partitions and with fold-over flaps that are shortened so that they no longer meet in the middle. And by getting its supplier to ship trigger spray tops for its cleaning product bottles in a reusable corrugated bulk tote that holds 5,000 trigger sprays, they saved 440,000 pounds of corrugated packaging annually. And they save 350,000 pounds of plastic annually by switching to a 24-hour production schedule for plastic bottles: the old schedule caused the machines to be shut down daily, and the rewarming process resulted in wasted plastic. Clorox also supports science education by encouraging its scientists to make classroom visits in the San Francisco Bay Area, and to be involved in Bay Area science fairs.

BASF, in its 2000 Environment, Safety, Health report, shows a predilection for planting trees, having planted its 50,000th tree on the banks of the Paraiba do Sul River in Brazil, in March 2000. Like Asahi Kasei, BASF is interested in reducing environmental costs and human risks of distribution. It has switched to rail transport at its Verbund site in Ludwigshafen, Germany, eliminating passage of 40,000 trucks through surrounding towns and villages.

The ABB Group 2000 Annual Sustainability Report notes that ABB offers direct financial support to a variety of local projects in Brazil including sanitation, medical checkups, and education; creates schools; and encourages employees to participate in social projects such as supplementing regular school classes of children from slum areas, and teaching arts and crafts—and donating the materials needed—to children, adults, the aged, and the physically impaired. It cites many other similar projects in China, Egypt, Poland, South Africa, and Europe.

Intel's 2000 EHS Performance Report documents a contribution of $14,500 to the Crumlin Children's Hospital in Ireland. Intel employees also provided the Israeli city of Qiryat Gat with technical and practical help in the form of survey collection and analysis, as well as cleaning up trash and planting trees. More than 60 Intel volunteers were involved in painting street safety markings in the Philippines, and more than 2,000 Intel Malaysia employees cleaned up a nine-kilometer stretch of coastline. In Oregon, Intel employees planted more than 4,000 trees, shrubs, and bulbs in public spaces.

Motorola, in its 2000 Global Corporate Citizenship Report, has a section on philanthropy and volunteerism in which it notes it has donated 17,000 new wireless phones and airtime to domestic violence shelters in the United States. Its employees pledged $7.2 million to the United Way in 2000, helped local communities in Brazil on a wastepaper recycling initiative that helps disabled people retain their dignity while working, and more.

Siemens 2000 Environmental Report provides many examples of environmental initiatives in the developing world, some involving process improvements and some external environmental improvements. Siemens counts among its environmental initiatives in Brazil the recycling of plastic trays, halving the consumption of water, using solar power to run a sewage plant, recycling used oil, lamps, and light bulbs, and depositing industrial waste in a landfill. Its employees also planted more than 2,000 trees in a small subtropical wet wood on the company campus and put on a motivational play to raise environmental awareness in local children.

Boise Cascade Corporation, in its 2000 Environmental, Health, and Safety Report announces the establishment of an annual $2,000 environmental research fellowship (based on a $50,000 donation) at Boise State University in Idaho. Its employees volunteer to help the Idaho Fish and Game Department plant bitterbrush to rehabilitate foothills burned by wildfires, and serve as volunteer members of the board of directors and technical committee of a program that oversees fish habitat rehabilitation projects. The company also manages trails, viewpoints, and historic landmarks on its timberlands, and manages an interpretive nature trail near its paper mill in Louisiana.

Georgia-Pacific Corporation's 2000 Environmental and Safety Report describes a Forest Management Assistant Program (Forest MAP) they developed to provide cooperative support to private forest landowners, and through its separate operating group, The Timber Company, is involved in many habitat partnerships on its 4.7 million acres across the United States. These include supporting a Wisconsin statewide habitat conservation plan to protect the Karner blue butterfly, and a variety of stream enhancement programs.

International Paper's 1999–2000 Environment, Health, and Safety Annual Report also takes credit for protecting the Karner blue butterfly in Wisconsin, as well as being a major sponsor of the National Wild Turkey

Federation's "Women in the Outdoors" program that educates women about outdoor activities. After acquiring the OAO Svetogorsk Paper Mill in Western Russia in January 1999, International Paper held a 10-day sustainable forestry education initiative to share forest stewardship and environmental best practices with the mill's foresters.

Alcoa, in its 2000 Annual Environment, Health, and Safety Report, touts planting half a million trees on five continents. It also says it engages in mine reclamation although it doesn't say anything about how—only that its solutions are productivity-based, whatever that might mean—and although it states that the areas it has used for mining bauxite (aluminum ore), coal, and lignite must be restored to a land use that is socially and ecologically sustainable, it doesn't make it clear what restoration has actually been accomplished.

The Corus Group, in its 2000 Environmental Report, like BASF, is moving some of its transportation, also in Germany, from roads to rail with the idea of reducing road travel by 4.4 million kilometers per year. In the UK, it has similarly used rail transport to eliminate 25,000 lorry journeys per year and ship transport to eliminate another 25,000. It is more explicit than Alcoa about land reclamation, citing a 1000-acre, £25m remediation of a site in Scotland that had been used for coal mining for 100 years prior to steelmaking, and now is available for further use. Corus also supports a variety of community and biodiversity projects ranging from contributing £50,000 to a bridge building project to provide access to a picturesque hidden valley and gardens, to supporting scientific studies of population trends and behavioral patterns of seals.

Nippon Steel, in its 2001 Environmental Report presents its successful efforts at energy savings, reduction of ozone layer depleting substances, and CO_2 emissions reductions as "initiatives for preservation of the global environment." Nippon Steel is also intensively engaged in reducing transportation impacts, arranging to ship its products in small steel vessels and ferry barges jointly with other steelmakers, and shifting from road to rail. It has also initiated a "green" buying drive which includes utilization of hybrid vehicles, using the unused side of once-used paper, and using recycled paper for printing and name cards.

Toyota, in its 2001 North America Environmental Report describes its Environmental Assistance Network initiative for Toyota and Lexus dealers with a private extranet Web site on waste stream management to help dealers comply with federal, state, and local regulatory agencies. It also takes half a page to point out that it sponsors a National Public Lands Day during which nearly 1,600 Toyota volunteers help renovate parks at 25 sites near Toyota facilities, that it supports NGOs such as the Nature Conservancy, that some of its employees in Kentucky participated in the annual "Fall Haul" roundup of household hazardous waste, and that it made grants of more than $1.8 million for various environment education programs.

Phillips Petroleum's 1998 Health, Environmental and Safety Report describes a joint partnership with the Okmulgee Area Development Corporation and the Oklahoma Department of Environmental Quality to clean up the former Okmulgee refinery site and turn it into an industrial park. The same report describes Phillips' cooperative effort with the Utah Division of Wildlife Resources, Utah Power, and North Ogden Junior High School to convert a 40-acre former refinery landfill and water treatment site into a bald eagle roosting site. It also describes a plan to donate Little Galloo Island, a major water bird site on Lake Ontario, to the State of New York; cooperative efforts with the Wildlife Habitat Council to turn a former copolymer plant site into a wildlife refuge and nesting area for great horned owls; implementation of a rotational mowing program at the Houston Chemical Complex to improve nesting for black-necked stilts (and save mowing effort at the same time); habitat improvements at Sweeny, Texas and Bartlesville, Oklahoma that appear to be volunteer efforts by some employees on the weekends; and joining of a consortium of corporate sponsors and government agencies restoring some habitat along the Rio Grande.

Chevron's 1997 Protecting People and the Environment report points out that Chevron has actively supported wildlife conservation and habitat restoration, has encouraged volunteerism, and has donated more than $7 million in the past five years to nonprofit conservation and environmental programs including planting 100,000 evergreens in Canada to restore land cleared for oil and gas production, and donating $60,000 to support reintroduction of California condors into wilderness, presumably in the vicinity of some of Chevron's operations.

ExxonMobil, in its 2001 Safety, Health, and Environment Progress Report discusses providing grants to three organizations involved in the battle against malaria in Africa where it has operations, but also treats as initiatives activities more directly related to its operations. For example, it has a formal Global Energy Management System Initiative under which energy management teams of as many as 30 internal technical and operating experts are dispatched to major refining and chemical sites to come up with ways to minimize energy use. Its gas conservation initiatives have reduced flaring of natural gas that is produced along with oil, resulting in both environmental benefits (lower CO_2 releases), and revenue (when the gas is sold).

AEP's System Environmental Performance Report 1997–1998 identifies a wide variety of initiatives, including leasing some of its 570 square miles of land, some of it reclaimed from prior surface coal mining, to cattle ranchers and farmers. Like most utilities in the United States with hydro-electric projects, it has developed park and camping sites, visitor centers, boat launches, fishing areas, and hiking trails associated with them.

RECOMMENDATIONS

Anything your company is doing that has positive environmental or social consequences—even, and maybe especially, if it also has positive business consequences—should find its way into your environmental or sustainability report. To prevent reader cynicism it is a good idea to be open about your motivation for undertaking these initiatives: it should not be embarrassing if they are required as part of project licensing or if they reduce risk of litigation. Meeting license requirements and reducing corporate risk are good management practices and should be showcased as such. It seems disingenuous to a knowledgeable reader when a report seems to imply that apparently required mitigations or activities obviously intended to reduce risk were undertaken simply out of the goodness of management's heart.

Some companies base their entire reports around anecdotes about initiatives. These reports seem a little frivolous to me. I would rather feel that a company is incorporating good environmental and social practices systematically into its core business and its products, even though it is also doing good works around the periphery.

13
Performance

Performance indicators result in performance data that is most effective when displayed graphically, and most informative when normalized—standardized to a meaningful index of the size of your company such as sales, number of employees, or amount of product. Normalization corrects the trends in performance indicators for simultaneous changes in the size of the company: If the company is growing rapidly it is not unexpected that emissions would also increase. The trend you want the graphs to show is not that emissions are going up, but that relative to company growth, they are stable or declining. Some complexity in data charts is easily assimilated, such as using stacked bar charts to show the partitioning of energy sources. Too much complexity will cause many readers to move on without processing the information.

RULE 8—PRESENT YOUR PERFORMANCE DATA CLEARLY AND GRAPHICALLY

What you choose to report you should report quantitatively. It should be presented in both absolute and relative terms, and it should be normalized in a way that makes sense for your industry. When the absolute numeric values of the data are important, or when the data are particularly voluminous, it is often good to use data tables. Generally, though, it is easier to grasp trends when data are presented graphically. If it is trends that matter more than the absolute values, graphical presentation alone may be sufficient, particularly if the graphs include numerical values as well. It is common for companies to illustrate trends in their own data, but the same graphs and tables can also be used to show industry trends. Whenever industry trends are available they should be used and explained.

Use Both Absolute and Relative Data and Put It into Perspective

It is perfectly reasonable to judge your performance by reference to some baseline. If you started intentionally decreasing energy usage in 1996 it is sensible to report current energy use in relative terms as a percentage of 1996 usage. But that doesn't tell the whole story. Maybe in 1996 you were already using half the energy of your competitors, so your reductions are not as impressive as theirs, but your absolute usage is lower. Or perhaps the opposite applies. Transparency requires you to provide both absolute and relative information so that your readers can put it into industry context even if you don't choose to.

This works the other way around too. In the Eli Lilly and Company example in chapter 11, we know that the absolute reduction of cardboard usage was 500,000 pounds per year, but Lilly doesn't tell us whether that is one percent or 99 percent of their previous cardboard usage. They also fail to explain the environmental consequences of not using 500,000 pounds of cardboard. Is this recycled paper, or is it trees that could have been saved?

Wherever Possible Normalize the Performance Indicators

Another way to put performance data into perspective is to normalize it. That is to say, to put it in terms of something else. How much energy is used per employee, per square foot of office space, per automobile produced? How much water is used per barrel of beer (for washing fermenters and cleaning up the brewery as well as for brewing the beer)? How many accidents per hours worked? These are the best way to make interindustry and intercompany comparisons. They need to be looked at with a critical eye— it is not unreasonable that a company in Finland would use more energy per employee for heating than one in California, or that a company in Houston would use more energy for cooling than its counterpart in San Francisco. But by proper selection of performance indicators—ones that distinguish between air conditioning and heating and manufacturing processes—it should be possible to demonstrate the quality of environmental performance.

Table 13.1 lists some example normalizing factors used in the reports listed in appendix C.

What to normalize data with is a big question. For lack of anything better Bristol-Myers Squibb decided to normalize everything to sales in their 2001 Sustainability Progress Report:

> *Normalizing data to production is not currently feasible for a company like Bristol-Myers Squibb because we produce such diverse products—from anti-cancer drugs to ostomy products to infant formula. In the interim, we have normalized data to worldwide and U.S. sales, as appropriate, and report in U.S. dollars. We acknowledge the shortcomings of this approach. Several factors, including inflation, currency fluctuations, and licensing agreements, can affect sales without impacting production levels or environmental operating results. Nonetheless, sales dollars apply to all our operations, at all of our divisions worldwide and represent the best normalizing measure currently available to us.*

Table 13.1 Examples of use of normalizing factors.

Accidents: accidents/200,000 h worked

Accidents: accidents/m miles driven

Accidents: reportable accidents/million hrs worked

Acid rain potential: kg sulfur oxide equivalents per tonne product

Attendance of safety training courses: people/year

Average barrels of oil used to generate 1000 MWh: barrels/MWh

Biochemical oxygen demand (BOD): pounds/unfinished tons

CO_2, anthropogenic emissions: g/tonne

CO_2, anthropogenic emissions: ml/m^3

CO_2 emitted from combustion of natural gas: % less than gasoline

CO_2 from energy use: kg/tonne coal

CO_2: kg/ton product

Coliform groups discharged: colonies/cm^3

Copper discharged: mg/liter

Costs, disability: dollars/employee

Crude waste emissions: lb of waste and emissions/300 lb barrel

Effluent flow: 1000 gallons/ton of product

Emissions: g/brake horsepower-hour

Energy conservation: energy usage/$U.S.

Energy consumption: Gigajoules/ton product

Energy consumption: MWh/employee

Fuel consumption: million Joules/$1000 sales

continued

	continued

Fuel economy of 3-way catalytic converter: % improvement over standard engine

Hazardous waste, total: kg/tonne of production

Hazardous waste: kg/ton

Liquid effluents–BOD: kg/1000 tonnes of crude processed

Nitrogen oxide: lbs/barrel of refined product

NO_x emissions: lbs/MWh

Odor, total reduced sulfur: lbs sulfur/air-dried ton pulp

Ozone-depleting compound releases: grams R-11 equivalents/tonne product

Ozone-depleting substances: kg/$1000 worldwide sales

Reportable incidents waste: lbs waste/lb product

Reportable incidents: fatalities/m hours worked

SARA 313 U.S. air releases: kg/ $1000 sales

SARA chemicals used: million kg /$ billion

SARA releases and transfers: lbs/barrel crude oil

SO_2 emissions from coal: tons/GWh

Solid waste disposed of: million kg/billion dollars

Solid waste reduction: cubic yards/100 tons production

Solid waste, reused or recycled: million kg /billion dollars

Sulfur dioxide: lbs/ton of product

Sulfur oxides: lbs/barrel of refined product

Toxic release rate, total: kg/tonne of production

TRI emissions and discharge: lbs/lb of waste and emissions

TRI primary manufacturing: lbs/ton of product

TRI releases indexed to U.S. sales: lbs/$1000 U.S. sales

Truck collision rate: collisions/m miles traveled

VOC, average emissions: kg/vehicle

Waste disposal: lbs landfilled/$1000 sales

Water use, average: gallons/kWh

Water use: gallons/lb product

Water use: liters/$1000 worldwide sales

Water used in manufacturing: gallons/ton of pulp and paper production

Wind power purchases: contracts/10,000 kWh

Worker's Compensation claims: claims/1,000 employees

Another aspect of normalization illustrated by Bristol-Myers Squibb's data is that if a business is changing in size, nonnormalized data may show a different trend from the absolute data. Bristol-Myers Squibb does not include absolute data in its 2001 Sustainability Progress Report, but it makes it available on the Web. Figure 13.1a shows the apparently stable fuel consumption since 1997 that appears in the printed report, normalized to sales. The absolute data from the Web site shown in Figure 13.1b show a continuing this analysis in the spring when you come for the review.

Thank you for agreeing to be part of this process. As far as I can tell you are one of very few academics interested in corporate environmental transparency. I am principally interested in the technical (ecological) effects of such transparency; it will be interesting to get a better-informed view of the economic effects. It will also be interesting to see what happens to transparency with *Nike v. Kasky*.

Hoping that you have had a good holiday season, and looking forward to meeting you in the spring, best regards,

J. Emil Morhardt

W. M. Keck Science Center, 925 North Mills Avenue, Claremont, California 91711-5916 (909) 621-8190 Fax (909) 621-8588
Member of The Claremont Colleges

CLAREMONT MCKENNA COLLEGE

Roberts Environmental Center

12/23/2002

Mark A. Cohen
Professor of Management
Director, Vanderbilt Center for Environmental Management Studies
Owen Graduate School of Management
Vanderbilt University
Nashville, TN 37203

Dear Mark:

Enclosed is the book we published in June summarizing the analysis my students and I have been doing of corporate environmental and sustainability reports, and introducing a new scoring system, the Pacific Sustainability Index, to grade them for environmental and social transparency and for reporting of performance. I thought that GRI shouldn't be the only game in town, though it looks like it will prevail eventually.

We have been using this system during the fall semester and have [not-quite-complete]

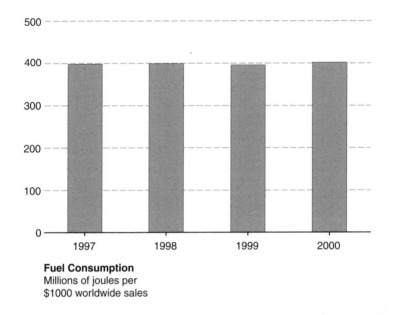

Figure 13.1a Simple bar chart.
Adapted with permission from the Bristol-Myers Squibb 2001 Sustainability Progress Report.

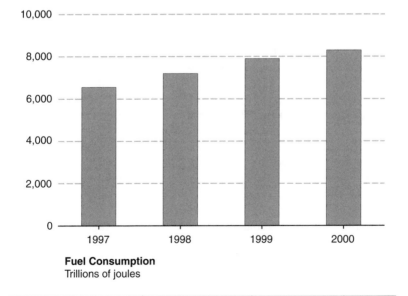

Figure 13.1b Simple bar chart.
Adapted with permission from the Bristol-Myers Squibb 2001 Sustainability Progress Report.

different story—fuel consumption has been steadily increasing and is 27 percent higher than in 1997. Not that this is bad: sales have increased by 27 percent so manufacturing activities and hence fuel consumption has also increased, but the immediate visual effect of the two graphs is quite different, and the story is clearer when they are both present.

Bristol-Myers Squibb opted for the simplest possible vertical bar chart of the type shown to display all of its data. This makes the report graphically elegant and easy to grasp, but at the price of including very little detail. All of Bristol-Myers Squibb's graphs represent either worldwide or U.S.-wide totals, and there is no subsetting of the data by, for example, type of fuel consumed.

How Complex Should Data Graphs Be?

This isn't rocket science. The complex graphs common to the sciences and engineering are off-putting to many potential readers, yet simple data graphs are far easier to grasp quickly than data in tables. One has to be really interested in the results to work through a data table while trends are immediately obvious using a graph. For some reason the social sciences seem to rely more heavily on tables than on graphs—the American Academy of Management Journal, for example, publishes technical articles involving extensive and complex statistical analyses, but seldom, if ever, prints a graph. In the sciences, almost every paper uses both graphs and tables. If the trend is the important thing, a graph is usually the data display of choice. If the absolute numerical data is important, for example if the reader might want to use it for something and the author would rather have her use the actual data than data extracted inaccurately from a graph, a table is useful.

Mitsubishi Electric, in its 2001 Environmental Sustainability Report, uses graphs more typical of the scientific and engineering literature than the simple bar charts used by Bristol-Myers Squibb. The most common type is illustrated in Figure 13.2a, which is a redrawn version of one of its simple bar graphs, overlaid with a second plot showing a separate trend line—two related plots in one. It is accompanied by the pie chart, also heavily used by Mitsubishi Electric, in Figure 13.2b that shows the source of the energy consumption plotted in Figure 13.2a. Mitsibushi Electric also makes heavy use of stacked bar charts, which provide information similar to the pie charts but also allow trend lines (see Figure 13.3).

In the world of environmental and sustainability reports, something usually not seen in science and engineering is evolving: a sort of combination of graph and table. The idea is to minimize the outward complexity of the scientific data graph embodied in the well-labeled horizontal and vertical axes, and present what in science would be tabular data on the face of the graph. The result is that trends are made obvious by the graph, and the data are right there accompanying the trend obviating the need for a table.

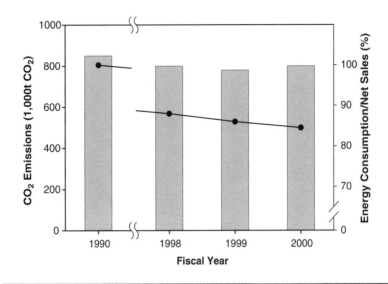

Figure 13.2a   Simple bar chart with trend line for second axis. By using the bars for one variable (CO_2) and the connected dots for a second one (energy consumption) the two trends can be compared.

Adapted with permission from the Mitsubishi Electric 2001 Environmental Sustainability Report.

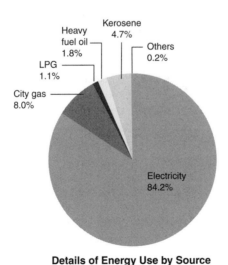

Details of Energy Use by Source

Figure 13.2b   Labeled pie chart. Pie charts are good for showing percentages of different components making up a total category such as energy use, CO_2 production, TRI releases, and water sources.

Adapted with permission from the Mitsubishi Electric 2001 Environmental Sustainability Report.

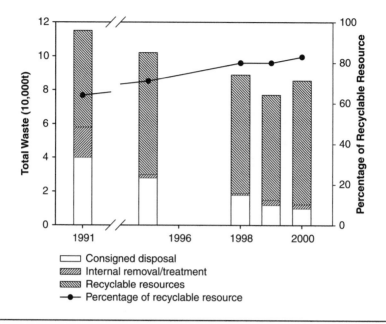

Consigned disposal
Internal removal/treatment
Recyclable resources
—●— Percentage of recyclable resource

Figure 13.3 Combination stacked bar chart and trend line with data points. Stacked bar charts, in addition to illustrating absolute values and trends, show the individual components of each bar.

Adapted with permission from the Mitsubishi Electric 2001 Environmental Sustainability Report.

Since the data are seldom, if ever, subjected to statistical analysis, there is no need for error bars and other complexities on the graphs so the presentation can be spare and graphically attractive. I have redrawn some examples following, but to get the full effect of the commonly used muted pastel shades, you will have to look at the company environmental Web sites or the printed reports themselves.

International Paper in its 1999–2000 Environment, Health, and Safety Annual Report uses another approach convenient for readers who are not used to looking at data charts. Vertical bars show the trends, but the values, rather than being shown on a vertical axis, are placed above the bars (Figure 13.4). This is a sort of hybrid between a table and a chart: the trends are readily discernable, but the data read like a table.

Mead's 2000 Sustainable Development Report uses horizontal bar charts to good effect. The one shown in Figure 13.5 is unusual in that it at first appears to be a stacked bar chart in which the length of each segment represents the full value for that variable. The immediate impression is

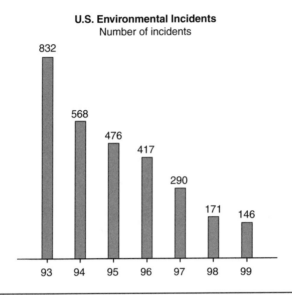

U.S. Environmental Incidents
Number of incidents

Figure 13.4   Vertical bar chart with numerical data but without vertical axis. The addition of numbers above the bars makes this chart read like a table while graphically illustrating trends.

Reprinted with permission of International Paper, from the International Paper Environment, Health, and Safety 1999–2000 Annual Report.

that in one of the two years shown companies had much higher OSHA incidence rates than in the other year. On closer inspection it is apparent that this is an *overlapped* bar chart in which there are two bars for each company, one on top of the other, each starting at zero. The longer of the two is underneath and sticks out at the right. The shorter bar represents either 1998 or 1999 data, which can be determined by the shading. The vertical ordering of the companies is determined by the 1999 data, so in some cases they are out of order for the 1998 data. This graph, by the way, is one of very few examples of companies comparing themselves directly to their competitors. OSHA Incidence Rates are one of the things that are unambiguously comparable between companies, but since the definition of an incident ranges from minor medical treatment to a fatality, some additional partitioning of the data would be extremely informative.

A grouped bar chart made up of the same data (Figure 13.6) is easier to read and the more conventional approach.

Phillips Petroleum plots its recordable injuries using a filled trend line with no vertical axis, and numbers associated with the data points

Mead and Its Competitors
1998 vs. 1999 OSHA Incidence Rate

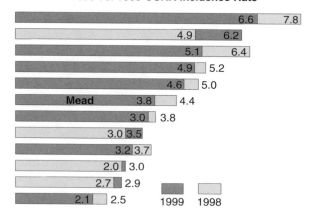

Figure **13.5** Horizontal overlapped bar chart with numerical data. The units are the number of employees who experienced occupational injuries and illnesses that resulted in medical treatment, days away from work, or restricted work, hearing threshold shifts, and fatalities per 200,000 hours worked. The overlap of the bars is unconventional and potentially confusing since it looks like a strangely shaded stacked bar chart.

Adapted with permission from The Mead Corporation 2000 Sustainable Development Report.

Mead and Its Competitors
1998 vs. 1999 OSHA Incidence Rate

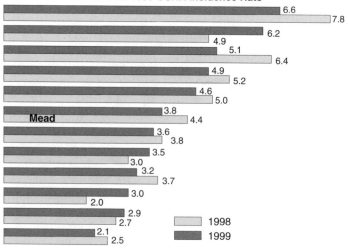

Figure **13.6** Data from Figure 13.5 reformatted as a stacked bar chart, making it more conventional and thus easier for most people to decipher.

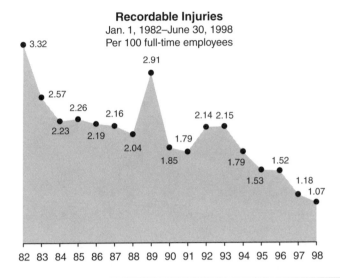

Figure 13.7 Trend line over filled area. This type of graph combines the virtues of a trend line, a bar chart, and a table.

Adapted with permission from the Phillips Petroleum Company 1998 Health, Environmental, and Safety Report.

(Figure 13.7). This format is easy to read and combines the qualities of trend lines, vertical bars, and a table in a single illustration.

Dow, in its Public Report—2000 Results uses a novel "spider web" diagram to give sustainable development results at a glance (Figure 13.8). The outside boundary represents the ideal situation with respect to any of the 21 topics; the shaded portion represents how well a representative Dow business is doing with respect to these variables.

Data Tables and the Web

If you want to present detailed data, there is no better way for users to access it than from a Web site. With a little thought it can be formatted into machine-readable tables so that users can download it and analyze it any way they wish. Furthermore, you can update it easily. Large data tables are generally incompatible with a graphically pleasing printed report, and few readers are likely to care about the detailed data anyway. Those that do care will appreciate being able to download the latest data, and if they want to analyze it, not having to re-enter it.

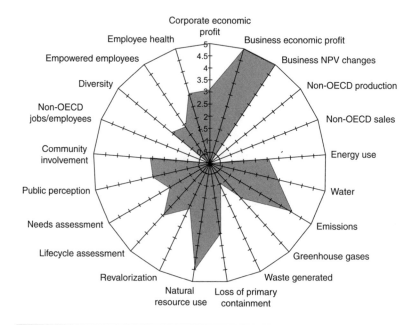

Figure 13.8 A "spider web" graph. The outer rim of the web indicates the ideal condition (undisclosed in the report) of each of the "sustainable development measures." The shaded area indicates how a representative Dow business is doing.

Adapted with permission from Dow Public Report—2000 Results.

Work Toward Comparing Yourself to Competitors

There must be strong institutional barriers and a substantial amount of reluctance to make this comparison, because very few reports even try. Most of the data you present, though, would make far more sense in the context of the performance of your peers. Hence the overwhelming success of the EPA Toxics Emissions Inventory in reducing emissions, flawed though it is as a reflection of actual risk. Interested parties can look up emissions data, make a comparison between companies, identify the poor performers, and confront or boycott them. The result has been substantial emissions reductions that, whether or not fully warranted by the damage of the emissions, are nevertheless generally a good thing. If your company is performing at average or better than average levels and is committed to good environmental and social performance, you ought to take credit for it. You will be nudging the industry forward and potentially doing good for yourself with stakeholders who care.

RECOMMENDATIONS

The heart of an environmental or sustainability report ought to be information on how well the company is performing. No amount of pleasant verbiage; color photographs of happy employees, sincere managers, and shipshape facilities; and third party awards and attestations of excellence can substitute for nice clean data. The data should include trends, and trends are best illustrated using data graphs. The graphs do not need to appear highly technical—done inventively they can become attractive graphic elements in their own rights—but they do need to contain useful information. The user should be able to extract data from them for analysis if so inclined, and the units in which the data are presented should be standardized within your industry as much as possible. Standardization includes normalization to sales, number of employees, number of widgets produced, or whatever makes the most sense. With the advent of the Web, the report does not need to present all the data needed for a detailed analysis: it just needs to point the reader to the data tables on your Web site.

14

Costs and Investments

Keeping track of environmental and social costs, investments, and subsequent recovery is called "environmental accounting." Such accounting is difficult because traditional financial accounting systems often fail to have the proper line items, and because it is not always clear whether an investment that results in environmental or social good is not just a regular business investment—landscaping factories, or reducing energy consumption, for example. Since environmental and social investments and expenses, at their best, also serve direct business purposes, there is little point in requiring that they be considered one or the other. For the purpose of an environmental or sustainability report it is best to report all costs and expenses that do environmental or social good.

RULE 9—DESCRIBE YOUR ENVIRONMENTAL AND SOCIAL COSTS AND INVESTMENTS, VOLUNTARY OR NOT

Keeping track of costs and investments made for environmental and social (rather than purely business) reasons ought to be routine practice of any company's accounting systems. One would expect readers of annual financial reports to be quite interested, if not necessarily sympathetic. Environmental and social expenditures, however, are not widely reported in much detail, either because they are difficult to account for, or because companies do not wish to report the details. The former is probably the principal reason. Some costs, like headquarters and operations health, safety, and environment staff salaries and expenses, are easy to identify. Others, though, like saving energy or maintaining low air emissions, are, in many respects, part of business as usual. If the company makes a one-time major investment like replacing all incandescent lights in a factory with fluorescent ones, that cost is easily identifiable, but if it starts using fluorescent lights preferentially in new construction, even though explicitly for the purpose of saving energy, it is more difficult to account for. If a new end-of-pipe treatment device is added to an existing factory, or if dust collectors are routinely operated, the cost is obvious. If an industrial process is gradually modified over the years to decrease emissions, how can its costs be accounted for?

Still, in a report devoted to environmental and social activities, it makes sense to estimate their costs and benefits. But which ones to select? Figure 14.1 is a list of specific examples of this type of metric from 73 corporate environmental reports, and will give a sense of the range of topics appearing in individual reports.

Amount invested in emission reduction project
Amount paid for 40,000 condensing boilers
Annual energy saved with upgraded lighting system
Annual environmental spending
Avoided treatment/disposal costs by substitution/recycling
Canadian fines and penalties
Capital expenditures for environmental manufacturing program
Civil penalties
Community investments in environmental projects
Compliance fines and penalties
Compliance costs
Cost of construction of recycling facility
Cost of depreciation and management for environmental facilities
Cost of energy efficiency program

continued

Figure 14.1   Environmental and social cost and investment metrics from the reports of 73 companies listed in appendix C.

Cost of operation, reduction since 1990
Costs of construction for environmental protection
Costs, disability
Costs, workers compensation
Current environmental expenditures
Disaster prevention costs
DSM (demand side management) program costs
EHS capital project spending
Energy conservation costs
Environmental and safety fines
Environmental audits
Environmental capital costs
Environmental capital expenditures
Environmental conservation costs and investments
Environmental damage cost
Environmental expenditures
Environmental expenditures (capital)
Environmental expenditures (expense)
Environmental personnel costs
Environmental protection costs
Environmental protection investments
Environmental staff, concurrent position
Environmental staff, divisions/departments
Environmental staff, headquarters
Environmental staff, R&D
Environment-related investigation expenses
Equipment investments since the 1970s
Expenses for implementation of environmental measures
Global environmental conservation costs and expenses
Global environmental conservation investments
Grant for Geothermal Heat Pump Initiatives from DOE
Green purchases
HSE expenses
HSE investments
Increase in chemical, pharmaceutical, and diagnostic production
    and mixing processes

continued

Figure 14.1   Environmental and social cost and investment metrics from the reports of 73 companies listed in appendix C *(continued).*

continued

Increase in energy and waste intensive chemical production
Investment in electric vehicles
Investment in upgraded burner systems at coal-fired plants
ISO 14001 implementation costs
Lifecycle assessment costs
Major refinery fire losses
Major refinery fire losses per crude throughput
Management activity costs, expenses
Management activity costs, investment
Notices of violation resulting in fines
Penalties
Personnel expenses of environmental preservation department
Photovoltaic purchases, 10 year record of
Pollution prevention cost, investments
Pollution prevention costs, expenses
Pollution-control-related investments
Pounds invested in environmental programs
Pounds invested in environmental protection
R&D costs, expenses
Reduction of environmental protection measure costs 1992–97
Research and development as percent of sales
Research projects for transport in major cities
Resource circulation costs, expenses
Resource circulation costs, investment
Safety and occupational hazard fines
Social activity costs, expenses
Social activity costs, investment
Spending on reforestation
Superfund liability costs since 1974
Supplemental environmental projects
Tax credits received for investing in scrubbers
Total spent on construction of control facilities
Total spent upgrading lighting systems at all facilities
Waste processing costs
Waste reduction efforts

Figure 14.1 Environmental and social cost and investment metrics from the reports of 73 companies listed in appendix C *(continued).*

The Significance of Environmental Accounting

DENSO Corporation, in its 2001 environmental report:

. . . regards environmental accounting as a tool for accomplishing the following three purposes.

1. *Identify costs and benefits in quantitative terms, so that future environmental protection activities can be more effective and management decision making can be improved*

2. *Boost the motivation of employees to pursue environmental activities*

3. *Broadly disclose information to stakeholders, so that shareholders and suppliers, in particular, can develop a clearer understanding of DENSO management*

Sony's 2001 Environmental Report says, "Sony recognizes the possibility of reconciling economic and ecological concerns—of achieving ongoing growth while minimizing environmental impact—through the appropriate application of environmental accounting."

Japanese firms in general appear to be more detailed in their environmental accounting than do those headquartered in other countries.

Industry Approaches to Environmental Accounting

Sony's 2001 Environmental Report estimates the individual costs of (1) energy and resources conservation in products; (2) recycling of container packaging, batteries, and so on; (3) pollution prevention; (4) energy and resource conservation at sites; (5) green purchasing; (6) environmental and risk management; and (7) communications and contributions to society, for a total of ¥22,742 million. These it weighs against savings from energy saved during product manufacture and use, decreasing weights of products, decreasing waste, lower water requirements, lower environmental risk, and a reduction of hazardous materials, which it calculates to be, using various conversion factors, ¥19,206 million, with the benefits offsetting 85 percent of the costs.

Toshiba's 2001 Environmental Report has an environmental accounting section similar to Sony's, itemizing environmental costs for itself and 46 domestic subsidiaries and affiliates and 28 overseas subsidiaries, for environmental aspects of general business activities, pollution prevention, preventing global effects (greenhouse gas), effective utilization of resources, green procurement/recycling, environmental education, environmental research and development, social activity costs (including landscaping of facilities), and environmental remediation. Total costs for FY2000 were ¥39,030 million. The economic benefits, both actual and assumed were ¥16,361 million, with the benefits offsetting 42 percent of the costs.

Mitsubishi Electric's 2001 Environmental Sustainability Report has a similar cost breakdown: pollution prevention, global environmental conservation, resource circulation (recycling and reuse), activities upstream and downstream of production, environmental management activities, research and development for environmental conservation, social activities (landscaping, support for volunteers, industry association membership), and costs of environmental damage and cleanup. These amounted to ¥19,500 million. Although Mitsubishi calculated a return from accumulated environmental measures of ¥67,700 million, this was ¥4,300 million less than for the previous year.

The Nippon Steel 2001 Environmental Report distinguishes between environment-related capital investments and expenses for environmental preservation. "Of the expenses, air pollution prevention cost, which claims the largest share, is a sum total of electricity expenses needed for the operation of the environmental dust collectors for keeping up air quality in the vicinity of the steelworks" and expenses for equipment maintenance and repairs. The report itemizes costs of countermeasures for air pollution, countermeasures for water pollution, energy saving, treatment of by-products (final disposal), treatment of waste (disposal), ISO 14001 certification, environment observation, personnel expenditures, R&D for eco-products, R&D for low environmental impact steelmaking process, increasing the greenery and advertisement, and SO_x levy.

DENSO Corporation's 2000 Environmental Report divides its environmental accounting expenditures between investments and costs and balances these against the cost savings and revenues it attributes to them. The costs include (1) primary business costs incurred in reducing the environmental impact generated by manufacturing, (2) upstream and downstream costs incurred through activities other than manufacturing, (3) administrative costs, (4) research and development costs, (5) social activities costs (of which there were none), and (6) environmental damage costs (of which there were also none). These amounted to a total of ¥15.8 billion. Offsetting these costs and investments were energy savings of ¥10 billion, reductions in waste disposal costs of ¥3 billion, and sales revenues of ¥15 billion for recycled iron, nonferrous metals, plastics, oil, and other materials for a total of ¥28 billion in revenues. By DENSO's calculations, environmental initiatives generated a profit of ¥13 billion.

RECOMMENDATIONS

Follow the solution used by many Japanese companies who are at the forefront in environmental accounting—for the purposes of an environmental or sustainability report, count anything that has a discernable environmental or social benefit as an environmental or social investment or expense, and count any savings or profits that result from current and previous investments an environmental or social profit. You can make your decisions of what to include transparent by itemizing rather than lumping. That way a reader who objects to landscaping as an environmental expense, or burning of sawmill residuals as an energy conservation tactic, can ignore them.

15

Goals and Targets

Presenting goals and targets for environmental and social performance is an important part of environmental and social management. Simply measuring and reporting indicators with no suggestion of what values ought to be achieved is timid, and not likely to result in much improvement. Some companies set goals that are already achieved, thus circumventing failure, but the best managers figure out what ideal performance is and strive toward it, setting concrete goals along the way. Current environmental and sustainability reports range from those with no discernable goals, to those including 30 or more explicit numerical ones. A report that has at least some numerical goals that will require some work to achieve reflects well on management.

RULE 10—SET CONCRETE NUMERICAL, ENVIRONMENTAL, AND SOCIAL GOALS AND COMMIT YOURSELF TO IMPROVEMENT

Some companies invoke sweeping explicit goals companywide, while others keep them general, or restrict them to local facilities. Some companies set goals that are quite ambitious, while others set goals that are in hand, or nearly so, before even being articulated. There seem to be broad intercompany—perhaps international—cultural differences that allow some companies to set high goals that are hard to attain and at which they may fail, and restrict others to goals that can certainly be achieved, guaranteeing success, but not great success.

I favor ambitious goals. Environmentally- and socially-conscious stakeholders want companies to perform significantly better, not just marginally better. It may well be that success is achieved incrementally, but the goals need not be incremental, at least not the overall goals. One way to set both lofty goals and achievable ones simultaneously is to set an ultimate goal and subdivide it into annual goals.

Explicit Goals and Targets

Appendix E is a list of a large number of goals extracted from 73 environmental and sustainability reports. I include it because it is helpful to get a broad overview of the types of goals companies set. One thing is clear from this list: goals are not standardized. Even within industrial sectors, there are very different ideas of what constitutes appropriate goals and targets. In appendix E, I have italicized the relatively few goals and targets that both are numerical and have a stated time frame, since these are the only ones against which performance can be judged. Some examples of both quantitative and nonquantitative goals from individual reports are included following.

Examples of Goals and Targets from Corporate Reports

BASF, in its 2000 Environment, Safety, Health report uses facility-specific goals and has 24 of them, though only eight of them have measurable outcomes. These include a 95% reduction in volatile organic carbon and carbon monoxide emissions, a 50% decrease in nitrate emissions, a 50% decrease in ammonium content of wastewater, a 23% reduction of CO_2 emissions, a chemical oxygen demand reduction of 10% in one plant and 50% in another, a 20% on-the-job accident reduction, and a 10% reduction in job-related skin and respiratory diseases.

ICI, in its 2000 Safety, Health, and Environment Web pages reports setting goals in 1995 for reducing releases of acidity to air and water by 50% by 2000. By 1997 they had exceeded these goals, and by 2000 had decreased the acidity releases by 79% relative to 1995. The goal for reductions in aquatic toxicity of 50% was surpassed even more by 90% reductions and an energy efficiency goal of 10% reduction was surpassed by a 16% reduction. But not all goals were so handily met. The goal of reducing hazardous air emissions by 50% was immediately achieved in 1996, but not achieved again until 2000, and the goal of reducing aquatic oxygen demand by 50% was not even approached by the 15% reduction in 2000. A number of other performance metrics for which no targets were set were also substantially improved and in retrospect should probably have had targets set.

Intel, in its 2000 EHS Performance Report, has five explicit numerical goals, four of which it has already surpassed. It has recycled 63% of U.S. hazardous waste (against a goal of 45%), 9% of non-U.S. hazardous waste (against a goal of 15%), 79% of U.S. solid waste (against a goal of 65%), and 40% of non-U.S. solid waste (against a goal of 35%). It also has a goal to maintain no increase in global VOC emissions, when in fact it had decreased them by 12% from the 1999 levels. Intel needs some new explicit goals.

Siemens' 2000 Environmental Report has four explicit goals each of them at a different German facility: (1) to extend the service life of cooling lubricants by 40% by the end of 2000, (2) to replace a chrome VI-based silver passivation process with a procedure generally recognized as safe, (3) to cut power requirements by 10% by the end of 2001 through the installation of energy-saving lighting, and (4) to reduce consumption of compressed air 10% by the end of 2002.

Sony's 2001 Environmental Report lists 33 goals, 14 of them with numerical targets, and many others with absolute targets. There are six energy-related targets, six resource input targets, four resource output targets, one water resource target, eight hazardous materials targets, and eight environmental management targets.

Unilever's 2000 Environmental Performance report uses a spider web diagram similar to Dow's (see Figure 13.8) to display simultaneously its goals (unlike the Dow diagram, the outer perimeter of Unilever's spider web diagram is the explicit goal rather than an idealized value) and performance (the interior polygons, one for 1996 and the other for 1999). This spider web is six-sided, including goals and performance for COD, SO_x, CO_2, total water used, hazardous waste, and nonhazardous waste, all normalized to weight of product. In addition, using a belt-and-suspenders approach, the report presents the yearly time series data for the six indicators both as a table and as a series of six bar graphs with the tabular data written beside them, and then presents them again in another series of six graphs as absolute rather than normalized data.

The Corus Group 2000 Environmental Report lists 11 environmental targets, some numeric including 95% certification to ISO 14001 by 2002, reducing emissions of perfluorocarbons from the primary aluminum production process by 50% between 1990 and 2005, reducing total energy consumption in the UK by 10% by 2010, reducing waste to landfill by

10% from 1999 levels by 2003, and increasing the amount of steel packaging waste recycled in the UK by 20% between 1999 and 2002. Some of the goals are fairly vague, such as undertaking appropriate risk assessments for any potentially contaminated land at Corus European sites, evaluating the potential for suppression of dioxin emissions from iron ore sintering, and identifying and assessing, where necessary, Corus's contribution to ambient air concentrations of fine dust particles (PM10s). One is a little frightening: install where necessary enhanced incoming scrap and product radiation detection equipment—where does radioactive scrap come from and who would have gotten the radioactive products?

Nippon Steel, in its 2001 Environmental Report, lists 16 priority targets, five of which are numeric: (1) reduce energy use by 4.4% between 1995 and 2010 (it had only been reduced by 0.6% by 2000), (2) reduce landfilled waste by 75% between 1990 and 2010 (to 100,000 tons per year—they had reached 148,000 tons in 2000), (3) establish a system for the steel industry to burn one million tons of plastic waste as an alternative fuel by 2010 (just starting, and this is an industrywide objective), (4) reduce benzene emissions 50% by 2003 (action plan started in 2001, no current results presented), and (5) reduce dioxin emissions by 30% between 1997 and 2002 (this target, based on a Japanese Iron and Steel Federation guideline of less than $1.0ng\text{-}TEQ/Nm^3$ was reached in 1998 and has been below it since). The remaining targets, such as "promote environmental communications" and "reduce generation of by-products and effectively utilize slag and dust" either are not measurable or provide little against which success can be measured.

Eli Lilly and Company's 1999 Environmental Health and Safety Report sets just one numerical environmental and two numerical social goals. The environmental goal is to reduce organic solvent emissions to the environment to 1% or less of the current total used by the year 2002. Will this be difficult to achieve? We do not know because Lilly reports neither its organic solvent usage nor its organic solvent emissions. Would it be good performance compared to other companies? No perspective is offered. One of the social goals is to reduce serious injuries to no more than 1 per 100 employees by the year 2001. We know this would be an improvement over the 1998 results of 1.6 per 100 employees or the 2000 goal of 2.0 per 100 employees, but we do not know if it is good by peer industry standards, or by any standards. The other social goal is to get all management practices in place by the end of 2000.

East Japan Railway Company's 2001 Annual Environmental Report states 11 explicit goals to be met by fiscal 2005, relative to fiscal 1990. These include a 20% reduction in CO_2 emissions from general business activities and a 30% reduction of CO_2 and 60% reduction of NO_X per unit of electricity generated at its thermal power plant; an energy-saving railcar ratio of 80%; a 15% reduction in energy consumption of trains relative to volume transported; an 85% reduction in large refrigerating machines using specific CFCs; recycling rates of 35% for waste generated at stations and on trains, 75% for waste generated in rolling stock workshops, and 85% for waste from construction projects; 100% usage of recycled paper in offices; and noise intensities less than 75dB in certain residential areas. None of these goals are yet achieved, but the report shows exactly how far the company has come with respect to them in fiscal 2000 and one gets the sense that it knows exactly what it needs to do to achieve them.

Chubu Electric Power's 2001 Environment Report (Web pages) has 12 numeric goals, many of which are highly precise and already, or very nearly already, met. They include 0.424 kg CO_2 emitted/kWh generated (having reached 0.427 kg CO_2/kWh in 1999), thermal efficiency of 41% or higher (1999 value was 41.52%), 80% facility utilization rate at nuclear power stations (1999 value was 82.7%), 5% transmission/distribution loss (1999 value was 4.9%), 0.07 g SO_x emitted/kWh (1999 value was 0.06 g SO_x/kWh) . . . you get the idea. Chubu is not reaching for anything with these goals they are not already almost achieving, but, on the other hand, these results may already be quite good. We do not know because the company has not compared its performance with respect to these metrics to its peers, at least in this report. For other metrics it has made this comparison: Chubu Electric Power has recorded the highest total thermal efficiency of thermal power stations in Japan for three consecutive years, as well as the lowest value of transmission/distribution loss. We would be better informed if it had made an attempt at such a comparison for all of the metrics.

RECOMMENDATIONS

It seems to me that companies should develop a set of at least 10 specific numerical goals that are ambitious but realistic. Setting fewer than 10 seems un-ambitious, and setting more, while admirable, seems unnecessary and sometimes confusing in the context of an environmental or sustainability report. For small, uncomplicated companies, some of the 10 goals might be components of a larger goal. A larger goal of reducing energy by 10 percent might be made up of separate goals to replace a certain number of incandescent lights with fluorescent ones, to turn lights off in unoccupied rooms 90 percent of the time, and to use 10 percent less energy for air conditioning and heating. For larger firms, a single goal might be the sum of many specific ones. Electricity reduction of 10 percent might be arrived at by hundreds of specific goals like those above in individual facilities.

Choose goals that are most appropriate for your industry, mimicking those of your competitors to facilitate third-party comparison. Explain how they were selected, how the levels were set, and why they are ambitious. Unless your performance is already well honed and you know exactly what you will be able to achieve, even with maximal effort, don't make them too precise.

III

Sustainability Report Evaluation and Scoring Systems

Part 3 describes and analyzes the existing report evaluation and scoring systems (chapter 16), most of which are used in this book to evaluate corporate reports, and introduces the Pacific Sustainability Index (chapter 17), a new scoring system introduced in this book.

16

Existing Environmental and Sustainability Report Scoring Systems

Since 1996 there have been formal attempts to grade corporate environmental reports and produce a numerical score. This chapter analyzes the most important existing scoring systems, showing how the topics they address are distributed relative to the topics of the 10 rules for writing highly effective environmental and sustainability reports.

───────────────

There are a variety of attempts in the academic literature and in reports by consulting firms to judge the quality of corporate environmental and sustainability reports. These include attempts to:

- Compare information in the reports with information from other sources to judge transparency and credibility

- Compile summary statistics about the number of pages devoted to different topics

- Compile summary statistics about the number of topics mentioned

- Evaluate the depth of coverage of the topics mentioned

Surprisingly, there has been little attempt to evaluate the quantitative environmental and sustainability *performance* discussed in the reports. The evaluations have been on the way in which performance has been reported rather than on the quality of the performance.

The three approaches discussed in detail in this chapter are scoring systems that judge transparency and comprehensiveness of reports by awarding points for mentioning specific topics, and increasing the number of points for increased depth of discussion. These are the Davis-Walling & Batterman scoring system (Davis-Walling & Batterman 1997), the Deloitte Touche Tohmatsu scoring system (Deloitte Touche Tohmatsu 1999), and the SustainAbility/UNEP scoring system (SustainAbility/UNEP 1996, SustainAbility/UNEP 1997, SustainAbility/UNEP 2000). All of these result in numerical scores of reporting comprehensiveness that allow comparison between companies and industrial sectors. The relative importance in each of these systems of the 10 generic environmental topics that make up the 10 rules for effective reporting is described in chapter 4. The results of their application to the environmental and sustainability reports of 40 of the world's largest industrial companies are presented in appendix B. This chapter supplies more detail about the way in which the systems were constructed and what the scores mean.

First, though, this chapter discusses examples of the other existing approaches to evaluating environmental and sustainability reports, including one that compares company reporting of negative environmental news with previous newspaper reports (Niskanen and Nieminen 2001), one that reports the percentage of companies that discuss particular environmental topics in their reports (KPMG 1997, KPMG 1999) and one that measures the percentage of space in corporate environmental and sustainability reports devoted to specific environmental topics (Lober et al. 1997).

DO COMPANIES FAITHFULLY REPORT NEGATIVE ENVIRONMENTAL NEWS?

One way to find out how useful the reports are is to compare what is independently known with what firms voluntarily disclose. In an empirical look at voluntary environmental disclosures from Finnish firms between 1985 and 1996, Niskanen and Nieminen (2001) compared positive and negative environmental news published about the companies in the newspaper with the information the firms themselves published. Between 1985 and 1992 the firms published no news at all about negative environmental events, but thereafter disclosed 41 percent of the negative information already in the newspaper, while reporting 86 percent of the positive environmental news. They concluded ". . . the environmental reporting of the sample firms cannot be considered objective, since the proportional share of negative events reported was negligible compared to the respective percentage for positive events." The pre-1992 absence of negative environmental disclosure by the companies largely predates any voluntary corporate environmental reporting and is thus not surprising. The significance of the post-1992 underreporting is also open to some question because standards for environmental reporting have been slowly evolving and some newsworthy "environmental" items may not have seemed appropriate in 1996 when the study ended, even though by 2001 standards they would have. The fact that 14 percent of positive environmental "news" also went unreported by companies reinforces this possibility, but it is human nature that newspaper reporters would be quicker to report negative corporate news than would corporate report writers. Still, corporate acceptance of full voluntary disclosure is certainly not yet universal, not least because it can sometimes increase risk and liability.

WHAT TYPES OF ENVIRONMENTAL TOPICS DO COMPANIES CHOOSE TO REPORT?

The Dutch consulting firm KPMG approached the top 100 companies in each of 11 countries in 1996 and 1999 (KPMG 1997, KPMG 1999) for their health and safety/environmental reports. In 1999, 267 of these companies produced such a report, 252 of which were analyzed by KPMG for the presence or absence of environmental policy statements, the inclusion of environmental topics within the policy statement, and quantitative environmental data. Topics noted within policy statements included employee involvement; natural resource conservation; legislative compliance; discharges to air, land, and water; health and safety; sustainable development; and local community issues. Figure 16.1 shows the distribution of topics, segregated into the topics of my 10 rules, and is heavily weighted toward environmental performance.

KPMG found that five of the seven policy topics increased substantially in policy statements between 1996 and 1999, that natural resource conservation remained unchanged at a relatively high 60 percent, but that mention of discharges to air, land, and water decreased from being in 64 percent of policy statements in 1996 to being in only 46 percent of them in 1999. This seems particularly odd because of all corporate environmental topics, the one most evident to most stakeholders would be expected to be discharges. KPMG also identified quantitative environmental data reported in six categories: waste disposal, air emissions, effluent discharges, energy conservation, environmental costs, and accidents and incidents. They found

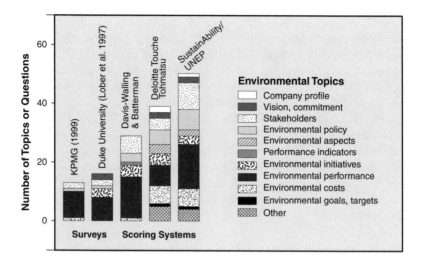

Figure 16.1 Number of topics addressed and questions asked in two surveys and three scoring systems for environmental and sustainability reports.

that reporting increased in all six categories from an average of 43 percent of reports in 1996 to 60 percent of reports in 1999.

Researchers at the Duke University Nicholas School of the Environment and Fuqua School of Business (Lober et al. 1997) measured the percentage of 106 reports from the Fortune 500 and the S&P 500 devoted to 16 topics selected from a variety of reporting guidelines and academic papers. These topics included a corporate policy statement, an environmental performance summary, information on waste reduction of various sorts, information on air, land stewardship, energy, global issues including biodiversity and ozone depletion, water, wetlands, letters from executives, monitoring and auditing, risk reduction, product stewardship, lifecycle analysis, and information about two categories of stakeholders: employees and local communities. Figure 16.1 shows the distribution of these topics. On average, over half of the report pages were devoted to corporate policy statements, summaries of environmental performance, and efforts at waste reduction, pollution prevention, recycling, and packaging.

These researchers also noted the percentage of reports having an additional 16 environmental characteristics, such as having an environmental policy statement, a letter from the company chairman, and awards and honors. Over 50 percent of the reports had these three characteristics, but fewer than 46 percent had any of the others.

All of these studies analyzed coverage of a small number of topics relative to what could reasonably have been included in a corporate environmental report, and characterized the reports collectively by country or industrial sector, rather than by individual company, but there is a small body of literature analyzing environmental reports by company, often addressing more topics.

THE DAVIS-WALLING AND BATTERMAN SCORING SYSTEM

In 1997, Paige Davis-Walling of GE Plastics and Stuart Batterman, a professor in the University of Michigan Department of Environmental Health Sciences, analyzed the 25 environmental reports produced in 1996 by Fortune 50 U.S. companies by extracting from them 29 topics that were found in at least four of them (Davis-Walling and Batterman 1997). They developed a scoring system that awarded 20 of the topics one point if addressed at all and awarded nine of the topics up to two points depending on level of detail. More than half of the potential total score is based on quantitative measures of environmental performance that include air emissions, reduction in use of ozone-depleting chemicals (ODCs), wastewater treatment, energy conservation, reductions in packaging and waste, recycling, and reuse of recycled materials. Figure 16.1 illustrates the number of questions devoted to the 10 generalized environmental topics. Missing entirely from Davis-Walling and Batterman's topics are a discussion of company profile, vision and commitment, aspects, and goals and targets. This system is heavily oriented toward existing results rather than a view toward the future, and, like the KPMG and Lober systems, there are no nonenvironmental topics, social or otherwise.

There are three main shortcomings of the Davis-Walling & Batterman system. First, it has few topics: only about half as many as the SustainAbility/UNEP system, about a third of the topics in the GRI 2000 guidelines, and about a fourth of the topics in the ISO 14031 guidelines. Second, all of the topics are based on what was being reported rather than what ought to have been reported, so it is entirely dependent on early thinking about the reporting process. Third, the topics are not very consistent internally. For example, reporting air emissions is worth two points, but there are no points for reporting other kinds of emissions or materials or energy use. There are points, however, for discussing wastewater treatment (rather than release), energy conservation (rather than energy use), and reductions in waste (rather than generation or disposal of it), use of ozone-depleting compounds, and packaging. Davis-Walling and Batterman were worried that since there was no way to check how comprehensive the reports were—what negative results might have been left out, for example, that their system could not ". . . be used to judge or evaluate a firm's environmental commitments, liabilities, and performance." They called for guidelines that ". . . specify a means to perform and report a comprehensive evaluation of a firm's environmental record and the environmental impacts of its products and services" with the idea that if comprehensive guidelines existed, then it would be more obvious if something were left out. Anticipating GRI 2000, and to an extent, the ISO 14031 Annex A list, they suggest that such a set of guidelines might become part of the ISO 14000 family of standards.

THE DELOITTE TOUCHE TOHMATSU SCORING SYSTEM

The Deloitte Touche Tohmatsu (1999) scoring system is derived from the SustainAbility/UNEP system (see next section) and is largely a subset of it although it treats its topics more generically. It is therefore applicable to more kinds of companies. For example the Deloitte Touche Tohmatsu system covers environmental performance with eight generic categories: (1) consumption (of energy, water, materials), (2) emissions (to air, water, soil), (3) waste (generated, reduced, recycled, disposed of), (4) packaging (types, amounts, handling, reduction), (5) transportation, (6) product stewardship (impacts during use and disposal), (7) land contamination and remediation, and (8) other, whereas the SustainAbility /UNEP system covers this same ground with the much more specific topics of (1) material use, (2) energy consumption, (3) water consumption, (4) land contamination and remediation, (5) waste minimization and management, (6) air emissions, (7) water effluents, (8) noise and odor, and (9) packaging.

Although it is more generic than the SustainAbility/UNEP system, the Deloitte Touche Tohmatsu system has much more explicit rules for scoring each topic. This is both a blessing and a problem. The blessing is that there need be very little subjectivity in arriving at a particular score. For example, for the topic of goals and targets, one point is allowed if there is a brief mention; two points are allowed if they are described in quantitative terms so that their achievement can be verified; three points are allowed if the achievement or nonachievement is described and the reasons for nonachievement are given; and four points are allowed if there is an even more detailed description. The problem is that the scorer must know what kinds of environmental aspects the company is likely to have. If a company reports on consumption of energy in detail it might seem appropriate to award it four points under the consumption topic even if the main consumption issue that the company should have been addressing was water or hazardous materials consumption.

THE SUSTAINABILITY/UNEP SCORING SYSTEM

The SustainAbility/UNEP scoring system is a joint effort of the UK consultancy SustainAbility and the United Nations Environment Programme (UNEP). This system is based on 50 topics that are somewhat less evenly spread over the 10 generic environmental topics than is the case in the Deloitte Touche Tohmatsu system, but like the Deloitte Touche Tohmatsu system, most of the generic topics are addressed to some degree. In this system there is particular emphasis on environmental performance, followed by stakeholders and environmental policy (see Figure 16.1). The SustainAbility/UNEP system uses 48 topics worth up to four points each depending on comprehensiveness of coverage, and two topics (awards received and charitable contributions made) worth one point each. Its assignment of up to four possible points is quite subjective, the only guidance given in 1997 being that ". . . '0' means that the area covered by the criterion is not discussed at all and '4' means that the reporting is comprehensive" (SustainAbility/UNEP 1997). In the 2000 report the scoring was modified slightly so that to achieve a score of four the topic must have been ". . . fully discussed in a comprehensive, integrated, and particularly innovative manner"(SustainAbility/UNEP 2000).

Like Davis-Walling and Batterman but unlike the Deloitte Touche Tohmatsu scoring system, the authors applied this system directly to corporate reports and published the results, in this case in their own commercial publications, which champion the high-scoring companies. They selected 40 companies in 1996 (SustainAbility/UNEP 1996), 100 companies in 1997 (SustainAbility/UNEP 1997), and, with revised scoring criteria, 50 companies in 2000 (SustainAbility/UNEP 2000). Many of the chosen companies were or became sponsors of the effort. The high visibility of these scores, popularized particularly in the UK in *Tomorrow* magazine, appears to have been a driving force in influencing large companies to prepare environmental and sustainability reports. SustainAbility has also supported the efforts of GRI to standardize the reporting systems.

THE GRI 2000 AND ISO 14031 ANNEX A SCORING SYSTEMS

The GRI 2000 guidelines and ISO 14031 Annex A list, both described in chapter 3, can be converted directly into scoring systems by isolating each of their topics and assigning potential scores to each of them. My students and I did just that and applied them to the environmental reports of 40 global companies. These guidelines have many more topics than do the scoring systems—the ISO 14031 list has four times as many topics as the SustainAbility/UNEP scoring system—and the scores from environmental reports tend to be much lower (Morhardt et al. submitted for publication). Figures 4.5, 4.6, and B.1 and B.2 in appendix B show the results of applying these systems to the reports from the 40 companies in much greater detail than was possible in the technical paper. Low scores based on the ISO 14031 list—an average score of only 13 percent of the total possible score (see Figure B.1 and [Morhardt et al., submitted for publication])—might be attributable to the fact that the list was not intended as a scoring system at all. It was intended to be a source of possible environmental metrics that a company could choose from. On close inspection, however, almost any company could readily address most of the topics on the list.

The low scores from the GRI 2000 scoring system are more problematic. The GRI guidelines are intended to be followed to the letter, and if they were, the GRI 2000 scoring system would award a perfect score. Remember, this is not a performance scoring system: it merely asks the question of whether the report writer addressed the topic in reasonable detail. Judging by the results, most companies are not on the same wavelength as the GRI. The highest-scoring report (Daimler-Chrysler 1999) got less than 40 percent of the total possible points and the average scores for all 40 reports were only 17.1 percent of the total possible points (see Figure 4.5 and Morhardt et al. [submitted for publication]). It also means that with a little effort at following the GRI guidelines, a score considerably higher than that achieved by most reports could be obtained.

CONCLUSIONS

The existing scoring systems differ over more than an order of magnitude in the number of topics that they address, but most of the topics fall into one or another of the 10 categories making up my 10 rules for effective environmental and sustainability reporting. Much of the difference is in how specific the topics are, and hence how specific the questions in the scoring system are. They also differ in weighting of topics, but most of the systems weight heavily in the direction of comprehensive reporting of environmental performance and processes intended to result in improved environmental performance. Few of the systems address the social considerations that make an environmental report into a sustainability report. Surprisingly, there is little emphasis on concrete goals and targets, which are an important part of any serious management effort, and there is no emphasis at all on quality of environmental or social performance. Why this should be the case is hard to understand. Even though it is difficult—some say practically impossible—to compare the overall environmental and social performance across companies and industrial sectors, nearly all companies use their environmental reports to compare their performance to their own previous performance. The existing scoring systems allow no credit for improvement, and no penalty for poor performance . . . only for reporting what the performance is. The existing systems that address social and economic issues also mix them in with environmental issues so that it is impossible to distinguish any differences in the two areas from the final score. This is problematic because although it may be desirable in some circles to report on social transparency, it is quite a different thing from environmental transparency, and companies who choose to be transparent in one should be able to get credit for it even if they choose not to address the other.

The Pacific Sustainability Index, described in the next chapter, attempts to solve some of these problems. Environmental and social comprehensiveness are scored entirely separately, and there is a separate process for scoring quality of performance independent of comprehensiveness of reporting.

17

The Pacific Sustainability Index: A New Scoring System for Environmental and Sustainability Reports

This chapter describes a new scoring system developed at the Roberts Environmental Center at Claremont McKenna College. It completely separates environmental and social scores and puts more emphasis than other scoring systems on providing a comprehensive overview of the company in relation to its industry peers. It goes beyond previous scoring systems by identifying and rewarding good environmental and social performance *in addition to comprehensiveness of reporting. This system is essentially a summarization and quantification of the ten rules, and can be used both as a checklist to be sure the rules are being followed when writing a report, and to score the reports of others. The scoring system in the form of a checklist is provided in appendix A.*

Previous scoring systems have incorporated environmental and social reporting into a single score and have awarded points only for inclusion of information (comprehensiveness or transparency) without judging the quality of environmental and social *performance*. These two aspects of the current systems are less than ideal because it should be possible to evaluate environmental and social reporting independently since environmental reporting is much more mature in most companies, and because no matter how comprehensive the reporting of environmental and social performance is, the thing that really matters is how good the performance itself is.

The Pacific Sustainability Index attempts to rectify these shortcomings by judging comprehensiveness of environmental and social reporting separately, and by judging quality of performance independently of the comprehensiveness of reporting it.

There are at least three advantages of this separation: (1) reporting of either environmental or social information is desirable and the absence of one should not diminish the credit a company gets for reporting the other, (2) comprehensiveness is to be desired and should be recognized, even if performance is lacking, and (3) good performance itself should be recognized and rewarded.

As with the previous systems discussed in chapter 16, the Pacific Sustainability Index can be used both to score finished reports, and as a diagnostic tool during the writing process. Applying it as a report is being written gives the writer a realistic picture of how effective the report is going to be and what to change to increase its effectiveness.

THE PACIFIC SUSTAINABILITY INDEX JUDGES COMPREHENSIVENESS OF REPORTING

The environmental and social comprehensiveness scoring systems in the Pacific Sustainability Index segregate environmental reporting issues into ten categories that correspond to the ten rules:

- Company profile

- Vision and commitment

- Stakeholders

- Policy

- Aspects

- Performance indicators

- Initiatives and mitigations

- Performance comprehensiveness

- Costs and investments

- Goals and targets

Details of the content appropriate to each of these categories are discussed in chapter 4.

THE PACIFIC SUSTAINABILITY INDEX ALSO JUDGES QUANTITATIVE PERFORMANCE

The environmental and social quantitative performance portions of the Pacific Sustainability Index scoring system include essentially the same topics as the performance section of the comprehensiveness scoring system, but award points for the quality of the numerical performance rather than for the comprehensiveness of coverage. Performance is judged both against the company's previous performance and against that of its peers, depending on the company's report to document average performance of peers and to compare it to the company's performance.

At this point in corporate reporting there is not much information available about peer performance and most current reports get relatively low performance scores as a result. Nevertheless, it seems inappropriate to judge performance either on an absolute level or on year-to-year performance alone. Different industrial sectors clearly vary in achievable performance on almost any given metric so an absolute target would guarantee that some sectors achieve better scores than others without effort, and prevent some sectors from ever achieving high scores. It seems better to try to compare the performance within the same sector, and of companies that regard themselves as peers. The companies themselves know whom they benchmark themselves against and are probably the best judges of who their peers are.

Judging solely on year-to-year improvement would penalize companies that have improved so much that they can just barely make further improvements. They should get performance credit if this improvement has placed them ahead of their peers even if they failed to improve since the previous reporting period.

SPECIFIC TOPICS IN THE PACIFIC SUSTAINABILITY INDEX

Figure 17.1 compares the number and distribution of topics of the Pacific Sustainability Index with the distribution of topics in three existing scoring systems and the GRI 2000 and ISO 14031 Annex A guidelines.

The total number of topics is almost identical to the GRI 2000 guidelines and the two systems are also similar in that they both have approximately 40 percent of their topics in nonenvironmental (primarily social)

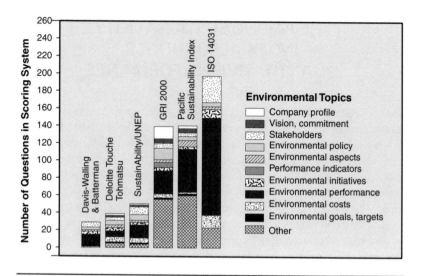

Figure 17.1 Number of questions in six scoring systems for environmental or sustainability reports, including the Pacific Sustainability Index and ones derived from the GRI 2000 and ISO 14031 Annex A guidelines.

categories, and both systems address all of the topics. The distribution of topics in the Pacific Sustainability Index is more heavily weighted toward performance, and, in particular, quantitative numerical performance, with fairly even coverage of the remaining topics, whereas the GRI 2000 guidelines emphasize company profile and environmental policy. The three scoring systems described in chapter 16 have far fewer topics whereas the ISO 14031 Annex A guidelines have more topics but in fewer categories restricted to environmental issues.

SCORING CRITERIA

Each topic in the comprehensiveness sections of the Pacific Sustainability Index is awarded a value of 1 if it is formally addressed but is restricted to specific divisions or facilities, or is not explained very clearly. It receives a value of 2 if the detail seems appropriate and is presented clearly. If not mentioned it receives a score of 0 which is averaged in to compute the final score. If the analyst judges that the topic is irrelevant for the company, the question is left blank and its possible points are not included in the maximum possible score for that particular report. Thus, questions with blank (null) scores are not considered when calculating the overall score as a percentage of the maximum possible score.

Each topic in the quantitative performance section is awarded one point if there is shown to be an improvement since the company's last report, two points if the performance is shown to be better than the average performance of the company's peers, or three points if the company both has improved since the last report and is better than the average of its peers. Thus, if a company is already performing well relative to its peers it gets credit for that level of performance even if it has not improved. Figure 17.2 shows how the points are distributed.

As a final stage in calculating the scores, the absolute scores for each of the four categories (environmental comprehensiveness, social comprehensiveness, environmental performance, and social performance) are normalized by dividing by the total possible score, taking into consideration null values (questions left blank), and multiplied by 100. The perfect score in each category, therefore, is 100.

There are more environmental topics that are awarded points than social ones, both in comprehensiveness, and in quantitative performance, and there are more comprehensiveness topics than performance topics. The percentages of each are shown in Figure 17.3.

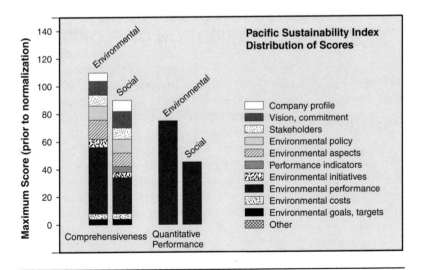

Figure 17.2 Distribution of maximum possible scores in the Pacific Sustainability Index (prior to normalizing each of them to achieve a maximum possible score of 100).

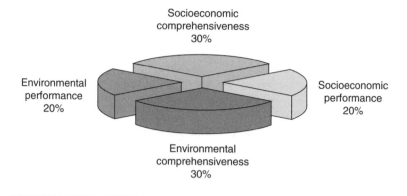

Figure 17.3 Distribution of topics in the Pacific Sustainability Index.

The complete scoring system in the form of a checklist is included as appendix A. The general rationale for the selection of most of the topics is included in Chapters 4 and 6 through 15, the ten rules for corporate environmental and sustainability reporting. A printable version of the appendix A checklist is available on the Roberts Environmental Center Web site http://www.roberts.mckenna.edu .

PACIFIC SUSTAINABILITY INDEX, INTERNAL DISTRIBUTION OF SCORES

In the first trial of the Pacific Sustainability Index, 30 environmental and sustainability reports (Figure 17.4) were scored and the average score for each topic determined. Figures 17.5 (environmental comprehensiveness topics), 17.6 (environmental performance topics), 17.7 (social comprehensiveness topics), and 17.8 (social performance topics) show the results. In these figures, the length of the bars represents the average score for each item for the 30 reports. The longer the bar, the more commonly was the issue addressed.

For environmental comprehensiveness (Figure 17.5, topics 1–55) the topics most often addressed were products, services, brands, markets, a visionary statement, environmental commitments, an environmental policy statement, discussion of voluntary certifications, environmental investments and initiatives, and explicit goals and targets. Among the least discussed topics were use of information from environmental stakeholders, and materials use in packaging.

The environmental performance scores (Figure 17.6, topics 56–80) were highest for emissions to air (both for greenhouse gases and for other

Amerada Hess 1999 Environment, Health, and Safety Report
Ashland, Inc. 1999 Environmental, Health, and Safety Annual Report
BMW 2001/2002 Sustainable Value Report
Boise-Cascade 1999 Environmental, Health, and Safety Report
Bosch 1998 Environmental Report
Conoco 2000 Safety, Health, and Environmental Highlights: Evolution towards Sustainable Growth
DENSO Corporation Environmental Report 2000
Eni 1999 Report: Health, Safety, and Environment
Georgia-Pacific Corporation Environmental and Safety Report 2000
Honda Environment and Technology
Indian Oil and Environment 1996
International Paper 1999–2000 Environment, Health, and Safety
Johnson Controls 2001 Environmental Web Pages
Kerr-McGee Corporation Report on Environment and Safety
Kimberly-Clark 2000 Environmental Ethic
Mazda 1996–2001 Environmental Action
Mazda Motor Corporation 2000 Environmental Report
Mead 2000 Sustainable Development Report
Murphy Oil Corporation 1995–1997 Meeting and Surpassing Environmental Standards
Navistar International 1999 Environmental, Health, and Safety Report
Oji Paper Co. 2000 Environmental Report
PSA Peugeot Citroen 1999 Environment Report
Renault 1999 Environmental Report
Repsol-YPF 1999 Environmental Report
Sinopec 1999—Environment, Safety, and Responsibility
Statoil HSE Accounting for 2000
Stora Enso 1999 Environmental Report
Toyota North American Environmental Report
Volvo Environmental Report 2000

Figure 17.4 Environmental and sustainability reports used to calculate the Pacific Sustainability Index scores in Figures 17.5, 17.6, 17.7, and 17.8.

air emissions), toxic emissions of all types, and water use. The least addressed environmental performance topics were fines and penalties and environmental performance of contractors.

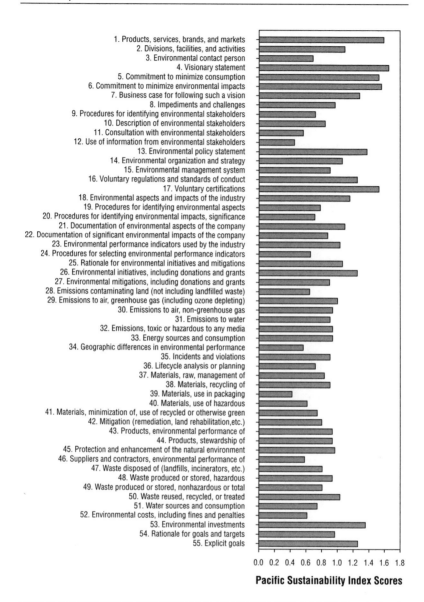

Pacific Sustainability Index Scores

Figure 17.5 Average scores for each environmental comprehensiveness topic (topics 1–55) for the reports listed in Figure 17.4. Maximum score is 2.0 for each topic. This figure gives a sense of how much effort is being put into reporting on each of the topics.

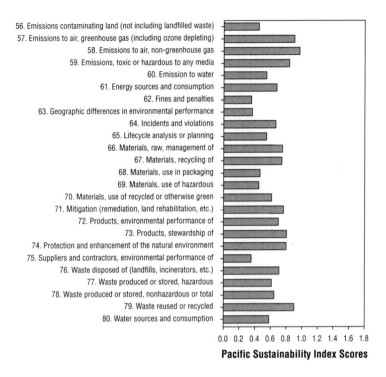

56. Emissions contaminating land (not including landfilled waste)
57. Emissions to air, greenhouse gas (including ozone depleting)
58. Emissions to air, non-greenhouse gas
59. Emissions, toxic or hazardous to any media
60. Emission to water
61. Energy sources and consumption
62. Fines and penalties
63. Geographic differences in environmental performance
64. Incidents and violations
65. Lifecycle analysis or planning
66. Materials, raw, management of
67. Materials, recycling of
68. Materials, use in packaging
69. Materials, use of hazardous
70. Materials, use of recycled or otherwise green
71. Mitigation (remediation, land rehabilitation, etc.)
72. Products, environmental performance of
73. Products, stewardship of
74. Protection and enhancement of the natural environment
75. Suppliers and contractors, environmental performance of
76. Waste disposed of (landfills, incinerators, etc.)
77. Waste produced or stored, hazardous
78. Waste produced or stored, nonhazardous or total
79. Waste reused or recycled
80. Water sources and consumption

0.0 0.2 0.4 0.6 0.8 1.0 1.2 1.4 1.6 1.8

Pacific Sustainability Index Scores

Figure 17.6   Average scores for each environmental performance topic (topics 56–80) for the reports listed in Figure 17.4. Maximum score is 3.0 for each topic. The average scores are all 1.0 or less, reflecting the fact that few companies comment on their own performance relative to that of their peers.

The social comprehensiveness scores were, on average, about half as large as the environmental comprehensiveness scores (Figure 17.7, topics 81–125), and were strongest when dealing with company financials, a visionary statement, and commitments to employees and stakeholders. Very few reports addressed the specific social issues regarding employee well-being contained in the SA8000 standard. These latter topics of employee well-being also comprise more than half the possible points in the social performance section of the Pacific Sustainability Index, and went largely unquantified in the corporate reports (Figure 17.8, topics 126–140). This is probably because companies and stakeholders alike take good performance in these matters for granted, and the largest companies—the ones producing most of the reports—are particularly likely to have internal standards that at least meet the SA8000 criteria. The good news is that for most companies, all of these issues can be addressed adequately in less than a page. There is little reason not to do so if stakeholders begin to expect it.

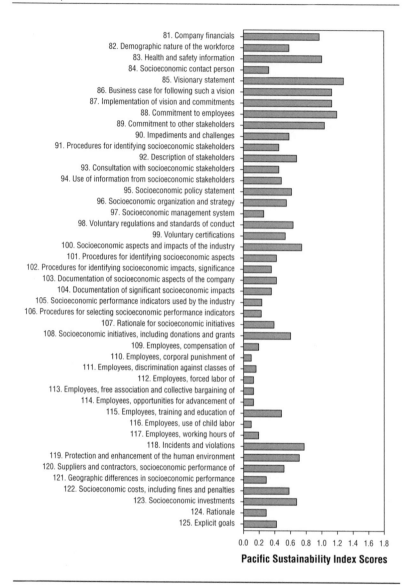

Figure 17.7   Average scores for each social comprehensiveness topic (topics 81–125) for the reports listed in Figure 17.4. Maximum score is 2.0 for each topic. This figure gives a sense of how much effort is being put into reporting on each of the topics.

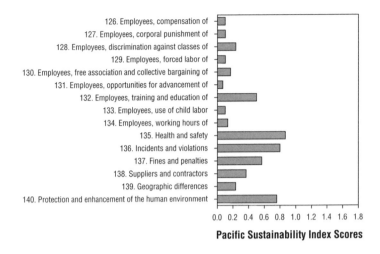

Pacific Sustainability Index Scores

Figure 17.8 Average scores for each social performance topic (topics 126–140) for the reports listed in Figure 17.4. Maximum score is 3.0 for each topic. The average scores are all 1.0 or less, reflecting the fact that few companies comment on their own performance relative to that of their peers.

CONCLUSIONS

The Pacific Sustainability Index is more transparent than other scoring systems because it separates environmental from social scores, and comprehensiveness from performance scores. It is much more detailed than the Deloitte Touche Tohmatsu, SustainAbility/UNEP, and Davis-Walling & Batterman systems and similar in comprehensiveness to scoring systems based on the GRI 2000 guidelines and the ISO 14031 Annex A guidelines. It also differs from all of the other systems in that none of the others scores quantitative performance. Using the Pacific Sustainability Index as a checklist will assure consideration of most of the environmental and social issues companies are currently addressing, and using it to score competitors' reports will provide a good indication of what the norm is for your industrial sector's environmental and sustainability reporting.

It is also worth remembering that people who read your environmental or sustainability report are likely to read those of other companies as well. As long as you are going to the trouble of producing such a report, you might as well be sure that it will be compared favorably.

18

Conclusions

It has become commonplace for the largest companies to produce periodic voluntary corporate environmental reports, and it is inevitable that they will push this practice down the supply chain, just as they are pushing environmental management systems, particularly ISO 14001, down the supply chain.

The absence of such reports from some large companies is noticeable to stakeholders who see the reports from their peer companies and stakeholders are beginning to expect that smaller companies will begin producing them too.

In addition to stakeholders' desires for comprehensive environmental reports, several organizations, particularly the Global Reporting Initiative, are urging the inclusion of social performance in environmental reports, converting them into "sustainability" reports. Many large companies have begun adding social information, and in 2001 the first wave of reports with "sustainability" in their titles arrived.

For companies already producing environmental or sustainability reports, this book has many ideas that could improve them. The state of the art is definitely in flux and many of the newer reports are better than their predecessors, in all sorts of ways.

For companies not yet producing some kind of environmental or sustainability report, it is time to consider doing so. For most companies a good first step is just a matter of reporting data they are already collecting for regulatory purposes; the act of reporting it need not be time-consuming, expensive, or in any way risky. Even some very large companies produce only photocopied handouts, and the cost of putting a few environmental or sustainability pages on the company Web site is nominal.

Of course the best reports, many of which are described in this book, can be quite involved and quite expensive, but the companies that produce them must believe they are valuable, or they would not continue. An inexpensive trial run with existing data should provide some sense of the value of environmental or sustainability reporting. If it happens that your peer companies are not yet producing such reports, it provides an opportunity to lead, and the possibility of achieving a competitive advantage.

The guidelines in this book should make the job straightforward, and should help make even the simplest report effective. The Pacific Sustainability Index provides a comprehensive checklist of topics that might be included, and can be used to monitor progress and benchmark reports of the competition. Finally, there are many suggestions throughout the text about how each of the topics can be presented effectively.

When you are finished, don't forget to send me a copy for analysis and inclusion on the Claremont McKenna College Roberts Environmental Center Web site (www.roberts.mckenna.edu).

J. Emil Morhardt, PhD
Roberts Professor of Environmental Biology
Roberts Environmental Center
Claremont McKenna College
Claremont, CA 91711-5916
E-mail: emorhardt@mckenna.edu
Phone: (909) 621-8190
Fax: (909) 621-8588

Appendix A

The Pacific Sustainability Index Scoring Sheet

The Pacific Sustainability Index is a system for scoring separately the environmental and social *comprehensiveness* of corporate environmental and sustainability reports, and, also separately, the environmental and social *performance* of the company as portrayed in the reports.

Comprehensiveness topics have a maximum score of two points each, based on the breadth and depth of discussion. Scores of 0, 1, and 2 are summed for a total score. Topics judged by the analyst to be irrelevant to the company in question should be left blank. The final environmental and social comprehensiveness scores are determined by dividing the total scores by the maximum possible score (2 × the sum of the non-blank topics) and multiplying by 100. Thus, irrelevant topics are not counted against a company's score. This latter feature prevents companies from being downgraded for failing to address issues which it makes no sense for them to address, but it also requires that the analyst be knowledgeable about what is relevant and what is not. While this adds a certain subjectivity to the scoring, most of the topics seem to be relevant to most companies, and the subjectivity seems a lesser evil than the alternative.

Performance topics have a maximum score of three points each. One point if the company has improved since the previous reporting period; two points if the company demonstrates that it is performing better than the average of its peers on that particular topic, whether or not it has improved since the previous reporting period; and three points if it has both improved and is performing a level better than its corporate peers. A score of zero is awarded if the company fails to address a relevant topic, or has not improved its performance since the last reporting period *and* is not performing better than its peers. As with the comprehensiveness scores, irrelevant topics are left blank. At this point, very few companies make an attempt to assess the performance of their peers, or provide data that lets peers make a similar assessment for themselves. Thus most performance scores for topics in current reports are 0 or 1, no more than one-third of the maximum possible. This still allows intercompany comparison of the total scores, but the overall performance scores are low.

We are already seeing, however, that companies that have been aggressively improving their performance for several years are finding it hard to continue to make yearly performance improvements reliably, while nevertheless performing well for their industries. Consequently, it seems preferable to allow them to achieve a good score if they are performing well, even if not improving, than to penalize them for making earlier aggressive improvements in performance that they are now not quite able to improve upon. Similarly, companies should be aware of how well they are doing relative to their peers—benchmarking themselves against them—and should get credit if they are doing better. I predict that performance scores will increase over time as good-performing companies seek to offset inabilities to make yearly improvements with the knowledge that they are nonetheless performing well compared to their peers.

Pacific Sustainability Index Scoring Sheet*

1. **Environmental Comprehensiveness:** Blank = not relevant, 0 = not mentioned, or only briefly mentioned, 1 = formally addressed but restricted to specific divisions or facilities, or not very clear, 2 = appropriate detail, clear presentation

A. Company Environmental Profile

Q#	Page#	Score	Topic	Question
1	☐	☐	Products, services, brands, and markets	Does the report identify the major types of products and services offered and the types of customers they are sold to? If the company produces branded goods and services, does it identify the most important ones?

continued

---

*Printable version in Adobe Acrobat format available on the Roberts Environmental Center Web site (www.roberts.mckenna.edu).

Q#	Page#	*Score*	*Topic*	*Question*
2	☐	☐	Divisions, facilities, and activities	Does the report identify the major divisions, subsidiaries, and facilities, and the business activities—such as manufacturing, research, and administration—taking place in them?
3	☐	☐	Environmental contact person	Does the report identify a technically knowledgeable person who is willing to answer questions and provide additional information? Does it include the person's name, title, address, e-mail address, and telephone number?

B. Environmental Vision and Commitment

Q#	Page#	*Score*	*Topic*	*Question*
4	☐	☐	Visionary statement	Does the report include a brief, clear, visionary statement expressing a corporate commitment to being the best it can be environmentally?
5	☐	☐	Commitment to minimize consumption	Does the report include specific commitments to minimize consumption appropriate to its industrial sector? These might include commitments to minimize energy, water, and materials consumption, to use recycled materials, and to recycle internally.
6	☐	☐	Commitment to minimize environmental impacts	Does the report include specific commitments to minimize environmental impacts appropriate its industrial sector? These might include commitments to minimize use of hazardous materials, and to minimize pollution and waste.
7	☐	☐	Business case for following such a vision	Does the report legitimize its environmental vision and commitments by explaining why they are beneficial from a business standpoint and are good for the company's own sustainability?
8	☐	☐	Impediments and challenges	Does the report realistically describe the impediments and challenges that it faces in attempting to realize its vision and commitments? Does it describe both its successes and failures?

continued

C. Environmental Stakeholders

Q#	Page#	Score	Topic	Question
9	☐	☐	Procedures for identifying environmental stakeholders	Does the report describe the process or rationale for identifying environmental stakeholders?
10	☐	☐	Description of environmental stakeholders	Does the report identify the company's environmental stakeholders?
11	☐	☐	Consultation with environmental stakeholders	Does the report describe the approaches and frequency of environmental stakeholder consultation?
12	☐	☐	Information obtained from consultation with environmental stakeholders and its use by the company	Does the report describe what information the company obtains through environmental stakeholder consultation? Does the report describe how the company uses the information derived from environmental stakeholder consultation?

D. Environmental Policy and Management

Q#	Page#	Score	Topic	Question
13	☐	☐	Environmental policy statement	Does the report include a formal statement of the company's environmental policy?
14	☐	☐	Environmental organization and strategy	Does the report describe the company's environmental management organization?
15	☐	☐	Environmental management system	Does the report describe how the company manages environmental information?
16	☐	☐	Voluntary regulations and standards of conduct	Does the report identify voluntary standards and regulations subscribed to by the company (Responsible Care, and so on), or indicate that none are subscribed to?
17	☐	☐	Voluntary certifications	Does the report describe the company's position and progress with respect to industry-standard environmental certifications appropriate to it (ISO 14001, EPA Green Lights, and so on)?

continued

E. Environmental Aspects and Impacts

Q#	Page#	*Score*	*Topic*	*Question*
18	☐	☐	Environmental aspects and impacts of the industry	Does the report describe the environmental aspects and impacts characteristic of its industry?
19	☐	☐	Procedures for identifying environmental aspects of the company	Does the report describe the company's procedures for identifying its environmental aspects?
20	☐	☐	Procedures for identifying environmental impacts and assessing their significance	Does the report describe its procedures for identifying the company's environmental impacts and assessing their significance?
21	☐	☐	Documentation of environmental aspects of the company	Does the report list and discuss the environmental aspects of the company?
22	☐	☐	Documentation of significant environmental impacts of the company	Does the report list and discuss the positive and negative environmental impacts of the company?

F. Environmental Performance Indicators

Q#	Page#	*Score*	*Topic*	*Question*
23	☐	☐	Environmental performance indicators used by the industry	Does the report describe the environmental performance indicators used by the industry and indicate the company's relation to that industry?
24	☐	☐	Procedures or rationale for selecting environmental performance indicators used by the company	Does the report define the procedures used by the company to select its environmental performance indicators?

continued

G. Environmental Initiatives and Mitigations

Q#	Page#	Score	Topic	Question
25	☐	☐	Rationale for environmental initiatives and mitigations	Does the report describe the reasoning behind selecting particular environmental initiatives and mitigations?
26	☐	☐	Environmental initiatives, including donations and grants	Does the report describe the company's environmental initiatives?
27	☐	☐	Environmental mitigations, including donations and grants	Does the report describe the company's environmental mitigations?

H. Environmental Performance Comprehensiveness

Q#	Page#	Score	Topic	Question
28	☐	☐	Emissions contaminating land (not including landfilled waste)	Does the report describe and quantify the emission of pollutants to land?
29	☐	☐	Emissions to air, greenhouse gas (including ozone depleting)	Does the report estimate total greenhouse gas emissions including those from purchased energy and non–energy-related activities?
30	☐	☐	Emissions to air, non–greenhouse gas	Does the report describe and quantify the emission of non–greenhouse gas pollutants to the air?
31	☐	☐	Emissions to water	Does the report describe and quantify the emission of pollutants to water?
32	☐	☐	Emissions, toxic or hazardous to any media	Does the report describe and quantify the emission of hazardous materials?
33	☐	☐	Energy sources and consumption	Does the report describe the company's energy sources and quantify its energy consumption?
34	☐	☐	Geographic differences in environmental performance	Does the report describe the company's environmental performance based on geographic location?

continued

Q#	Page#	Score	Topic	Question
35	☐	☐	Incidents and violations	Does the report describe the company's environmental incidents, accidents, and violations, or state that there have not been any?
36	☐	☐	Life cycle analysis or planning	Does the report describe the aspects of the company's operations, products, and services that are appropriate for life cycle consideration?
37	☐	☐	Materials, raw, management of	Does the report describe and quantify the company's management of its raw materials? (Leave blank if it just purchases them.)
38	☐	☐	Materials, recycling of	Does the report describe and quantify the company's recycling of materials during manufacturing?
39	☐	☐	Materials, use in packaging	Does the report describe and quantify the company's use of packaging materials?
40	☐	☐	Materials, use of hazardous	Does the report describe and quantify the company's use of hazardous materials and why they are necessary?
41	☐	☐	Materials, minimization of, use of recycled or otherwise green	Does the report describe and quantify the company's use of recycled materials?
42	☐	☐	Mitigation (remediation, land rehabilitation, and so on)	Does the report describe and quantify the company's efforts at environmental mitigation?
43	☐	☐	Products, environmental performance of	Does the report describe and quantify the environmental performance of the company's products?
44	☐	☐	Products, stewardship of	Does the report describe and quantify the company's efforts to assure the environmental performance of its products throughout their lifecycles?
45	☐	☐	Protection and enhancement of the natural environment	Does the report describe and quantify the company's efforts to enhance the natural environment?

continued

Q#	Page#	*Score*	*Topic*	*Question*
46	☐	☐	Suppliers and contractors, environmental performance of	Does the report describe the degree to which the company imposes its environmental standards on suppliers and contractors?
47	☐	☐	Waste disposed of (landfills, incinerators, and so on)	Does the report describe and quantify the company's waste disposal practices?
48	☐	☐	Waste produced or stored, hazardous	Does the report describe and quantify the hazardous waste produced by the company that must be disposed of?
49	☐	☐	Waste produced or stored, nonhazardous or total	Does the report describe and quantify the nonhazardous waste produced by the company that must be disposed of?
50	☐	☐	Waste reused, recycled, or treated	Does the report describe the company's efforts to see that its waste is reused or recycled, either as a part of its operations or by external contractors or customers?
51	☐	☐	Water sources and consumption	Does the report describe the company's water sources and quantify its water consumption

I. Environmental Costs and Investments

Q#	Page#	*Score*	*Topic*	*Question*
52	☐	☐	Environmental costs, including fines and penalties	Does the report describe costs that have been imposed on it by environmental regulations and fines (if any) for non-compliance?
53	☐	☐	Environmental investments	Does the report describe investments in the environment such as research and development, acquisition of non-required environmental technology, and company and employee environmental initiatives?

continued

J. Environmental Goals and Targets

Q#	Page#	Score	Topic	Question
54	☐	☐	Rationale for goals and targets	Does the report provide a rationale for selecting particular environmental goals and targets?
55	☐	☐	Explicit goals	Does the report contain environmental goals and targets that are both explicit and appropriately comprehensive?

2. Quantitative Environmental Performance: Blank = not relevant, 0 = no data or no improvement, 1 = improvement since last report, 2 = performance better than peer average, 3 = improvement since last report and performance better than peer average

Quantitative Environmental Performance (if more than one metric is presented, use an average score)

Q#	Page#	Score	Topic	Question
56	☐	☐	Emissions contaminating land (not including landfilled waste)	Are fewer pollutants leaking, being spilled, or otherwise being released to land?
57	☐	☐	Emissions to air, greenhouse gas (including ozone depleting)	Is less greenhouse gas being emitted, including that from the generation of purchased energy?
58	☐	☐	Emissions to air, non–greenhouse gas	Are fewer non–greenhouse gas pollutants being released to the air?
59	☐	☐	Emissions, toxic or hazardous to any media	Are fewer toxic or hazardous emissions being made?
60	☐	☐	Emissions to water	Are fewer pollutants being released to water?
61	☐	☐	Energy sources and consumption	Is less energy being used? Are greener sources being added?
62	☐	☐	Fines and penalties	Are there fewer fines and penalties?

continued

Q#	Page#	Score	Topic	Question
63	☐	☐	Geographic differences in environmental performance	Are there fewer geographic differences in environmental policy and practice within the company?
64	☐	☐	Incidents and violations	Are there fewer environmental incidents and violations?
65	☐	☐	Lifecycle analysis or planning	Are more processes and products subject to life cycle analysis?
66	☐	☐	Materials, raw, management of	If the company manages its own natural resources, is it doing it better? (Blank if it doesn't manage natural resources.)
67	☐	☐	Materials, recycling of	Are more materials being recycled during manufacturing?
68	☐	☐	Materials, use in packaging	Is packaging being reduced or recycled? Are greener forms being substituted?
69	☐	☐	Materials, use of hazardous	Is use of hazardous materials being reduced?
70	☐	☐	Materials, use of recycled or otherwise green	Is more recycled material being used in products? Are greener sources being used?
71	☐	☐	Mitigation (remediation, land rehabilitation,etc.)	Is environmental mitigation improving? (Blank if there is nothing to mitigate.)
72	☐	☐	Products, environmental performance of	Is environmental performance of products improving?
73	☐	☐	Products, stewardship of	Is lifecycle stewardship being applied to more products, or more comprehensively?
74	☐	☐	Protection and enhancement of the natural environment	Is the company doing more to protect and enhance the natural environment?
75	☐	☐	Suppliers and contractors, environmental performance of	Are the company's environmental policies and practices being more strongly required of suppliers and contractors?

continued

Q#	Page#	*Score*	Topic	*Question*
76	☐	☐	Waste disposed of (landfills, incinerators, and so on)	Is less waste being disposed of? (i.e. less being produced, or more being treated or recycled)
77	☐	☐	Waste produced or stored, hazardous	Is less hazardous waste being produced?
78	☐	☐	Waste produced or stored, nonhazardous or total	Is less nonhazardous waste or less total waste being produced?
79	☐	☐	Waste reused or recycled	Is more waste being reused or recycled?
80	☐	☐	Water sources and consumption	Is less water being used? Are greener sources or recycling being added?

---

3. **Socioeconomic Comprehensiveness:** Blank = not relevant, 0 = not mentioned, or only briefly mentioned, 1 = formally addressed but restricted to specific divisions or facilities, or not very clear, 2 = appropriate detail, clear presentation

---

A. **Company Socioeconomic Profile**

Q#	Page#	*Score*	Topic	*Question*
81	☐	☐	Company financials	Does the report provide enough financial information to clarify its size and profitability, and the way this is distributed geographically?
82	☐	☐	Demographic nature of the workforce	Does the report characterize its employees in a way that makes it possible for the reader to envision working conditions in the company? This might include the numbers of employees and their geographic distribution, and the level of employee education.
83	☐	☐	Health and safety information	Does the report include relevant health and safety information such as numbers of lost workdays, accidents, and deaths? If appropriate to the industrial sector, does it describe health and safety training for employees?

continued

Q#	Page#	*Score*	Topic	Question
84	☐	☐	Socioeconomic contact person	Does the report identify a technically knowledgeable person who is willing to answer questions and provide additional information? Does it include the person's name, title, address, e-mail address, and telephone number?

B. Socioeconomic Vision and Commitment

Q#	Page#	*Score*	Topic	Question
85	☐	☐	Visionary statement	Does the report include in its visionary statement expressions of a corporate commitment to being the best it can be for its employees, shareholders, its other stakeholders, and for society as a whole?
86	☐	☐	Business case for following such a vision	Does the report legitimize its socioeconomic vision and commitments by explaining why they are beneficial from a business standpoint and are good for the company's own sustainability?
87	☐	☐	Implementation of vision and commitments	Does the report emphasize how the socioeconomic vision and commitments are being implemented in the company?
88	☐	☐	Commitment to employees	Does the report include specific commitments to its employees appropriate to its industrial sector? These might include commitments to health and safety training and precautions, and to technical and business training and education.
89	☐	☐	Commitment to other stakeholders	Does the report include specific commitments to other stakeholders such as shareholders, local communities, industry trade organizations, and nongovernmental organizations?
90	☐	☐	Impediments and challenges	Does the report realistically describe the impediments and challenges that it faces in attempting to realize its vision and commitments? Does it describe both its successes and failures?

continued

C. Socioeconomic Stakeholders

Q#	Page#	*Score*	*Topic*	*Question*
91	☐	☐	Procedures for identifying socioeconomic stakeholders	Does the report describe the process or rationale for identifying socioeconomic stakeholders?
92	☐	☐	Description of stakeholders	Does the report identify the company's socioeconomic stakeholders?
93	☐	☐	Consultation with socioeconomic stakeholders	Does the report describe the approaches and frequency of socioeconomic stakeholder consultation?
94	☐	☐	Information obtained from consultation with socioeconomic stakeholders and its use by the company	Does the report describe what information the company obtains through socioeconomic stakeholder consultation? Does the report describe how the company uses the information?

D. Socioeconomic Policy and Management

Q#	Page#	*Score*	*Topic*	*Question*
95	☐	☐	Socioeconomic policy statement	Does the report include a formal statement of the company's socioeconomic policy?
96	☐	☐	Socioeconomic organization and strategy	Does the report describe the company's socioeconomic management organization including its health and safety management?
97	☐	☐	Socioeconomic management system	Does the report describe how the company manages socioeconomic information?
98	☐	☐	Voluntary regulations and standards of conduct	Does the report identify voluntary standards and regulations subscribed to by the company?
99	☐	☐	Voluntary certifications	Does the report describe the company's position and progress with respect to industry-standard socioeconomic certifications appropriate to it (for example, SA8000)?

continued

E. Socioeconomic Aspects and Impacts

Q#	Page#	*Score*	*Topic*	*Question*
100	☐	☐	Socioeconomic aspects and impacts of the industry	Does the report describe the socioeconomic aspects and impacts characteristic of its industry?
101	☐	☐	Procedures for identifying socioeconomic aspects of the company	Does the report describe the company's procedures for identifying its socioeconomic aspects?
102	☐	☐	Procedures for identifying socioeconomic impacts and assessing their significance	Does the report describe its procedures for identifying the company's socioeconomic impacts and assessing their significance?
103	☐	☐	Documentation of socioeconomic aspects of the company	Does the report list and discuss the socioeconomic aspects of the company?
104	☐	☐	Documentation of significant socioeconomic impacts of the company	Does the report list and discuss the positive and negative socioeconomic impacts of the company?

F. Socioeconomic Performance Indicators

Q#	Page#	*Score*	*Topic*	*Question*
105	☐	☐	Socioeconomic performance indicators used by the industry	Does the report describe the socioeconomic performance indicators used by the industry and indicate the company's relation to that industry?
106	☐	☐	Procedures for selecting socioeconomic performance indicators used by the company	Does the report define the procedures used by the company to select its socioeconomic performance indicators?

continued

G. Socioeconomic Initiatives

Q#	Page#	Score	Topic	Question
107	☐	☐	Rationale for socioeconomic initiatives	Does the report describe the reasoning behind selecting particular socioeconomic initiatives?
108	☐	☐	Socioeconomic initiatives, including donations and grants	Does the report describe the company's socioeconomic initiatives and quantify their results?

H. Socioeconomic Performance Comprehensiveness

Q#	Page#	Score	Topic	Question
109	☐	☐	Employees, compensation of	Does the report describe the company's procedures and commitment to ensure that its wages meet minimum legal standards wherever it operates?
110	☐	☐	Employees, corporal punishment of	Does the report describe the company's procedures and commitment not to engage in corporal punishment or other forms of abuse?
111	☐	☐	Employees, discrimination against classes of	Does the report describe the company's procedures and commitment to fully nondiscriminatory practices?
112	☐	☐	Employees, forced labor of	Does the report describe the company's procedures and commitment not to utilize forced labor directly or through its suppliers?
113	☐	☐	Employees, free association and collective bargaining of	Does the report describe the company's procedures and commitment to encourage freedom of employee association, and to support employee's legal rights to join trade unions or to otherwise bargain collectively?
114	☐	☐	Employees, opportunities for advancement of	Does the report describe the company's efforts to facilitate the advancement of women and minorities to management positions?
115	☐	☐	Employees, training and education of	Does the report describe the company's efforts to support internal and external education?

continued

Q#	Page#	Score	Topic	Question
116	☐	☐	Employees, use of child labor	Does the report describe the company's procedures and commitment not to utilize child labor directly or through its suppliers?
117	☐	☐	Employees, working hours of	Does the report describe the company's procedures and commitment to assure that it complies with all working hours legislation?
118	☐	☐	Incidents and violations	Does the report describe the company's socioeconomic, health, and safety incidents and violations, or state that there were none?
119	☐	☐	Protection and enhance of the human environment	Does the report describe the company's efforts to enhance the socioeconomic human environment, for example in surrounding communities?
120	☐	☐	Suppliers and contractors, and socioeconomic performance of	Does the report describe the degree to which the company imposes its socioeconomic standards on suppliers and contractors?
121	☐	☐	Geographic differences in socioeconomic performance	Does the report describe the company's comparative socioeconomic performance based on geographic location?

I. Socioeconomic Costs and Investments

Q#	Page#	Score	Topic	Question
122	☐	☐	Socioeconomic costs, including fines and penalties	Does the report describe costs that have been imposed on it by socioeconomic regulations and fines (if any) for non-compliance?
123	☐	☐	Socioeconomic investments	Does the report describe investments in socioeconomic improvements?

J. Socioeconomic Goals and Targets

Q#	Page#	Score	Topic	Question
124	☐	☐	Rationale	Does the report provide a rationale for selecting particular socioeconomic goals and targets?

continued

Q#	Page#	*Score*	*Topic*	*Question*
125	☐	☐	Explicit goals	Does the report contain socioeconomic goals and targets that are both explicit and appropriately comprehensive?

4. Quantitative Socioeconomic Performance: Blank = not relevant, 0 = no data or no improvement, 1 = improvement since last report, 2 = performance better than peer average, 3 = improvement since last report and performance better than peer average

Quantitative Socioeconomic Performance (if more than one metric is presented, use an average score)

Q#	Page#	*Score*	*Topic*	*Question*
126	☐	☐	Employees, compensation of	Do more wages meet minimum legal standards?
127	☐	☐	Employees, corporal punishment of	Are more measures in place to limit the possibility of corporal punishment or other forms of abuse?
128	☐	☐	Employees, discrimination against classes of	Are more nondiscriminatory practices being used?
129	☐	☐	Employees, forced labor of	Are better procedures in place to prevent forced labor directly or through suppliers?
130	☐	☐	Employees, free association and collective bargaining of	Are better procedures in place to encourage freedom of employee association, and to support employees' legal rights to join trade unions or to otherwise bargain collectively?
131	☐	☐	Employees, opportunities for advancement of	Are there more women and minorities in management positions?
132	☐	☐	Employees, training and education of	Is there more internal and external education?
133	☐	☐	Employees, use of child labor	Is there better control of child labor than before?

continued

continued

Q#	Page#	Score	Topic	Question
134	☐	☐	Employees, working hours of	Are better procedures in place to assure that the company complies with all working hours legislation?
135	☐	☐	Health and safety	Are there fewer lost workdays, injuries, deaths?
136	☐	☐	Incidents and violations	Are there fewer incidents and violations?
137	☐	☐	Fines and penalties	Are there fewer socioeconomic fines and penalties?
138	☐	☐	Suppliers and contractors	Are more suppliers and contractors required to adopt the company's socioeconomic standards on suppliers and contractors?
139	☐	☐	Geographic differences	Are there fewer socioeconomic performance differences based on geographic location?
140	☐	☐	Protection and enhancement of the human environment	Is the company doing more to enhance the human environment?

Appendix B

How 40 of the Largest Corporations Score on Their Environmental and Sustainability Reports

The best way to get a quantitative sense of what types of information companies put into their reports, and how complete their coverage is, is to score them. My students and I used the GRI 2000 guidelines, ISO 14031 Annex A list of topics, and the SustainAbility/ UNEP, Deloitte Touche Tohmatsu, and Davis-Walling & Batterman scoring systems to score the 1998–1999 environmental and sustainability reports of 40 of the world's largest companies. We picked the ten largest companies with Web-based reports in the electronics, motor vehicles and parts, petroleum refining, and gas and electric utilities sectors. These results are displayed in chapter 4 (Figures 4.5 and 4.6 for the GRI 2000 scoring system) and in this appendix (for the ISO 14031, SustainAbility/UNEP, Deloitte Touche Tohmatsu, and Davis-Walling & Batterman scoring systems) in a series of ten graphics, a pair for each of the scoring systems. The first of each pair shows the actual score to allow comparison of overall performance between companies. The actual scores are normalized to a maximum total score of 100: if all of the available points in the scoring system had been awarded, the score would have been 100. The lengths of the sections of bar representing each topic show the actual score awarded for each topic. The second graphic of each pair shows each score adjusted to 100 to cause the length of the bar representing each topic to represent the percentage of the report made up of that topic.

Inspection of these graphics reveals several things:

- The scores from the GRI 2000 and ISO 14031 scoring systems are much lower than the scores from the other three systems

- Not all of the scoring systems score all ten topics—a high score in some of them does not take into consideration material in the topics not included

- The amount of coverage of specific topics is quite variable among companies

- There are noticeable differences in average score between industrial sectors

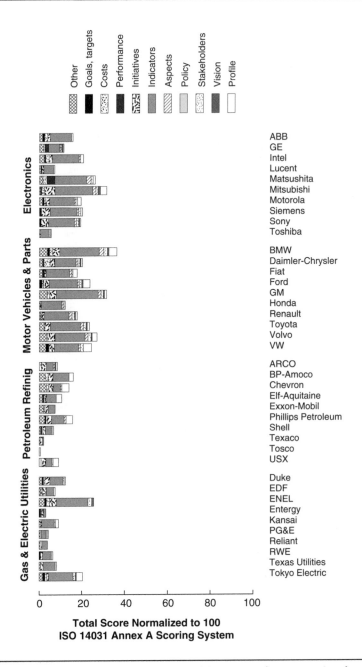

Figure B.1   Scores of environmental or sustainability reports of 40 corporations from a scoring system based on the ISO 14031 Annex A guidelines.

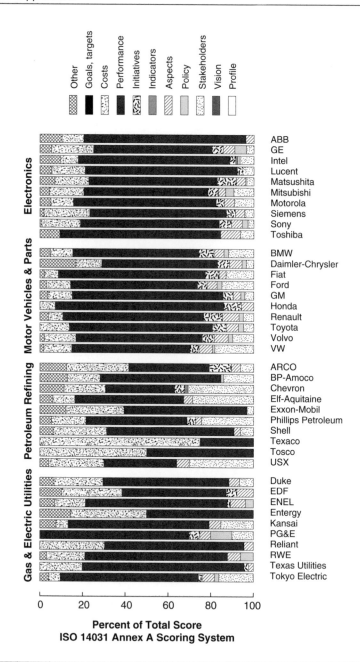

Figure B.2 Distribution of topics in the environmental or sustainability reports of 40 corporations from a scoring system based on the ISO 14031 Annex A guidelines.

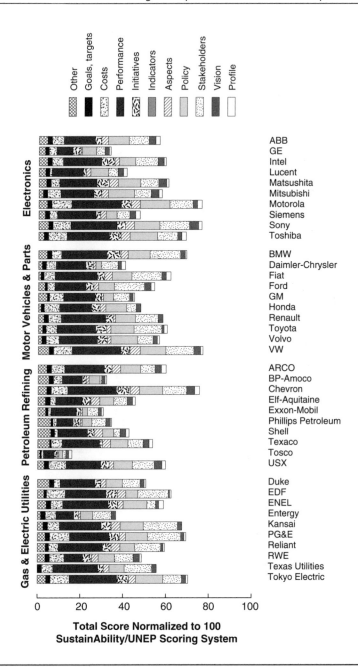

Figure B.3   Scores of environmental or sustainability reports of 40 corporations from the SustainAbility/UNEP scoring system.

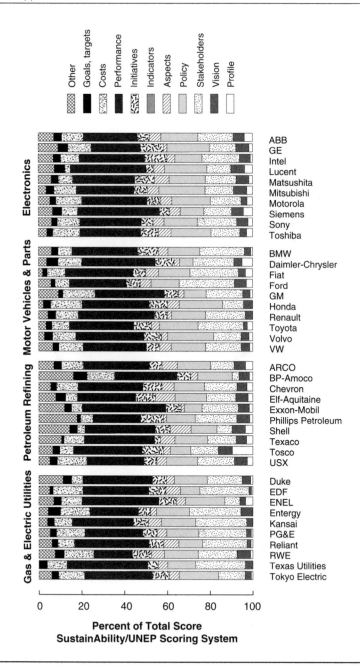

Figure B.4   Distribution of topics in the environmental or sustainability reports of 40 corporations from the SustainAbility/UNEP scoring system.

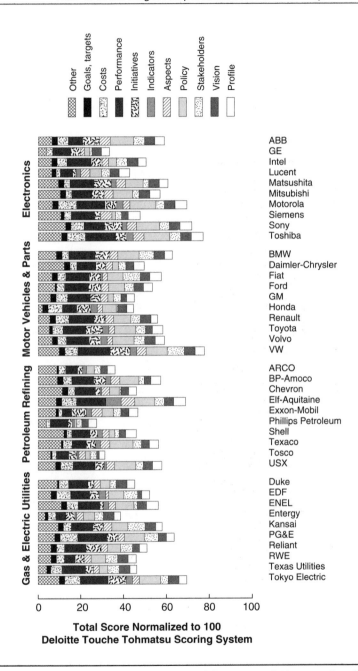

Total Score Normalized to 100
Deloitte Touche Tohmatsu Scoring System

Figure B.5 Scores of environmental or sustainability reports of 40 corporations from the Deloitte Touche Tohmatsu scoring system.

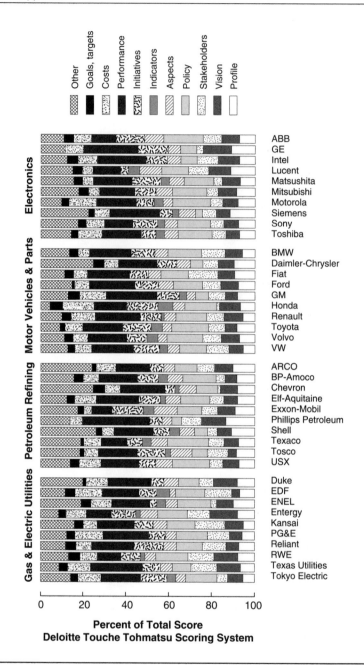

Percent of Total Score
Deloitte Touche Tohmatsu Scoring System

Figure B.6   Distribution of topics in the environmental or sustainability reports of 40 corporations from the Deloitte Touche Tohmatsu scoring system.

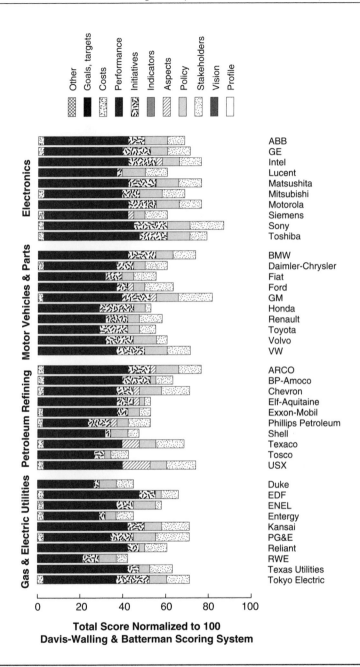

Figure B.7 Scores of environmental or sustainability reports of 40 corporations from the Davis-Walling & Batterman scoring system.

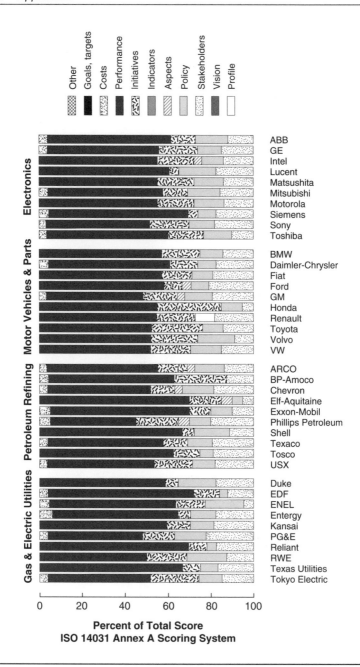

Percent of Total Score
ISO 14031 Annex A Scoring System

Figure B.8 Distribution of topics in the environmental or sustainability reports of 40 corporations from the Davis-Walling & Batterman scoring system.

Appendix C
Reports Used for Metrics, Performance Indicators, Goals, and Targets

Data appear in appendixes D and E.

ABB 1999 Environmental Report

Abbott Laboratories, 1999 Environmental, Health, and Safety Report

AEP System 1997–1998 Environmental Performance Report

Amerada Hess 1999 Environment, Health, and Safety Report

American Home Products Corporation 2000 Environmental and Safety Report

ARCO 1998 Environment, Health, and Safety Report

Ashland 1999 Environmental, Health, and Safety Annual Report

AstraZeneca 1999 Safety, Health, and Environment Report

Aventis 1999 Environment, Health, and Safety Progress Report

Bayer AG 1999 Responsible Care Report

BMW 2001/2002 Sustainable Value Report

Boise Cascade 1999 Environmental, Health, and Safety Report

Bosch 1998 Environmental Report

Briggs & Stratton 1996 Environmental Report

Bristol-Myers Squibb 1999 Report on Environmental Health and Safety Progress: On the Path to Sustainable Development

Canon 1999 "Ecology" Environmental Report

Centrica (1999) and the Environment

Chubu Environment Report

Conoco 2000 Safety, Health, and Environmental Highlights: Evolution towards Sustainable Growth

Coors Brewing Company 1999 Environmental, Health, and Safety Progress Report

Cytec Industries: scattered pages from Cytec's Web site

Danone Group 1999 Social Responsibility Report

DENSO Corporation 2000 Environmental Report

Diageo 1999 Environmental Report

Dominion Environmental Responsibility

Dow Progress Report on Environment, Health, and Safety: Goals for 2005

DTE 1999 Environmental Programs

DuPont 2000 Sustainable Growth Progress Report

Eli Lilly and Company 1999 Environmental, Health, and Safety Report

Eni 1999 Report: Health, Safety, and Environment

First Energy Corporation Environmental Report

FPL 2000 Environmental Report

Georgia-Pacific Corporation Environmental and Safety Report 2000

H. J. Heinz Company 1999 Environmental Health and Safety Report

Indian Oil and Environment 1996

International Paper 1999–2000 Environment, Health, and Safety Annual Report

ITT Industries 1999 Environment Report

John Deere 1999 Environment, Health, and Safety Report

Johnson & Johnson 1999 Environmental, Health, and Safety Report: Healthy People, Healthy Planet

Johnson Controls 2001 Environmental Web pages

Kawasaki Heavy Industries, Environmental Report

Kyushu Environmental Action Report

Louisiana-Pacific 2000 Environmental Performance, Policy, and Management System Report

Mannesmann AG 1998 Environmental Report

Mazda 1996–2001 Environmental Action

Mazda Motor Corporation 2000 Environmental Report

Mead 2000 Sustainable Development Report

Merck & Company 1999 Environment, Health, and Safety Progress Report

Murphy Oil Corporation 1995–1997 Meeting and Surpassing Environmental Standards

Navistar International 1999 Environmental, Health, and Safety Report

Nestle 2000 Environmental Progress Report Highlights

Northeast Utilities 1999 Environmental, Safety, and Ethics Performance Report

Novartis 2000 Innovation and Accountability: Novartis Health, Safety, Environment Report: Sustainability and the UN Global Compact

Oji Paper Company, 2000 Environmental Report

Olin Corporation 2000 Responsible Care

PepsiCo 2000 Environmental Commitment

Pfizer 1999 Environmental, Health, and Safety Report: Safeguarding Health, Promoting Safety, and Preserving the Environment

PPG Industries 2001 Environment, Health, and Safety Progress Report

PSA Peugeot Citroen 1999 Environment Report

Renault 1999 Environmental Report

Repsol-YPF 1999 Environmental Report

Roche 1999 Safety and Environmental Protection at Roche: Group Report

Schering-Plough Corporation 1998 Setting the Global Standard, Report on Environment, Health, and Safety

Smith International, 1999 Environmental Report

Statoil HSE Accounting for 2000

Stora Enso 1999 Environmental Report

Sunoco 1999 Health, Environment, and Safety Review

Thyssen-Krupp. Stahl AG 1999 Environmental Report

Timkin Company FY 1999 Environmental Report

Tohoku Electric Power Company 2000 Summary of Global Environmental Action Report

Unilever 2000 Environmental Performance Report

Westvaco 2000 Environmental, Safety, and Health Report

Willamette Industries 1999 Environmental Commitment and Summary

Appendix D

Environmental and Social Metrics

These metrics were extracted from the reports listed in appendix C.

AUDITS AND INSPECTIONS (ENVIRONMENTAL)

Audits of environmental facilities

BMP implementation

Compliance audits

Environmental audits

Environmental multimedia audits

Follow-up audits

Government agency inspections

Government enforcement actions

Number of storage tanks tested for integrity

On-time completion of audit items

Status of audit findings

Total facilities receiving audits

Total laboratory analyses performed at nuclear plant

Total number of audits—facilities and timberlands

Total samples collected at nuclear plant

Water quality analyses

AUDITS AND INSPECTIONS (SOCIAL)

Annual safety inspections

Audits of health and safety facilities

Percentage of work hours in industry top quartile

Safety, health, and environmental reviews

AWARDS AND RECOGNITION (ENVIRONMENTAL)

Cash awards for environmental ideas

Clean Car Salute Award

Company/organization recycler of the year

Corporate conscience award for environmental stewardship

Excellence in Environmental Engineering Award

Green Power Leadership Award

Overall corporate scores earned

Promise to the Earth Award

Rewarded environmental ideas

Star of Energy Efficiency Award

Total shares awarded to environmental ideas from employees

Waste reduction awards program recipient

AWARDS AND RECOGNITION (SOCIAL)

Chairman's Safety Award winners

CERTIFICATIONS AND CODES OF CONDUCT

Completed ISO 14001 internal auditor training

Facilities certified

Health and safety

Pollution prevention

Product stewardship

Responsible Care—process safety

Responsible Care community awareness

Responsible Care distribution

Responsible Care emergency response

Total certified energy administrators

Total certified pollution control administrators

Total certified radiation handling coordinators

CUSTOMERS, INCREASES IN ECOEFFICIENCY OF

Average customer energy use, residential

Average customer energy use, commercial

Average customer energy use, industrial

Customer project energy reduction (1991–1995)

Customers advised with audits

Demand reduction through customer programs

Elderly people assisted by "Help the Aged" program

Gas boilers installed in customer homes

Households provided with light bulbs

Insulation measures installed

Inverters installed

Low-energy light bulbs installed in customer homes

Number of subsidized photovoltaic installations

CUSTOMERS, NUMBERS OR COMPOSITION OF

Customer accounts, percent commercial

Customer accounts, percent industrial

Customer accounts, percent residential

Customer accounts, total accounts

Customer accounts, total population served

Natural gas customers

Number of customers

People served

Retail customers served

DONATIONS, GRANTS (ENVIRONMENTAL)

Donation to Rachel Carson Homestead

Grants and contributions (1995–1998)

DONATIONS, GRANTS (SOCIAL)

Corporate foundation and corporate contributions

Corporate foundation volunteer activities

EMISSIONS CONTAMINATING LAND (NOT LANDFILLED)

Mercury released to land

EMISSIONS TO AIR, GREENHOUSE GAS

Avoided CO_2 emissions with "Green Lights"

Avoided emissions of CO_2

Carbon monoxide

CFC emissions

CFC use reduction

CFC-11 NPO

CFC-12 NPO

CH_4 emissions

Chlorofluorocarbons (CFC-11 equivalents)

CO emissions

CO emissions reduction in procurement and production

CO emissions reduction in sales

CO_2

CO_2 (1992–1999) decrease

CO_2 absorption ability

CO_2 absorption fixing

CO_2 avoidance

CO_2 emission from transport

CO_2 emissions averages versus national/regional averages

CO_2 emissions by district heating

CO_2 emissions by electricity

CO_2 emissions by gas

CO_2 emissions by oil

CO_2 emissions from different power sources

CO_2 emissions from fossil fuel use

CO_2 emissions per power consumption unit

CO_2 emissions reduction

CO_2 equivalents from CFC/halon emissions

CO_2 from waste

CO_2 per unit produced

CO_2 prevented through use of cogeneration

CO_2 reduced with "Energy Partnership"

CO_2 reductions from energy conservation

CO_2 reductions from plant efficiencies

CO_2 reductions from renewable resources

CO_2 reductions from tree planting/forest preservation

CO_2 reductions from use of nuclear power

CO_2 released during gas production

CO_2 sequestered since 1991

CO_2 vented

Contribution to greenhouse effect worldwide

Customer project CO_2 reduction

Freon

Gas flared

Gas vented

Global greenhouse gases

Global warming potential

Greenhouse gas

HCFC-225 use

Methane emissions

Ozone depletion potential (ODP)

Ozone-depleting compound releases

Ozone-depleting substance loss—CFCs

Ozone-depleting substance loss—HCFCs

Ozone-depleting substance reduction

Reduction in use of CFC-12 NPO

Sequestered carbon from tree planting efforts

SF6 emission reduction (recovery rate)

SF6 recovery rate

Total equivalent warming impact (TEWI) of HCF-134a

Total greenhouse gas emissions (versus past values)

EMISSIONS TO AIR, NON–GREENHOUSE GAS

1,2,4 TMB

Acid rain potential

Aluminum file dust

Ash

Avoided NO_2 emissions with "Green Lights"

Avoided SO_2 emissions with "Green Lights"

Boiler/utilities sulfur oxides

Carbon disulfide

Carbonyl sulfide

Chemical emissions

CO, NO, SO_2 and particulates (total)

Curnene

Dust emissions

Ethylbenzene

Ethylene

HCL

Heavy metals total (Ni, Cu, Pb, Cr, Cd, Hg)

Hexane

History of emissions versus net fossil generation

Hydrochloric acid

International comparison of SO_X/NO_X emissions

Methanol

Molybdenum trioxide

n-Butyl alcohol

Nickel

Nickel compounds

Nitrate compounds

Nitrogen

Nitrogen gases emissions

Nitrogen oxides

NO Emissions

NO emissions reductions

NO_2 emission

NO_2 emission intensity

NO_2 emissions averages versus national/regional averages

NO_2 reduced with "Energy Partnership"

Noise

Noncontained releases

Nonhalogenated VOC emissions

NO_X emissions

NO_X emissions from transport

NO_X reduction

Overall emissions to air

Particles, dust

Particulate emissions

Phosphorous

PM emissions

Propylene

Rate of NO_2 emissions of coal burned

Rate of SO_2 emissions of coal burned

Reduction of dust

Reduction of nitrogen oxide

Reduction of NO_2 with environmental facilities

Reduction of NO_X since 1990

Reduction of NO_X with new boiler annually

Reduction of SO_2 with environmental facilities

Reduction of SO_2 with new boiler annually

SO_2 emissions

SO_2 emission averages versus national/regional averages

SO_2 emissions reduction

SO_2 reduced with "Energy Partnership"

SO_2 removed with scrubbers

Solid particulates

SO_X

SO_X emissions from transport

SO_X reductions

Sulfur emissions

Sulfuric acid

Total boiler/utilities sulfur oxides

VOCs emitted during manufacturing

Voluntary reductions

Wood products facility air quality measures (NO)

Wood products facility air quality measures (particulate matter)

EMISSIONS TO WATER

Adsorbable organic halide

Ammonia

Ammonia in wastewater

Antimony compounds

Biochemical oxygen demand

Cadmium discharged

Chlorides in wastewater

Chemical oxygen demand (COD)

COD discharged

COD in wastewater

Coliform groups discharged

Cooling water and process effluent

Copper discharged

Discharge of suspended solids

Dissolved inorganic salts

Effluent discharge

Effluent flow

Fluorine discharged

Heat discharged to water from thermal plants

Heavy metals total (Ni, Cu, Pb, Cr, Cd, Hg)

Hydrocarbons in wastewater

Individual and collective septic tanks

Mud and cutting discharges

Nickel

Nitrate, ammonium, and phosphorus total

Nitrogen

Nitrogen and phosphorus load per sales volume

Oil and grease

Oil discharges to water

Oil discharged

Oil in buffer cell water

Oil in produced water

Oxidants

Phenol discharged

Phenols in wastewater

Phosphate

Phosphorous compounds

PM emissions

Pthalates

Pulp and paper water use and quality measures (total suspended solids [TSS], biological oxygen demand [BOD])

Pulp and paper mill biochemical oxygen and total suspended solids discharges

Reduction in COD

Reduction in level of impurities in outflow

Soluble manganese discharged

Soluble iron discharged

Soluble salts

Specific salt load per sales volume

Sulfides

Sulphates in wastewater

Surface water

Suspended in wastewater

Suspended solids discharged

Suspended solids discharged to ground water

Total chemical oxygen demand

Total chromium

Total iron discharged

Total nitrogen discharged

Total organic carbon (1992–1999) decrease

Total organic carbon (after site treatment)

Total organic carbon (after site treatment) to sewer

Total organic carbon emissions to natural waters increase

Total phosphorous discharged

Total suspended solids (TSS)

Total water discharged

TSS discharges to water

Volume of wastewater

Wastewater discharged at refineries

Wastewater generated

Wastewater noncompliance

Wastewater, on-site treatment

Water/Injected

Wood products facility water use and quality measures (BOD)

Wood products facility water use and quality measures (TSS)

Wood products facility water use and quality

Zinc discharged

EMISSIONS, TOXIC OR HAZARDOUS, TO ANY MEDIA

1,1,1 TCA

1,2,4 TMB

1,3 Butadiene

33/50 chemicals

Air emissions

Ammonia

Anthracene

Asbestos

Average VOCs

Benzene

Canadian National Pollutant Release

Carbon tetrachloride

Chlorine

Cobalt

Cyclohexane

Decrease in toxic emissions over decade

Emissions of priority compounds

EPA 33/50 voluntary toxic reduction

Ethylbenzene

From production plants

Global air carcinogenic emissions

Global air toxin emissions

Halogenated solvents

Halogenated VOC emissions

Heavy metals emissions

Highly hazardous substances released to air

Highly hazardous substances released to water

Hydrazine releases

Lead

Lead emissions

Mercury released to air

Mercury released to water

Methylene chloride emissions

MTBE

Naphthalene

n-hexane

Para-xylene

Percent materials recycled from all plants

Percent TRI of total coal burned

Phenol

Polycyclic aromatic compounds

Reduced emissions from engine painting process over past decade

Reduced mercury emissions

SARA 313 toxic releases

SARA 313 U.S. air releases

SARA 313 U.S. transfers to off-site energy recovery/disposal

SARA releases treated on-site: refineries

Solvent air emissions

Solvent emissions

Solvents

Suspect carcinogens

Tetrachloroethylene

Toluene

Total 33/50 releases and transfers

Total emissions of 18 TRI chemicals to land, air, and water

Total factory chemical emissions

Total organic carbon emissions

Total releases and transfers

Total releases to air, water and land

Total SARA releases and transfers

Total solvent emissions

Toxics release inventory (TRI) emissions and discharge

TRI (refinery releases)

TRI (transportation)

TRI air emissions

TRI decrease

TRI primary manufacturing

TRI releases

TRI releases indexed to U.S. sales

TRI total NPO

TRI/NPRI air releases

Trichlorotrifluoroethane releases

Tris phosphate releases

Tris phosphate transfers

VOC emissions

VOC emissions (chlorinated)

VOC emissions (non-chlorinated)

VOC waste

VOCs

VOCs (halogenated)

VOCs (nonhalogenated)

VOCs emitted during manufacturing

VOCs released to air

VOCs released to air and water

VOCs released to water

VOCs/toxic air releases

Wood products facility air quality measures (VOC)

Xylene

EMPLOYEES, COMPENSATION OF

Bonus payments

Personnel costs

Profit sharing dividends

EMPLOYEES, NUMBERS OR COMPOSITION OF

Contractor frequency

Eco-leaders assigned to promote green activities

Employee frequency

Employee wages, salaries, benefits

Employees

Employees working for environmental protection

Energy control managers

Environmental stewards employed

Full-time environmental program

Handicapped workers

Health Safety Environment (HSE) personnel

Number of employees

Part-time environmental program employees

Personnel in production

Research and development staff

Total employed

EMPLOYEES, TRAINING AND EDUCATION OF

Attendance of safety training courses

Education

Employees who received training

Energy management certification

Environment Month activities

Environmental audit assistance
certification

Environmental education system

Environmental inspector training
course

Environmental internal audit
certification

Environmental training hours

Environmental workshops
sponsored

Hours of safety training

Instructors hired since 1995

Internal environmental auditor
training course

Number of employees trained

Pollution prevention administrator

Pollution prevention management
certification

Roundwood to mills from trained
loggers

State implementation program
support

Specially managed
industrial waste
disposal administrator

Students reached by workshop
information

Training contacts made
throughout system

Waste disposal facilities
technician

Wood provided by trained
loggers

EMPLOYEES, WORKING HOURS OF

Hours worked

Volunteer hours

ENERGY SOURCES AND CONSUMPTION

All energy use broken down by
facility

Amount from substations

Amount of electricity generated
from coal

Amount of energy saved

Annual savings of
cogeneration units

Average barrels of oil used to
generate 1000 MWh

Average customer energy use,
industrial

Average fuel consumption of new vehicles

Avoided emissions due to DSM program

Coal

Coal BTUs used in equivalent barrels of oil

Company use converted to barrels of oil

Composition of electricity sales

Consumption per sales volume

Corporate energy produced by cogeneration

Crude oil equivalent

Disposal of hazardous waste— energy recovery on-site

District heating

Electricity consumed

Electricity produced

Electricity

Electricity (all facilities)

Electricity consumption

Electricity produced for washing machines

Electricity use reduction (1994–1998)

Emissions from fuel use reduction

Energy

Energy conservation

Energy conservation costs

Energy consumed per barrel

Energy consumption

Energy consumption per employee

Energy consumption per unit produced

Energy consumption, coal

Energy consumption, district heating

Energy consumption, gas

Energy consumption, oil

Energy derived from hydro

Energy derived from natural gas

Energy derived from oil

Energy derived from wind

Energy Efficiency Forum participation

Energy from wind power projects

Energy produced from nuclear power

Energy rate

Energy rate reduction

Energy saved with "Energy Partnership"

Energy saving attributed to Demand Side Management (DSM) programs

Energy sources, coal

Energy sources, natural gas

Energy sources, nuclear

Energy sources, oil

Energy sources, purchased power

External power use

Extralight oil

Fuel BTUs used in equivalent barrels of oil

Fuel consumption

Fuel oil

Fuel use reduction (1995–1998)

Gas

Gas BTUs used in equivalent barrels of oil

Generated electricity

Global energy consumption

Heat

Heating oil

Heavy or waste oil

History/trends of electricity sales

Incineration plants

Liquefied petroleum gases

Load leveling; bottom up (development of night load)

Mineral oil

Natural gas

Natural gas and LPG (all facilities)

Natural gas/fuel gas

Net purchase steam

Nuclear BTUs used in equivalent barrels of oil

Nuclear power utilization

Number of landfill gas-to-energy plants

Number of LPG vehicles in Canada

Office power consumption

Oil recycled

Oil BTUs used in equivalent barrels of oil

Other liquid fuels

Output increase with revamp of existing hydroelectric facilities

Participants in DSM programs

Percent of energy generated from biomass fuel

Power produced by gas

Power purchased from new energy

Propane

Propane/butane

Proportion of electrical power supplied internally

Proportions of carbon and hydrogen in various fossil fuels

Purchased electricity

Purchased power

Purchased solar power versus 1998 values

Purchased steam

Purchased wind power
versus 1998

Recovered energy

Reduced demand for energy
in last two decades

Reduction in peak demand
from DSM

Remote heating

Residual fuel

Saved energy costs (1990–2010)

Steam

Supply capacity

Ten-year record of wind
power purchase

Thermal efficiency

Thermal efficiency of
cogeneration

Thermal efficiency of electricity
from combustion

Third party use of electricity

Total coal annual use

Total coal burned

Total consumption of fuel in
production

Total energy consumption per ton
of production

Total fuel use (versus 1999 values)

Total use for production and
heating

Transmission/distribution loss of
kWh generated

Volume of energy usage

Waste solvents

Wood recycled

FACILITIES AND EQUIPMENT, ENVIRONMENTAL

Amount of facilities with
upgraded lighting systems

Electric vehicle mileage since 1980s

Energy efficient compressors

Energy efficient light fixtures

Facilities engaged in recycling
activity

Fuel cell sites

Generation capacity using
clean fuels

Number of facilities no longer
considered "large quantity
generators"

Number of LPG vehicles in U.S.

Number of waste minimization
methods

Plants with NO_x burners installed

Production equipment/processes

Thermal power efficiency

Thermal power stations

Total used in closed-circuit systems increase

Transformers with PCB oil

Various highlights predicted from merger with CSW

Waste management sites

FACILITIES, INFRASTRUCTURE AND EQUIPMENT

Additional capacity installed for summer

Boilers

Fuel cell facility capacity

Generating capacity, increase

Generating capacity, total

Geothermal capacity

Geothermal power stations

Hydro power capacity

Hydro power stations

Internal combustion power capacity

Internal combustion power stations

Km of pipeline

Maximum capacity

Miles of distribution lines

Miles of transmission lines

Nuclear power capacity

Nuclear power facilities

Number of facilities

Number of general waste incinerators

Number of industrial waste incinerators

Number of LPG service stations in U.S.

Number of substations

Passenger fleet equipped with CFC-free AC systems

Photovoltaic power generating capacity

Pipelines

Pipelines for oil transportation

Power purchased from new energy

Railroad cars in fleet

River barges in fleet

Solar power facility capacity

Solar power sites

Storage tanks

Thermal power capacity

Thermal storage system capacity

Total distribution line length

Total facilities, square feet

Total generating capacity

Total installed capacity

Total installed cogeneration

Total power capacity

Total system capacity

Total transmission line length

Wind power facility capacity

Wind power generating capacity

Wind power sites

FINANCIAL PERFORMANCE

Amount by which prices are lower than U.S. averages

Annual revenues

Average decrease in residential rates

Average shares outstanding

Capital

Debt/equity ratio

Diluted earnings per share

Dividend per share

Dividends paid

Earnings

Earnings per share

Economic value added

EHS operating expenses

Income

Net earnings increase

Net income

Net income—normalized

Number of shareholders

Number of shares issued

Operating income

Operating profit

Operating revenues

Rate decrease since 1985

Research and development

Research and development increase since 1998

Retained in the group

Return on capital employed

Revenues

Sales

Sales—diagnostics

Sales—total

Sales—vitamins and fine chemicals

Taxes

Total assets

Total production

Total revenue

FINES AND PENALTIES (ENVIRONMENTAL)

Air permit exceedances

Canadian fines and penalties

Civil penalties

Compliance fines and penalties

Environmental and safety fines

Fines and penalties

Notices of violation resulting
   in fines

Number of consent decrees

Penalties

Total cost of fines

Total fines paid (1994–1998)

Total value of fines

Violations resulting in fines
   (1994–1998)

FINES AND PENALTIES (SOCIAL)

Penalties

Safety and occupational
   hazard fines

Total value of fines

GENERAL, NON-SPECIFIC

Land use analysis—
   building area

Land use analysis—green area

Land use analysis—other
   sealed areas

Land use analysis—property area

INCIDENTS AND VIOLATIONS, ENVIRONMENTAL

Accident rate

Amount of material spilled

Amount of oil spilled

Causes of incidents—
   human error

Chemical spills

Chemical spills—volume

Class 1 spills

Class 2 spills

Class 3 spills

Environmental incidents

Environmental, process, and transportation incidents

Incidents

Loss of primary contaminants

Major refinery fire losses

Net amount of water taken from outside for use

Number of notices of (federal and state) violations

Occupational accidents per million working hours

Oil spills

Oil and oil products discharged in spill

Oil spills

Oil spills reported

Overall compliance record of tested water

Reduction in fires (1991–1999)

Reduction of noncompliance events (1995–1999)

Removed impacted groundwater

Reportable incidents, air

Reportable incidents, annual total

Reportable incidents, other

Reportable incidents, waste

Reportable incidents, water

Reportable release rate

Reportable spills

Spills

Total compliance data

Total federal violations

Total incidents and prosecutions (versus 1999 values)

Total state violations

Total volume

Transportation related

Transportation-related release

Type of incident—exothermic

Type of incident—fire/explosion

Type of incident—substance release

Type of incident—technical failure

U.S. environmental incidents

Violations received (1994–1998)

Wastewater exceedances

Wastewater incidents

Wastewater noncompliance

Water quality analyses exceeding regulatory limits

INCIDENTS AND VIOLATIONS, HEALTH AND SAFETY

Accident severity

Accidents

Accidents—burns

Accidents—cuts

Accidents—manual handling

Accidents—other

Accidents—slips, trips, and falls

Accidents—vehicles

Accidents—total

Average duration of claims
(1996–1998) reduction

Calendar days out/1000
employees (1996–1998)
reduction

Causes of incidents—natural
phenomena

Causes of incidents—process

Causes of incidents—technical
error

Costs, disability

Decline in injuries, ergonomics-
related from 1994–1999

Fatalities

Fines and penalties

Frequency of industrial accidents

Frequency of occupational
accidents reduction

Frequency rate

Incident frequency rate

Incidents with products at
customer facilities

Injury and illness incident rate

Injury frequency rate

Injury severity rate

Lost time (global)

Lost time (U.S.)

Lost time accident rate

Lost time case rate

Lost time incident frequency

Lost time incident rate

Lost time incident rate (U.S.)

Lost time injury and illness index

Lost time injury frequency rate

Lost workday case rate

Lost workday case rate reduction
(1995–1998)

Lost workday rate

Lost workdays—worldwide

Lost workdays (global)

Lost workdays (U.S.)

Lost-time accident rate

Lost-time days rate

Lost-time incident rate

Lost-time injury rate

Motor vehicle incident rate

Non–work related care

Number of events

Occupational accidents

Occupational accidents with fatal outcome

Occupational illness—internal organs

Occupational illness—skin

Occupational illness cases

Occupational illness cases— hearing

Occupational illness cases— noise induced hearing loss

Occupational illness cases—other

Occupational illness cases— other illnesses

Occupational illness cases— other musculoskeletal

Occupational illness cases— poisoning

Occupational illness cases— respiratory

Occupational illness cases— stress related

Occupational illness cases— travel illness

Occupational illness cases— upper limb disorder

Occupational illness cases per million working hours

Occupational illness—lungs

Occupational illness— musculoskeletal system

Oil recycled

OSHA incidents rate

OSHA inspections

OSHA penalties paid

OSHA recordable frequency

OSHA recordable incident rate

OSHA recordable rate

Recordable case rate

Recordable incidence rate

Recordable injury rate

Reduction in fires (1991–1999)

Reduction in lost time incident case rate and total incident case rate (1991–1999)

Reduction of employee high blood pressure (1996–1998)

Reduction of employee high cholesterol (1996–1998)

Reduction of employee smoking (1996–1998)

Reportable case rates reduction (1995–1998)

Responsible Care—process safety

Robbery rates

Safety performance

Safety record

Serious incident frequency

Serious injury and illness
cases (global)

Serious injury and illness
cases (U.S.)

Severity of occupational
accidents increase

Severity rate

Sickness absence

Total case incident rate

Total illnesses/injuries
recordable rate

Total incident case rate

Total recordable injury frequency

Total staff days worked

Truck collision rate

U.S. lost workday incidence
rate (LWIR)

U.S. total incidence rate (TRI)

Voluntary glucose and cholesterol
test participation

Workers compensation claims

Working days lost due to
occupational accidents

Working days lost due to
occupational illness

INITIATIVES (ENVIRONMENTAL)

Employees volunteering in
Pencil Pals

Environment Month activities

Saplings grown and donated
to public

Waste minimization studies
conducted

Investments, required and voluntary

Research projects for transport
in major cities

INVESTMENTS, REQUIRED
AND VOLUNTARY

Amount expenses rose to in 1998
for environmental protection

Amount invested in emission
reduction project

Amount made from sale of
by-products (wood, scrap
metal, and so on)

Amount paid for 40,000
condensing boilers

Annual costs

Annual energy saved with
upgraded lighting system

Annual environmental spending

Avoided treatment/disposal costs
by substitution/recycling-
capital expenditure

Capital expenditures for
environmental manufacturing
program

Community investments in
environmental projects

Compliance costs

Cost for waste processing

Cost of construction of
recycling facility

Cost of depreciation and
management for
environmental facilities

Cost of energy efficiency program

Cost of ISO 14001
implementation

Cost of lifecycle assessment

Cost of operation, reduction
since 1990

Cost of reclamation of
spent solvent

Cost of waste reduction efforts

Cost of wastewater processing

Costs in service area—expenses

Costs in service area—investments

Costs saved with geothermal
systems

Costs, amount of construction
costs for environmental
protection

Costs, annually

Costs, construction

Costs, total since 1970

Current environmental
expenditures

Demand side management (DSM)
program costs

Disaster prevention costs

Energy conservation costs

Environmental audits

Environmental capital costs

Environmental capital
expenditures

Environmental capital spending

Environmental conservation costs
and investments

Environmental damage cost

Environmental expenditures

Environmental expenditures—
capital

Environmental expenditures—
expense

Environmental expenditures—
operating expenses

Environmental investments in the
plant to date

Environmental operating costs

Environmental penalties

Environmental personnel

Environmental protection costs

Environmental protection
investments

Environmental staff, concurrent
position

Environmental staff,
divisions/departments

Environmental staff, headquarters

Environmental staff, R&D

Environment-related investigation
expenses

Equipment investments since
the 1970s

Expenses for implementation of
environmental measures

Expenses for implementation
of environmental
measures, ongoing

Global environmental
conservation costs, expenses

Global environmental
conservation costs, investment

Grant for geothermal heat pump
initiatives from DOE

Green purchases

Increase in energy- and waste-
intensive chemical production

Investment in electric vehicles

Investment in Exhaust Gas
Research Center

Investment in upgraded burner
systems at coal-fired plants

Major refinery fire losses

Major refinery fire losses per
crude throughput

Management activity costs—
expenses

Management activity costs—
investment

Number of active remediation
projects at the end of
each year

Operating and maintenance
expenditures

Other environment assurance items

Personnel expenses
of environmental
preservation department

Pollution prevention costs—
expenses

Pollution prevention costs—
investments

Pollution-control-related
investments

Pounds invested in environmental
programs

R&D costs—expenses

Reduction of environmental
protection measure costs
1992–97

Reduction of hazardous and nonhazardous waste

Research and development

Research and development, as percent of sales

Research expenses

Resource circulation costs, expenses

Resource circulation costs, investment

S&E operating costs increase

Social activity costs, expenses

Social activity costs, investment

Spending on reforestation

Superfund liability costs since 1974

Supplemental environmental projects

Tax credits received for investing in scrubbers

Ten-year record of photovoltaic purchase

Total cost of fines

Total environmental investments

Total expenses

Total spent on construction of control facilities

Total spent on construction of control facilities since 1969

Total spent upgrading lighting systems at all facilities

MANAGEMENT SYSTEM (ENVIRONMENTAL)

Divisions with systems in place to implement EHS Codes of Practice

Facilities working with "Energy Partnership"

Percent of power plants with pollution prevention plans

Staffed service centers with pollution prevention plans

Technologies implemented to control pollution

Waste streams developed with waste reduction strategy

MANAGEMENT SYSTEM (SOCIAL)

Health and safety guidelines

Health awareness team, number of employees reached

MATERIALS, RAW (MANAGEMENT OF)

Annual acres harvested

Forestland managed

Forestland owned

Forest management assistance
program participation

Harvested acres

Timberland

Land developed

Land managed in Belize

Planted acres of Canadian
timberland

Planted acres of U.S. timberland

Reforestation acreage in Bolivia

Seedlings grown in nurseries

Seedlings planted

Seedlings planted abroad

Seedlings planted in U.S.

Seedlings produced

MATERIALS, RAW (SOURCES, RESERVES OF)

Acids and alkalis

Non-water-mixable cooling
lubricants

Oil and greases

Paints and coating materials

Paper, purchased

Property area

Proved oil and gas reserves

Surface cleaning agents

Wood inventory

MATERIALS, RECYCLING OF

Aluminum cans recycled

Aluminum scrap

Cardboard recycled

Catalysts recycled

Energy recovered through
recycling

Filter dust and slurries recycled

Industrial waste recycling volume

Mean recycling rate

Metal recycled

Number of times cooling water
is recycled

Office and computer paper
recycled

Office paper recycled

Off-site (coal ash, dust, wastepaper) recycled

Oil recycled

On-site (scrap metal, foundry sand, plastic) recycled

Paper recycled

Percent materials recycled from all plants

Plastic containers recycled

Polypropylene recycled

Post-consumer recycled material use

Post-consumer soft drink container recycling rate

Proportion (by weight) of vehicle recycled

Proportion of bumper composed of thermoplastic polypropylene

PVC reused

Ratio of recycled paper used

Ratio of recycled toilet paper used

Raw materials recycled

Steel cans recycled

Sand recycled

Scrap metal recycled

Spent carbon recycled

Spent caustic recycled

Steel recycled

Target for number of plastics used in materials

Tires recycled

Total sand reused

Use of recycled materials

Used metal drums recycled

Used motor oil recycled

Volume of recycled materials

Wood recycled

MATERIALS, USE IN PACKAGING

Cardboard used in packaging

Plastic packaging use

Cumulative reduction (1992–1999) of packaging

Packaging indicator

Packaging use

Reductions in aluminum can packaging since 1972

Reduction in cardboard volume

Reduction in glass bottle packaging since 1972

Reduction in plastic bottle packaging since 1972

Total plastic packaging use

Weight of packaging

MATERIALS, USE OF HAZARDOUS

1,2,4 TMB

Amount of lead in new cars

Cadmium

CFC Class I

CFC Class II

CFCs and halons total consumption reduction

CFCs and halons total inventory

CFCs and halons total inventory reduction

Chlorohydrocarbons

Chloroparaffine

Consumption of specific freons

Consumption of specified CFCs

Dichloromethane

Fungicides

Insecticides

Lead

Mercury

New solvent purchased

Nickel compounds

Nonylphenoletoxylate

Paint thinner

PBB and PBDE

PCBs replaced

Pthalates

PVC used

Reduction in use of CFC-11 NPO (1989–1997)

Reduction of toluene use

Reduction of xylene

SF6

Solvent in water-based coating

Specified halons consumption

Toluene

Transformers with PCB oil

Xylene

Zinc compounds

MATERIALS, USE OF RECYCLED OR OTHERWISE

Aluminum used/year

Amount of backing paper from urethane foam

Amount of recycled paper used for photocopies

Amount of wallboard created with reused gypsum

Chemicals–water reused

Corrugated use

Recovered fiber used

Recovered paper consumption

Recycled asphalt

Recycled material usage

Recycled materials, metals

Recycled materials, office paper and cardboard

Recycled materials, porcelain and concrete

Recycled materials, scrap wood

Recycled paper used

Treated crude oil

MITIGATION (REMEDIATION, LAND RECLAMATION)

Acres of swamp preserved

Acres replanted

Amount of land restored to wetland

Annual visitors to reclaimed land

Available funding for tree projects

Biologically diverse land preservation

Coal tar impacted soils and debris removed

Contaminated sites to be cleaned

Contaminated sites transferred or closed

Debris cleaned up

Free product removed from impacted soils

Impact sites responsible for

Land designated recreational

Land ownership, green areas

Land ownership, total acreage

Number of sites

Reclaimed surface mine land

Remediation sites

Removed coal tar and debris from impacted soil

Total land certified as urban wildlife sanctuary

Trees of 40 different varieties planted

Trees planted at power plant

Trees planted at old mining land

Trees planted on-site

Trees planted with DOE's Climate Challenge Program

Underground storage tank site remediations—closed

Underground storage tank site remediations—new

Visitors on recreation land

Visitors touring swamp

OTHER (ENVIRONMENTAL)

Amount of important domestic production

Animals used

Business travel—commercial (versus 1999 values)

Business travel—private car (versus 1999 values)

Cars transported by boat to the domestic market

Citizen complaints

Environmental portfolio ranking

Facilities integrated in the benchmarking process

Number of households using products

Number of products/services used

PCB capacitors removed

States with our projects

Total mileage (versus 1999 values)

Total people contacting ethics office

PRODUCTS, AMOUNTS OR VOLUMES OF

All-time system peak load, summer

Annual peak load, summer

Annual peak load, winter

Average customer energy use, commercial

Average customer energy use, industrial

Electric vehicles produced

Electricity generated

Electricity sold

Generation from wind power projects

Global production

Manufactured engines

Net megawatts in operation, from hydro

Net megawatts in operation, from natural gas

Net megawatts in operation, from oil

Net megawatts in operation, from other

Net megawatts in operation, from wind

Net production of hydrocarbons

Number of automobiles produced

Power produced by nuclear

Power produced by oil

Power produced by renewables

U.S. auto production

PRODUCTS, COMPOSITION OF

Changes in amount of nuclear
power operations since 1994

Diesel, cetane number, content

Diesel, density

Diesel, polyaromatics content

Diesel, sulfur content

Diesel, volume pressure

Generation by clean
fuels/renewable sources

Percent made of water

Recycled content of
aluminum cans

Recycled content of
corrugated packaging

Recycled content of glass bottles

Recycled content of paperboard

Recycled content in
packaging trays

Unleaded gas—aromatics content

Unleaded gas—benzene content

Unleaded gas—olefins content

Unleaded gas—sulphur content

Unleaded gas—volume pressure

PRODUCTS, ENVIRONMENTAL PERFORMANCE OF

Amount of hydrogen that can be
stored as gaseous hydrogen

Amount of hydrogen that can be
stored as liquid hydrogen

Amount of hydrogen that can be
stored in titanium hydride

Aromatic HC (benzene) from
petrol + LPG system

Aromatic HC (benzene) from
petrol + natural gas for
vehicles (LPG) system

Average fuel consumption of
1,000 kg vehicle

Average fuel consumption of
new vehicles

CNG truck cruising range

CO emissions with a high-pressure
direct injection engine (HDI)

CO from petrol + LPG system

CO from petrol + NGV system

CO_2 emissions with a high-
pressure direct inject engine

CO_2 emitted from new vehicles

CO_2 from low-emissions vehicle

CO_2 from petrol + LPG system

CO from super ultra-low-
emissions vehicle

CO from ultra-low-emissions
vehicle

Energy efficient air conditioners

Energy per unit weight of hydrogen

Energy per vehicle produced

Facility-utilization rate at
nuclear station

Fuel consumption of new vehicles

Fuel economy of 3-way catalytic
converter for lean burn engines

HC (including methane) from
petrol + LPG system

HC (including methane) from
petrol +NGV system

HC + NO_x from petrol +
LPG system

HC + NO_x from petrol +
NGV system

HC emissions

HC from low-emissions vehicle

HC from super ultra-low-
emissions vehicle

HC from ultra-low-
emissions vehicle

Inhalation products with
CFC propellants

Installed geothermal systems
in business

Installed geothermal systems
in homes

Level of unburned hydrocarbons
(HC) with an HDI engine

Line loss decreases with higher
volt transmission line

Load leveling, peak shift

Low-emission vehicles

Maximum speed for electric
vehicle

Miles per gallon

Noise, maximum levels for new
vehicles in EU

NO_x emission levels for
diesel engines

NO_x emissions

NO_x from low-emission vehicle

NO_x from petrol + LPG system

NO_x from petrol + NGV system

NO_x from super ultra-low-
emissions vehicle

NO_x from ultra-low-
emissions vehicle

Number of LPG service stations

Number of LPG vehicles

Particulate emission levels
for diesel engines
(industrywide)

Particulate emissions with an
HDI engine

Percent made of soluble oil

Rate of transmission loss

Total number of four-wheeled
vehicles in use today

Total thermal efficiency at thermal plants

Transmission/distribution loss

Vehicles using gasoline or diesel fuel

Volume of compressed natural gas (CNG)

Weight of safety equipment post-1980s

PRODUCTS, STEWARDSHIP OF

Batteries

Cardboard used in packaging

Filters

Number of bumpers collected

Proportion of vehicle recycled

Reconditioned power tools

Reconditioned starters and alternators

Reconditioned truck, bus, and construction equipment parts value

Recyclability rates

Recycled plastic

Remanufactured products

Total collected

Tires

PROTECTION AND ENHANCEMENT OF THE HUMAN ENVIRONMENT

PROTECTION AND ENHANCEMENT OF THE ENVIRONMENT

Crocodile hatchlings in cooling canals

Cumulative fish species in watershed enhancement creeks

Large trees planted

Manatees seeking refuge in warm water around power plants

Plants donated from 1985–1999

Plants donated in 1999

Seedlings distributed to customers

Trees donated to schools and municipalities

SALES OF PRODUCTS AND SERVICES

Annual sales

Electricity sales

Gallons of gasoline on the market

Geothermal residential systems installed

Households provided with insulation

Rebates given to "School Energy" schools

Sales—fragrances and flavors

Sales—pharmaceuticals

Sales increase since 1998

Sales volume

Sales, net

Schools in "School Energy" program

Total energy supplied

STAKEHOLDER INVOLVEMENT (ENVIRONMENTAL)

Community partnerships

School involvement

Trucking Across America, participation

SUPPLIERS AND CONTRACTORS, ENVIRONMENTAL

Number encouraged to adopt EHS policies/practices

Total S&E expenditure

WASTE DISPOSED OF (LANDFILLS, INCINERATORS)

Asbestos disposed

By-products and waste

Chemical waste—incinerated

Chemical waste—landfilled

Coal ash disposed

Coal ash disposed versus national/regional averages

Construction materials disposed

Contaminated sand

Deepwell disposal of
hazardous waste

Demolition waste

Disposal of hazardous waste—
incineration

Disposal of hazardous waste—
landfill

Disposal of nonhazardous waste—
incineration

Disposal of nonhazardous waste—
landfill

Disposed (including landfilling)

General waste—incinerated

General waste—landfilled

Gypsum disposed

Hazardous waste off-site transfer

Hazardous waste tip

Hydrazine transfers

Incinerated

Incinerated, bio/chemical treated,
or deep injected

Buried

Landfarm

Landfill

Manganese transfers

Mercury released to off-site
transfer

Nonhazardous waste disposal
reduction

Nonhazardous waste disposed

Off-site

Off-site waste oil shipments

Paint sludge incinerated to
recover energy

Pounds of waste

Public landfill

Requires monitoring

Sludge disposed

Solid waste recycled

Solid waste landfilled

Solid waste, U.S. disposed

Solid waste, non-U.S. disposed

Solid waste, total

Total waste sent to landfill rate—
worldwide

Waste disposed

Waste disposed on-site

Waste for removal

Waste incinerated off-site

Waste landfilled off-site

Waste material to landfill

Waste metal chips disposed

Waste products

Wood products facility
landfilled waste

Wood products facility waste
incinerated

WASTE PRODUCED OR STORED, HAZARDOUS

Methanol

Methytert-butyl ether

Methylethyl ketone

Mixed waste (radioactive
  and hazardous)

Mixed waste produced

Naphthalene

n-hexane

Nickel compounds

Packing waste classified
  as hazardous

PAC's category

Paint sludge, total generated

PCBs

Phenol

Phosphoric acid

Propionaldehyde

Propylene

Radioactive dosage

Radioactive liquid waste reduction

Radioactive liquid waste reduction
  since 1993

Radioactive waste reduction at
  nuclear plant since 1992

Reduction in fires (1991–1999)

Reduction of hazardous waste
  produced

Routine refinery hazardous waste

Solvents

Special waste, sulfuric acid

Tetrachloroethylene

Toluene

Total hazardous waste

Total hazardous waste
  per production

Total hazardous waste—
  worldwide

Total mercury released

U.S. hazardous waste management

Wood products facility
  hazardous waste

Xylene

Zinc compounds

WASTE PRODUCED OR STORED, NONHAZARDOUS

Adopt-a-Highway litter removal

Amount of gypsum in total waste

Amount of scrap metal in
  total waste

Amount of sludge in total waste

Amount of total waste from
  concrete poles

Amount of total waste produced
  by coal ash

Annual coke production

By-products and waste

CCPs produced from FGD

Chemical waste—total

Chemical waste—valorized

Chemical waste (1992–1999) decrease

Chemical waste increase

Coal ash generated

Combustion by-products

Compostable waste

Construction materials generated

Crude waste/emissions

Discarded concrete poles

Divisions of waste (sorted into)

Fly ash removed with electrostatic precipitators

Free product removed

General waste—total

Global nonhazardous waste

Gypsum produced

Heavy oil ash disposed

Heavy oil ash generated

Household waste

Inert waste

Liquid industrial waste reduction

Liquid industrial waste reduction since 1992

Mixed waste reduced (by sorting)

Nonhazardous waste

Nonhazardous waste including external disposal

Non-U.S. generation

Operated refineries, waste and emissions

Ordinary waste

Packing waste recycled

Paint sludge total generated

Pollution reduction 1990–2010

Production amount when exceeded requires a hazardous waste contingency plan

Reduction in processed waste

Reduction of coal ash

Reduction of waste materials to landfill

Reduction volume

Refinery residuals

Scrap metal produced

Sludge generated

Sludge produced

Solid waste recycled

Solid waste (general trash) increase

Solid waste disposed (1994–1999), decrease in U.S. facilities

Solid waste generated

Solid waste reduction since 1991

Solid waste reuse or recycling in U.S. facilities increase (1994–1999)

Solid waste, total

Subdivisions of waste

Systemwide yard waste reduction

Total chemical waste

Total coal combustion products

Total nonhazardous waste

Total refinery hazardous waste

Total waste

Total waste disposed

Total waste generated

Total waste generation rate—worldwide

Total waste paper

Total waste per unit produced

Used oil generation reductions

Used oil reduction since 1994

Waste from steel business

Waste generation

Waste metal chips generated

Waste reduction, total industrial waste removed from stream

Waste reduction, total solid waste volume

Waste removed from waste streams at 13 facilities

Wastewater generated

WASTE REUSED, RECYCLED, OR TREATED

Aerosol cans diverted from landfill

Amount of coal ash reused

Amount of gypsum recycled

Amount of recycled paper

Amount of sludge recycled

Avoided spending on paint disposal due to recycling

Bottom ash used for floating road

Cardboard recycled

CCPs recycled

Coal ash recycled

Coal ash utilization rate

Coal ash recycling rate versus 1998

Combustion by-products recycled

Concrete/asphalt recycled

Concrete pole recycling versus 1998

Concrete poles recycled

Construction materials recycled

Contracted recycling

Corrugated cardboard recycled

Disposal of nonhazardous waste—recycling

Dry cell batteries recycled

Ferrous metals recycled

FGD material used to line acidic mining refuse

Fluorescent bulbs recycled

General waste—recycling

Glass recycled

Gypsum recycled

Gypsum utilization rate

Gypsum wallboard/rock reclaimed

Hazardous waste recycled

Hazardous waste recycled (versus 1999 values)

Heavy oil ash recycled

Holiday greeting cards recycled

Improvement of SF6 recovery rate versus1998

Increase in paper recycled since 1998

Industrial waste recycling rate

Industrial waste reused

Large truck tires recycled

Lead acid batteries recycled

Liquid waste recycled

Metals recycled

Newspaper/magazines recycled

Nonferrous metals recycled

Nonhazardous waste recycled

Nonhazardous waste recycling increase (1994–1998)

Office paper and cardboard recycled

Office paper recycled

Off-site (ash and dust) recycled

Off-site energy recovery or disposal reduction (1988–1997)

Old documents recycled twice a year

On-site (scrap metal, foundry sand, plastic) recycled

Packing waste recycled

Paint sludge treated in special center

Paper recycled

Photographic calendars recycled

Plastic recycled

Power generated from waste versus 1998

Quantity recycled off-site

Quantity recycled on-site

Quantity treated off-site

Quantity treated on-site

Quantity used for energy recovery off-site

Rate of recycled hazardous wastes

Recycled office waste

Recycled or sold waste

Recycling rate of coal ash

Recycling rate of gypsum

Reused waste

Reused water at refineries

Salvaged materials (scrap metal)

Scrap copper recycled

Scrap metal recycled

Scrap metal recycling rate

Scrap wood recycled

Seabees produced using 650 tons of fly ash

Sludge recycled

Sludge recycling rate

Solid waste recycled

Solid waste, non-U.S. reused or recycled

Solid waste, U.S. reused or recycled

Streetlight lamps recycled

Total generated/reused

Total paint recycled

Total paper products recycled

Total waste recycled

Total waste recycled (versus 1999 values)

Treated on-site (nonhazardous)

Treated/disposed offsite (non-hazardous)

Trichloro trifluoroethane transfers

Types of waste reused

U.S. recovered fiber purchased

U.S. solid waste reduction

Use of old corrugated containers

Used oil recycled

Used paper collection boxes

Waste metal chips recycled

Waste porcelain and concrete recycled

Waste recycled

Waste recycled off-site

Waste recycled on-site

Waste treated off-site

Waste treated on-site

Wastepaper recovery rate

Water recovery factor

Water treatment sludge recycled

Wood products facility burned for energy waste

Wood products facility waste applied for soil amendment

Wood products facility waste reused/recycled

Wood chips recycled

Wooden crossarms recycled

Wooden poles recycled

WATER SOURCES AND CONSUMPTION

Amount of water treated daily

As product ingredient

Average cooling water used per kWh produced

Average gallons of water used in manufacturing

City water

Clean water discharged

Consumption of cooling water

Consumption of process water

Cooling water

Drinking water

Drinking water reduction

Factory water

Global water consumption

Own supply

Process wastewater

Process wastewater per unit produced

Process water input

Process water output

Processing and washing

Pulp and paper mill water use

Purchased from public supply

Removed impacted groundwater

Surface water consumed

Total water consumed (broken down by facility)

Total water consumed

U.S. facilities use (1994–1999) decrease, water

Wastewater consumption/water input

Wastewater total

Water consumed—chemicals

Water consumed—liquefied petroleum gases

Water consumed—refining

Water consumption

Water consumption (1992–1999) decrease

Water consumption including fresh water

Water consumption used in production of each vehicle

Water consumption/water input

Water passing through hydro plants

Water produced

Water produced for washing machines

Water usage

Water usage, daily

Water use

Water use reduction (1994–1998)

Water utilized by thermal plants

Well water consumed

Appendix E
Goals and Targets

These goals and targets were extracted from the reports listed in appendix C. The ones that are both quantitative and have a deadline are italicized, unfortunately a small minority, and are the real goals and targets. These are the ones I encourage you to emulate. Vagueness is not a virtue in setting goals.

AUDITS AND INSPECTIONS (ENVIRONMENTAL)

100% manufacturing sites audited by the end of 2000

Audit, appropriately, all operations and practices for compliance with the spirit as well as the letter of all applicable laws, regulations, and internal requirements

Maintain an independent corporate environmental, health, and safety, and transportation audit program

Produce standardized energy audits for all units

Verify compliance with external and internal requirements through audits

CERTIFICATIONS AND CODES OF CONDUCT (ENVIRONMENTAL)

Support implementation of UN Global Compact, particularly regarding our business partners

Meet Responsible Care Standards

CERTIFICATIONS AND CODES OF CONDUCT (SOCIAL)

Increase the number of facilities accepted into OSHA's Voluntary Protection Program

CUSTOMERS, INCREASES IN ECOEFFICIENCY OF

Contact customers with details of implications of new Climate Change Levy

Launch a series of home energy efficiency schemes to achieve savings of 5100 GWh by 2002

Vehicle Fuels are aiming to continue their growth with refueling points and encouragement of CNG use

EMISSIONS TO AIR, GREENHOUSE GAS (INCLUDING OZONE DEPLETING)

A 10 percent reduction in manufacturing plant CO_2 emissions compared with 1990 levels by 2010

Compile a GHG inventory by FY2004

Continue reforestation (carbon sink) project in Brazil

Determine potential for long-term CO_2 reduction

Eleven target levels of global warming indicators to be achieved by 2003

Eliminate ozone-depleting substances

Eliminate the use of all CFCs in units containing greater than 10 kg of gas by January 1, 2001

Eliminate the use of PFCs, HFCs, and SF6 greenhouse gases by the end of 1999

Extinguish 80 percent of flares by year's end

Further reduce carbon dioxide emissions

Improve distribution efficiency to reduce CO_2 emissions

Introduce and increase the use of low-emission vehicles

Minimize handling and use of chemicals that can harm the Earth's protective ozone layer

Reduce CO_2 emissions

Reduce CO_2 emissions by 25 percent from 1995 to 2008

Reduce CO_2 unit energy consumption more than 1 percent per year and maintain use at 1990 levels in 2000

Reduce discharge of greenhouse gases

Reduce emissions of CO_2 from energy use

Reduce emissions of greenhouse gases

Reduce further CO_2 emissions

Reduce greenhouse gases to 1990 levels

Reduce the use of gases that exacerbate global warming

Reduction of greenhouse gases in compliance with protection of endangered rain forests in Belize

Sequester and avoid 9.55 million tons of CO_2 emissions in 2000

To reduce the amount of CO_2 it releases per unit output

EMISSIONS TO AIR, NON-GREENHOUSE GAS

Actively seek to prevent pollution by minimizing our emissions to the environment paying particular attention to on-site land

By year-end 2000, achieve a 30 percent reduction in odor-causing emissions from U.S. sites, 1993 base year

Continue efforts to reduce atmospheric emission levels

Continue reducing organic emissions, particularly of halogenated VOCs

Further reduce air and water emissions for global operations

Further reduce emissions of nitrogen oxides and sulfur dioxide per unit of energy used through eco-efficient modernization of the energy generation facilities

Further reduce the amount of organic compounds emitted per production unit

Low emission paint operations—introduction of powder clear-coat technology, and new pretreatment area

Lower emissions despite production increases

No increase in halogenated VOC emission, despite production increases

Reduce amount of emissions to air

Reduce emissions of VOCs, which contribute to smog

Reduce impact of emissions

Reduce nitrogen oxide emissions by about 16,500 tons per year using selective catalytic reduction systems

Reduce SO₂ emissions, specifically by implementing scrubbers in 2002

Reduce SO₂ emissions, specifically by implementing scrubbers

Reduce sulfur dioxide emissions by 95 percent by 2002 using scrubbers

Reduce VOC emissions to 4 kg/vehicle by 2007

Reduce volume of shredder dust

To achieve zero emissions from incinerators

Zero emissions

EMISSIONS TO WATER

By year-end 2000, achieve a 30 percent reduction BOD from U.S. pulp and paper mills, 1993 base year

Eliminate all potentially harmful metals from wastewater

Improve water quality

Intensify efforts to reduce heavy metal emissions and significantly reduce the load emitted into receiving waters

Reduce discharges of hazardous chemicals and heavy metals, which can contaminate drinking water sources and harm wildlife

Reduce hazardous substances in plant effluent and promote closed-loop systems

Reduce organic solvent emissions to the environment to 1 percent or less of the total used by the year 2002

Reduce the amount of waste and wastewater generated per pound of production by 50 percent

Refine wastewater treatment to prevent water pollution

To improve wastewater treatment so that all water can be reused in manufacturing

Use best available methods to clean water

Work to avoid drug substance releases into aquatic environment from manufacturing activities

EMISSIONS, TOXIC OR HAZARDOUS, TO ANY MEDIA

By year-end 2000, achieve a 40 percent reduction in TRI releases from U.S. sites, 1990 base level

By year-end 2000, achieve an 85 percent reduction in ITP releases from U.S. sites, 1988 base year

Eliminate or minimize environmental pollution from the conduct of industry operations

Elimination of solvent emissions

Reduce body-painting emissions of volatile organic compounds (VOCs) to less than 30 g/m^2 for all paint shops

Reduce toxic chemicals emitted by each vehicle assembly plant to 1.0 kg/vehicle or less

Minimize and strive to eliminate the release of any pollutant that may cause environmental damage to the air, water, or earth or its inhabitants

Pursue alternatives to replace or reduce the use of TRI chemicals

Reduce dioxin emissions by 90 percent by 2005

Reduce emissions

Reduce releases of 17 toxic chemicals by 50 percent by the year 2000

Reduce SARA releases within five years by 25 percent from the 1998 base-year level

Reduce volume of hazardous chemical substances released by more than 20 percent by the end of 2000 (based on 1996 standards)

To reduce total emissions by 40 percent in two of their facilities

We will reduce and make continual progress toward eliminating the release of any substance that may cause environmental damage to the air, water, or the earth or its inhabitants

Zero hazardous air pollutants

EMPLOYEES, COMPENSATION OF

Create a balanced work situation, attractive package for employees

EMPLOYEES, CORPORAL PUNISHMENT OF

EMPLOYEES, HEALTH AND SAFETY OF

Achieve zero accidents that result in injuries to employees

Consider more carefully workplace ergonomics and noise and dust contamination at workplaces where powder is handled, particularly in new projects

Create programs that promote the well-being of employees and protect public health

Eliminate the root causes of workplace accidents and environmental incidents

Maintaining a healthy environment and a safe workplace

Minimize health hazards associated with generation, transmission, distribution, and use of electricity

Minimize industrial accidents and work-related ill health

Prevent finger and hand injury

Provide a safe and healthy workplace throughout the business

Provide pacesetting, cost-effective health and wellness services that develop self-responsibility and improve the health and well-being of employees

Reduce injuries and illness per 200,000 work hours by 90 percent

Reduce safety, health, and environmental risks to employees and the communities through safe technologies, facilities, and operating procedures, and by being prepared for emergencies

Reduce total recordable injury rate

EMPLOYEES, TRAINING AND EDUCATION OF

Improve overall driving skill, increase driver accountability, demonstrate environmental leadership credentials, and increase miles per gallon across the fleet

Develop and implement new employee environment, health, and safety (EHS) orientation program at manufacturing sites

Educate and engage employees in the company's efforts to optimize health, safety, and environmental performance, and provide other stakeholders with relevant information on these efforts

Educate employees and the community about the importance of individual and corporate environmental responsibility

Employee awareness of their role in environmental control must be ensured through training and employee meetings

Encourage safe practices by employees on and off the job through formal training and procedures

Support training at all levels, through regional seminars, specific EHS courses and interactive training tools

Increase management support and education, so that employees incorporate environmental quality in their conduct of business

Instill high environmental values in all employees

Integrate environmental compliance into the daily work of every employee

Promote awareness of environmental protection and health and safety precautions among all employees and provide appropriate training to those responsible for implementing environmental control measures

Promote EHS awareness of all employees and stakeholders by training, advising, and encouraging

Promote employee training and awareness-building activities

Provision of technical, financial, manpower, and training resources

Raise environmental awareness among personnel

Raise staff awareness in certain areas to reduce the high proportion of accidents caused by human error during routine operations

Roll out employee communication program to: inform employees about environmental Web site, facilitate how they can contribute to improving environmental performance, show them how to assist customers in environmental issues

Set training requirements for employees with environmental responsibilities

Support further development of knowledge culture—employee home pages, promote in-house knowledge

Support training at all levels, through regional seminars, specific EHS courses and interactive training tools

To create a workplace free from occupational injuries and illness

To enlighten employees on environmental issues

ENERGY SOURCES AND CONSUMPTION

Actively promote research for energy efficiency improvement, global environment problems, and load factor improvement

Actively pursue the use of renewable energy sources at new facilities

Conserve energy and natural resources

Reduce energy use by 2 percent

Cut energy consumption to net sales by more than 30 percent by the end of 2000 (based on 1990 standards)

Decrease consumption of fossil fuels

Decrease environmental impact by promoting natural gas use

Design facilities and equipment with energy-conserving features

Develop alternative energies

Develop alternative energy sources and bearers

Develop technologies that generate electricity in an environmentally sound manner

Efficient use of energy

Establish and monitor appropriate targets for energy reductions by January 1, 2001

Expanding landfill gas recovery programs in southeastern Michigan and throughout U.S.

Generate 2/3 of energy through biomass fuels

Implement efficiency improvements at fossil-fueled plants

Implement systems to define quantitative energy targets by 2002

Improve energy efficiency

Improve energy efficiency by 10 percent

Improve utilization rates of existing nuclear power generating facilities

Increase utilization of nuclear power plant

Increased application for small-scale generation systems like fuel cells and solar units

Innovate alternative energies

Make wider use of renewable energies

Reduce energy usage by 15 percent per unit of production, from the 2000 base year

More efficient energy use

Operate all facilities and manufacturing processes with energy-efficient practices

Promote the efficient use of energy resources through cost-effective conservation and energy management programs

Promotion of liquefied natural gas (LNG) use which does not emit SO_2 or generate particulates

Provide technical assistance for environmental preservation and power generation efficiency improvement by increasing the thermal efficiency of thermal power stations in developing countries

Pursue energy conservation and efficiency improvements in operations and promote conservation practices and investments at customer level

Pursue hydrogen power, from manufacturing to storage and use

Reduce building energy use by 15 percent by 2005

Reduce energy consumption

Reduce energy use per pound of production by 20 percent

Reduce fuel use by 5 percent by 2005

Reduce the consumption of natural resources and energy

Reduce use of fuel

Reducing energy usage and overall costs

Research and develop a clean, renewable energy source

Stabilize energy consumption to FY 1990 level by FY 2000

Support installation of further solar power generation and wind power generation

To save energy

To use renewable forms of energy whenever practical

Use new energy sources more effectively while giving due consideration to the surroundings

We will conserve energy and improve the energy efficiency of our internal operations and of the goods and services we sell

We will make every effort to use environmentally safe and sustainable energy sources

We will invest in improved energy efficiency and conservation in our operations

We will make every effort to use environmentally responsible and sustainable energy sources to meet our needs

Facilities and equipment, environmental characteristics of

Establish procedures to test and deactivate underground tanks and piping systems by the end of 2000

Prohibit the operational use of underground tanks and piping systems by the end of 2000

Reduce or eliminate the need for mercury thermometers

FINES AND PENALTIES (ENVIRONMENTAL)

Remain committed to full compliance with all laws and regulations of local, state, and federal governments that affect operations

GENERAL, NON-SPECIFIC

Achieve environmental excellence

Achieve sustainable development

Adhere to the highest standards of environmental quality

Adhere to the strictest of standards

Aggressively seek new ways to provide customers the services they need with even less impact on the environment

Apply our continuous improvement philosophy to our environmental performance

Balance the automotive society we are developing with nature

Be a responsible corporate citizen

Be the best at environmental, health, and safety performance

Becoming a sustainable corporation

By practicing resource reduction, innovative packaging, recycling and reusing materials, we will minimize the creation of waste, especially hazardous waste, in providing products and services to our customers

Conduct business responsibly

Conduct business with respect and care for the environment and without compromising the health and safety of people around the world

Conserve resources and continuous improvement in emissions and waste minimization

Constant improvement

Continue to improve the quality of life on the planet in a safe, healthy, and environmentally responsible manner

Continued profitable growth, strong finances, high productivity, and fruitful research and development, leading to competitive superiority

Continuous improvement for the present and future well-being of people and the environment

Continuously reduce the use of materials or practices that may have a negative impact on human health and the environment

Contribute to global sustainable development

Deliver on environment, health, and safety promises

Develop an environmental strategy to address forest-related environmental issues

Encourage and support the group's environmental protection activities

Ensure an environmentally responsible workplace

Ensure exemplary environmental programs and performance worldwide

Environmental impact must be decreased by the efficient use of energy, raw materials, water, and packaging

Impact minimization

Impact minimization of the environment

Improve environmental performance

Include environmental, health, and safety considerations as an integral part of the planning and development of business, products, facilities, and manufacturing processes in order to meet policy

Integrate environment, health, and safety issues into all business activities, from research and discovery through manufacturing to distribution and sales

Integrate environmental awareness and responsibility into core business processes

Integrate health, safety, and environmental concepts into business and operations planning and decision making

Know that sound environment, health, and safety programs ultimately create value for customers

Learn more about environmental issues

Maintain a responsible role in managing natural resources

Maintain a safe and healthy workplace and environment

Maintain momentum built up over the last few years to make sure not to lose its focus on the environment during restructuring

Maintain open channels of communication with employees, government agencies, public officials, the media, and the public to meet their information needs in regard to energy and environmental issues

Make every operating location a better place to live and work

Make sustainable use of renewable natural resources

Ongoing adjustment to regulations

Our operations should never pose a significant risk to human health or the environment

Prevention of pollution (air, water, waste, noise, vibration, and so on)

Produce and distribute electricity in a reliable, safe, cost-effective, and environmentally acceptable manner

Produce medicines while adhering to worldwide environmental goals

Promote environment-friendly production activities

Promote global standards for safe and environmentally sound operations

Promptly correct any conditions known to result in significant health, safety, or environmental impact

Protect the environment

Protect the global environment

Provide personal respect, fair compensation, and honest and equitable treatment for all employees

Provide quality products

Recognizing and adapting to the social aims of current and future generations

Reduce environmental impacts

Reevaluate society's relationship with the automobile

Remain responsive to evolving environment, health, and safety needs based on changing science, regulations, and social conditions

Respect the ecosystem and the earth's resources

Stay ahead of regulatory standards and customer expectations

Strive to set the standard for environment, health, and safety performance

Sustainability

Sustainable corporate management—implementation of sustainable, quality strategy, procurement strategy and guidelines, and expand stakeholder dialogue

Sustainable corporation, communities, and world

Target levels set for 18 environmental indicators to be achieved by 2003

Target levels set for all environmental indicators with current statistics for 2003

The creation of shareholder and societal value while minimizing our environmental footprint

The goal is zero, aimed at achieving zero recordable injuries, zero environmental incidents, zero manufacturing process incidents, and zero distribution incidents

To assist the company in setting environmental targets for 2000/2001 and monitor and report performance against them

To attain environmental excellence

To be acknowledged as an environment, health, and safety leader in Life Science

To be fully accountable for environmental considerations in corporate planning and decision making

To be open and honest about company operations

To be the safest and most environmentally conscious transporter of oil in the utilities industry

To become one of the best companies in the world

To conduct business in an environmentally responsible manner and be a good neighbor

To continually reduce the environmental impact in manufacturing measured by the statistics given in the metrics section

To effectively deal with sources of environmental problems and develop and maintain facilities and equipment to maintain the environment

To integrate environment, health, and safety into business strategies and processes

To make us a world-class company in environment, health and safety, and sustainable forestry

To make products that contribute to environmental protection

To measure energy consumption, draw up management indicators, set up numerical targets and promote 1 percent electricity reduction in electricity consumption

To play a useful role in the development of society

To preserve environment, protect health and well-being of employees and customers

To promote environment-friendly production activities

To reduce the burden on the environment and gather and utilize technological capabilities to protect the environment

To seek the most effective ways to protect and enhance the environment while providing reliable electricity at a competitive cost

To take care of customers' daily essentials, making their lives easier

To use all resources economically and ecologically, also to make production even more efficient and less costly

Utilize the best environmental practices in all products and processes

We will continuously analyze and improve our practices, processes, and products to reduce their risk and impact through the product lifecycle

We will continuously improve our practices in light of advances in technology and new understandings in safety, health, and environmental science

We will extract, make, use, handle, package, transport, and dispose of our materials safely and in an environmentally responsible manner

Zero harm to people or the environment

Zero pollution

Zero pollution in the long term

GEOGRAPHIC DIFFERENCES IN ENVIRONMENTAL PERFORMANCE

Uphold same standards throughout the world

INCIDENTS AND VIOLATIONS, ENVIRONMENTAL (SPILLS, FIRES, ACCIDENTAL RELEASES, AND SO ON)

Achieve a companywide recordable incident rate of less than one

Avoid accidents and incidents

Develop plans for further strategic risk reduction

Eliminate all environmental incidents

Manage environmental cleanups effectively

Number of reportable environmental incidents in 2000 not to exceed one

Protect state water by preventing oil spills and responding quickly to spills occurring during transportation

Reduce loss of primary containment incidents (leaks, breaks, and spills) by 90 percent

Reduce the number of reportable accidental releases of chemicals to the environment

Respond quickly and effectively to accidents and incidents

Strengthen emergency preparedness and fire safety programs worldwide, and expand the applicability of our environment, health, and safety guidelines to locations other than manufacturing and research sites

INCIDENTS AND VIOLATIONS, HEALTH AND SAFETY OR OTHER SOCIAL

Achieve an OSHA Incidence Rate of 3.4

Continue reducing lost-time accident rate to 1.0

Create an injury-free workplace

Improve health and safety performances

Improve injuries rate to 1:10

Lower recordable injury rate to 1.22 percent

Maintain a safe and healthy work environment with zero accidents

Maintain lost-time accident rate under 0.9

Reduce lost-time accident rate to 0.5

Reduce lost-time accident rate to less than 0.5

Reduce lost-time accident rate to less than one

Reduce process safety incidents (fires, explosions, and significant chemical releases) by 90 percent

Reduce serious injuries to no more than one per 100 employees by the year 2001

Reduce total recordable illness/injury rate 75 percent (to 1.3 illnesses/injuries per 100 employees per year) by 2000

To have all sites meet the expectations for OSHA VPP status

To reduce injury rates to 2.0 by year 2000

Zero accidents or losses or occupation illnesses

Zero accidents worldwide

Zero injuries

Zero injuries, fires, gas leaks, or material damage

Zero work-related illness and injuries

LIFECYCLE ANALYSIS OR PLANNING

Exercise innovation in optimizing product lifecycle design in manufacturing processes and end of products

To incorporate eco-efficiency in product design by extending the application of lifecycle assessment and developing new tools for use by product developers

MANAGEMENT SYSTEM (ENVIRONMENTAL)

100 percent implementation of existing environment, health, and safety guidelines

ABIS waste information system to compile data on costs and waste control

Accreditation of the new environmental management system to ISO 14001 by the end of 2000

Achieve ISO 14001 certification at all vehicle and parts distribution centers by FY 2005

Acquire ISO 14001 certification for all domestic production points by FY 2000

Acquisition of ISO 14001 certification at all domestic and overseas locations and at six affiliated companies

Address environment, health, and safety issues and impacts in all practices, processes, and products to align business with public expectations

All business areas should have their environmental management systems certified with ISO 14001 no later than December 31, 2001

All European sites to achieve ISO 14001 certification by the end of 2000

All management practices are to be in place by the end of 1999, with the exception of the Process Safety Code; the Process Safety Code practices will be in place by the end of 2000

Analyze and manage the environment, health, and safety risks of the business

Analyze and manage the environment, health, and safety risks of the businesses throughout product lifecycle and assess and manage the environmental impacts from past practices

Annual EMS objectives and targets must be set to drive continuous improvement in environmental performance, manufacturing efficiencies and shareholder value

Annually complete the CERES Report, which will be made available to the public

Apply global environment, health, and safety management system consistently for the safety and health of the environment

Attain ISO 14001 certification for all assembly plants by 2000

Build upon the systems for sharing environment, health, and safety information, analyzing environment, health, and safety problems, and managing environment, health, and safety programs

By the end of 2000, achieve certification to ISO 14001 for offshore operations

By the end of 2000, develop business performance ratio indicators for the key environmental impacts as recommended in GRI

Centralized data system for monitoring environment-related systems

Certify environmental management system in accordance with ISO 14001 Standard

Complete the data gathering for the 2000 baseline and eliminate the gaps identified in performance data tables

Complete the update of guidelines, addressing more sustainable development issues such as water use and climate change

Compliance with applicable legal requirements is the minimum standard for operating performance

Comply with all applicable laws and company policies and standards designed to protect human health, safety, and the environment

Comply with all environmental laws and regulations

Comply with all laws and regulations established to protect the environment as well as the health and safety of workers

Comply with laws and regulations

Comply with the AF&PA SFI program

Continue environmental progress by going beyond minimum requirements of compliance

Develop and establish internal guidelines for good environmental practices and good safety practices that will apply to company operations

Develop more effective management systems

Disclose environmental report via Internet

Disclose information on manufacturing environment

Disclose information on product environment

Each affiliate is required to establish an environmental management system

Each production unit shall comply with the minimum level specified in the production requirements

Each production unit shall implement active improvement measures based on the actual situation

Environmental product declarations (EPDs) shall be developed for key products

Ensure sustainable compliance

Ensure that board of directors is fully informed about pertinent environmental issues

Ensure that the policy, standards, and management system is communicated, understood, and accepted across all company units

Ensure that the reporting system is fully operational

Environmental management systems cover all production units

Establish and maintain operating procedures and programs that support the corporate environmental protection policy

Establish environment, health, and safety management systems for improved compliance (no fines)

Expansion of the scope of environmental reports to cover all consolidated subsidiaries by 2003

Focus on communication of the environment, health, and safety reporting requirements to help understand more fully the underlying causes of work-related health and safety issues

Focus on individual production units

Fully implement Codes of Management Practices globally by 1997

Implement balanced scorecard at corporate level

Have all manufacturing facilities in the world certified under ISO 14001 by year-end 2001

Have all thermal and nuclear power stations obtain ISO 14001 certification by the end of FY 2000

Implement a nationwide waste tracking program and set nationwide waste reduction targets by FY 2003

Implement an environmental management system which meets the requirements of ISO 14001 across current key business activities by 2005

Implement balanced scorecard at corporate level

Implement new environment, health, and safety tasks triggered by business reorganization

Implement programs for self-monitoring, assessing, and reporting to ensure continual improvement

Implement the necessary systems to ensure certification under ISO 14001

Implement third-party EHS management system (audits, risk portfolios)

Implementation of EHS Codes of Practice, safety performance in top 25 percent of peers, and incorporation of product lifecycle criteria into new product development by 2000

Inclusion of environmental criteria in general business management

Incorporate principles of sustainable development and eco-efficiency into business strategies

Increase environmental impact information availability

Integrate companywide environmental protection activities (coordinated by the Environmental Committee)

Integrate newly acquired sites into EHS culture and systems

Introduction of an environmental management system

ISO 14001 certification for all consolidated manufacturing subsidiaries by 2002

Manage compliance and the development and implementation of environmental, health, and safety policies and programs under the guidance of its Corporate Environmental and Safety Council

Manage EHS effectively by developing, implementing, and maintaining a state-of-the-art EHS integrated management system including requirements, guidelines, and standards

Measure and manage EHS performance and develop annual EHS objectives for continuous, sustainable improvement

Meet or exceed all applicable laws and regulations

Meet or surpass the requirements of environmental laws and regulations

Produce an environmental report on the Internet by the end of 2000

Publish an environmental report specific to North American manufacturing in spring 2001

Roll out AA Drivesmart programme to the rest of the group by the end of 2001

Standardize all timberlands and manufacturing to the ISO 14001 EMS by 2005

Strengthen voluntary management standards

Systematic management of environmental performance

To comply with all environmental laws and regulations that apply to our business

To continually assess environmental management and performance policies and procedures

To create consistent environmental management systems to manage environmental risk

To further expand environmental data processing system and increase the responsibility of every employee towards the environment and future generations

To get remaining main divisions certified to ISO 14001 by March 31, 2002

To have every facility meet environmental standards and goals

To have ISO 14001 certification within the next three to four years

To implement an environment management system

To improve efficiency of environmental management system, and against the background of the group's global activities, further enhance information management

To institute our own environmental control standards as appropriate and necessary

To introduce green purchasing, environmental accounting, and other environmentally protective solutions

To provide employees anywhere in the world with easy-to-follow, step-by-step environmental guidelines, so that we can keep the air, water, and land clean wherever we conduct our business

Total compliance with environmental laws

Update environmental Web site as often as possible rather than annually

We will conduct an annual self-evaluation of our progress in implementing these CERES Principles

We will implement these principles and sustain a process that ensures that the board of directors and chief executive officer are fully informed about pertinent environmental issues and are fully responsible for environmental policy

We will promptly and responsibly correct conditions we have caused that endanger health, safety, or the environment

We will support the timely creation of generally accepted environmental audit procedures

Work to comply with latest external regulation noises

Work with government toward the development and implementation of equitable and effective environmental policy

MATERIALS, RAW (MANAGEMENT OF)

Aggressive reforestation

Design processes that are efficient in use of natural resources

Increase the number of acres of forested land managed for sustained yield to 100 percent of owned acres

Make the most of available raw materials, waste nothing

Manage all forests in a sustainable way

Manage all forests with ecosystem-based Multiple Use Forest

Manage and harvest timber in a way that respects other forest benefits

Manage forest resources to enhance future productivity

Practice sustainable forestry

Practice sustainable forestry to sustain timberlands for future generations

To conserve resources

MATERIALS, RAW (SOURCES, RESERVES, OR CHARACTERISTICS OF)

Decrease the waste of natural resources in manufacturing

To source all fish from sustainable sources by 2005

MATERIALS, RECYCLING OF

Develop technologies and systems that enable energy and resource conservation and recycling

Promote energy and resource conservation activities and recycling at overseas plants

To maximize recycling

Utilize every portion of a log

MATERIALS, USE IN PACKAGING

Implement a technology transfer database for sharing packaging innovations across all company divisions

Implement returnable-packaging program at parts distribution facilities by FY 2005, and increase returnable-packaging and direct shipment programs to vehicle distribution centers

Packaging reduction

Reuse packaging materials

Source reduction—eliminate or minimize the mass of packaging per unit of product

MATERIALS, USE OF HAZARDOUS

Confirm the elimination of the use of PCB-containing fluids in concentrations greater than 50 ppm and total weights greater than 28 g by January 1, 2001

Continue to pursue the replacement or reduction of TRI chemical usage

Continued pursuit of alternatives to replace or reduce the use of TRI-listed chemicals.

Eliminate all elemental chlorine and hypochlorite

Eliminating hazardous materials

Employ production processes that do not require the use of chlorinated solvents

Establish a release volume control system for hazardous chemical substances by the end of 1999

Phase out use of PCBs

Promote further reductions in the use of hazardous substances in products

Reduce amount of hazardous materials used in maintenance

Reduce and eliminate the use of purchased products that pose environmental hazards such as PCBs and CFCs

Reduce chemical usage

Reduce use of materials with environmental loading (lead) as: 2000—half or less of 1996 level and, 2005—one third or less of 1996 level

Step up efforts to substitute all CFCs and halons

MATERIALS, USE OF RECYCLED OR OTHERWISE GREEN

Develop and make more use of coal ash reuse projects

Implement green procurement of parts and materials by 2000

Increase recycled materials content

Increase the use of recovered fiber in our pulp and paper operations

Increase use of recycled material

Increase use of recycled paper

Promote green purchasing

Promote the use of recycled waste materials within manufacturing processes

Reduce operation costs by reusing materials and recycling as many materials as possible

OTHER (ENVIRONMENTAL)

Completely remove PCB capacitors from public access areas by 2005

Conserve nonrenewable resources through efficient use and careful planning

Dealers shall undertake customer-oriented environmental activities

Develop plans for further strategic risk reduction

Develop technologies that solve ongoing environmental problems outside industry

Developing quantifiable and challenging source reduction targets

Environmental responsibility

Extend the environmental impact study of teleworking to 150 staff and publish a report on the results of the study in spring 2001

Improve knowledge of energy and water consumption in key areas

Improve the efficiency of operations around the world

Improve the thermal efficiency of thermal power generation and reduce transmission/distribution loss

Improve worldwide risk portfolio and environmental data reporting

Increase paperless activities by increased computerization

Initiate a recycling-oriented society

Monitor and account for environmental impacts on a consistent basis

Promote the construction of nuclear power plants as the pillar of energy source diversification

Reduce noise pollution

Reduce the number of road accidents by refurbishing the transportation system, and developing new technologies

Reduce the volume of paper used

Research new technologies to ensure knowledge of latest environmental issues and technologies

Responsibility of all employees in environmental performance

Roll out environment impact study to all of our 150 teleworkers and report results during 2001

Take a holistic view of transportation to make it smoother, safer, and more comfortable

Teach young people to give them the tools to provide a greener and cleaner future for each of us

To achieve a score of over 75 percent on their Self Assessment Questionnaire, companywide.

To ensure that external noise measured at the nearest residential property does not exceed 60 dB(A)

To provide reliable energy at a pace equal to Florida's incredible growth rate

Understanding and fulfilling legal duties

Upgrade facilities to avoid sensory pollution

We will conserve nonrenewable natural resources through efficient use and careful planning

We will make sustainable use of renewable natural resources, such as water, soils, and forests

Work to develop new products and processes that have minimal impact on the environment and are inherently safe

OTHER (SOCIAL)

Continue to strengthen commitment to discovering new and valuable therapies for complex diseases and devising innovative solutions to global health issues

Encourage environmental education by linking 100 "Solar Schools" photovoltaic systems to Web site

Health and safety first

Improve urban mobility

In selecting our board of directors, we will consider demonstrated environmental commitment as a factor

Increase employee access to and use of e-HR (electronic human resources)—Web-based system

Increase level of employee satisfaction with regular full-scale employee surveys

Operate facilities in a manner harmonious with the local community

To be number one in customer satisfaction in the markets we choose to serve

To conduct business with the highest ethical standard

To the extent feasible, we will redress injuries we have caused to persons or damage we have caused to the environment and will restore the environment

We will make sustainable use of renewable natural resources, such as water, soils, and forests

PRODUCTS, AMOUNTS OR VOLUMES OF

Develop an infrastructure for widespread delivery of alternative fuels

Improve product yields

PRODUCTS, COMPOSITION OF

Create lighter products with petroleum-based carbon fiber

Eliminate the use of or find alternatives for hazardous substances contained in products by 2000

Expand the use of easy-to-recycle thermoplastics

Improve product yields from raw materials

Increase cetane number to eight from 45 in product

Limit the use of new, nonrecycled refrigerants for air conditioners

Lower benzene content in product

Promote manufacturing of larger components

Reduce lead in new Mazdas to a third of 1996 levels by 2006

Reduce number of plastics used for interiors to three or four

Reduce the number of plastics used in manufacturing

Reduce the weight of components

Take positive steps toward a more flexible electricity rate (for example, time of use rate and midnight power rate options) and innovative marketing

PRODUCTS, ENVIRONMENTAL PERFORMANCE OF

Achieve 2 million geothermal heat pump installations and increase annual installations to 400,000 by 2005

Aggressive implementation of designs to meet 2010 mileage standards in fuel efficiency

Aggressive implementation of low-emission designs for gas emission

Clean energy vehicles: introduce strategic products that take into account multifaceted development projects and market characteristics

Commence mass production of a fuel-cell vehicle before 2010

Continue development of electric vehicle program

Continue to develop clean-energy vehicles, including LNG, LPG, and fuel-cell electric vehicles

Continue to investigate and examine for rural electrification in developing countries by utilizing renewable energies

Deliver environmentally adapted and competitive products

Design and develop energy-efficient vehicle and engine products

Develop clean processes and products

Develop technologies to reduce exhaust emission levels from gasoline and diesel vehicles

Establish a prior assessment system for recyclability from the design stage

Exhaust emissions: promote appropriate emissions reductions responses considering needs of specific environments

Fuel efficiency: meet or exceed corporate average fuel economy (CAFÉ) standards

Fuel efficiency: secure top levels of efficiency for all vehicle classes by meeting or exceeding corporate average fuel economy (CAFÉ) standards

Improve cost and cruising range of alternative fuel vehicles

Improve fuel efficiency

Improve the energy efficiency of products by more than 35 percent by the end of 2000

In 2002 all Honda vehicles will be certified as low-emission vehicles (LEV)

Increase customer satisfaction through added safety and convenience

Make high-efficiency fuel cells for electric vehicles commercially available

Meet the 2010 mileage standards in design of cars

New development in transportation equipment and related fuels

Production of electric vehicle

Products and services of a specific 'environmental' design shall be available

Promote research and development in recycling vehicles

Reduce average CO_2 of all vehicles to 140g/km by 2008, and to 120g/km by 2012

Reduce the exhaust emissions of current engines

Reduce vehicle fuel consumption

Reduce vehicle fuel use by five percent by 2005 against the 2000 normalized baseline

Secure top levels of efficiency in all vehicle classes by leading the full-line manufacturers in meeting or exceeding corporate average fuel economy (CAFÉ) standards

Set reduction targets for fuel consumption, exhaust emissions, and other areas of product environmental impact

Specify use of materials in products and manufacturing that optimize energy utilization

To continue to look for cost-effective, clean power generation when acquiring new generation facilities and managing our existing power plants

To equip all buses with the cutting-edge factory-fitted exhaust filters, and emission control system

To increase the market for natural gas/bio gas buses

To perfect the electric-hybrid project

Utilize alternative fuels consistent with cost-effectiveness and customer preferences

We will inform our customers of the environmental impacts of our products or services and try to correct unsafe use

We will maximize the energy efficiency of products and services we produce and sell

We will reduce and where possible eliminate the use, manufacture, or sale of products and services that cause environmental damage or health or safety hazards

PRODUCTS, STEWARDSHIP OF

90 percent recyclable and/or reusable by 2002

Aggressive promotion of commercially-recovered bumpers

At least 90 percent of new models manufactured in 2002 and later to be recyclable

Build a recovery and recycling system for used products

Build a supply system for remanufactured products

By 2002, raise the recyclable proportion of the new Mazda to over 90 percent (by weight)

Cradle to grave product stewardship

Eliminate joints, facilitating the extraction of potentially harmful liquids or gases

Environmentally compatible recycling of vehicles and components

Help prepare for widespread electrovoltaic usage with continued use of EV testing site

Improve the ratio of reuse and recycling of used products to more than 90 percent by the end of 2000

Increase reuse of parts

Recycle 15,000 units in 2001

Respond to market needs and the problem of end-of-life cars

Set up systems for reclaiming and recycling, like reclamation of replaced bumpers

Standardize materials for major resin components

To recycle 95 percent of the total weight of end-of-life vehicles by the year 2015

Trial black box technology to find out how our vehicles are used

PROTECTION AND ENHANCEMENT OF THE HUMAN ENVIRONMENT

Create products that improve quality of life

Improve the living environment in local communities

Integrate factories within the living environment

Protect the community

PROTECTION AND ENHANCEMENT OF THE NATURAL ENVIRONMENT

Care of land, air, water, and all living things

Continue to seek new partnerships and opportunities to improve the local environments around facilities and to protect the global environment for the good of future generations

Create and operate schemes for conservation

Create green spaces at factories

Develop and establish afforestation technology

Employ practical land-management and conservation techniques to conserve soils and forests at facilities

Give full consideration to the protection of ecosystems and natural resources

Improve quality of life and preserve natural resources

Maintain and enhance fisheries in specific bodies of water affected by our power stations

Make global contributions to environmental preservation through the World Bank

Minimize the negative effects and to improve processes and products to reduce any adverse impact on the environment

Plant 10,000 trees in Michigan by end of 2000

Preserve 1700 acres of biologically diverse land by 2001

Protect wetlands and wildlife habitats surrounding facilities

Protecting the environment, in all of its diversity, through the prudent use of resources

Provide habitat diversity

Strive to minimize the impacts of our operations on the environment

Supply timber to our mills while protecting and enhancing the forest ecosystem

Support aims to conduct afforestation on ruined land and to promote environmental awareness in Myanmar

Support repopulation efforts of endangered species found on-site

Take every possible measure to preserve local environments

To correct conditions we have caused that have damaged the environment

To restore and maintain the natural environment in which our facilities are located and where our employees and customers live

We will safeguard all habitats affected by our operations and will protect open spaces and wilderness, while preserving biodiversity

Where a determination has been made that the environment is adversely affected by our actions, we will make every effort to restore the environment and to compensate fairly those persons who are directly adversely affected

Work to encourage a general understanding of the environment and to foster good stewardship

STAKEHOLDER INVOLVEMENT (ENVIRONMENTAL)

Broaden public dialogue about sustainable forestry

Communicate lessons to be learned from past incidents; the main focus will be on rapid notification of the various interested parties within the group

Develop community involvement plans to inform our communities about our operations, products, and environmental programs

Develop employee communication programs to raise awareness of environmental issues

Dynamic disclosure of environmental data to all stakeholders

Environmental cooperation

Establish superior community trust relationships

Expanding network of environmental protection activities to local communities and international communities to advanced sustainable development efforts

For customers and shareholders to always view us as one of the best manufacturing companies in the world

Further external partnerships with academic institutions and government organizations

Implement appropriate environment, health, and safety reporting processes—both internally and externally—to enhance confidence and acceptance by employees and stakeholders

Increase community involvement

Inform appropriate officials, contractors, employees, and public about significant environmental and safety hazards known by us to be related to our facilities

Internal and external environmental communications and relations with the community

Involve employees and community residents as volunteers

Keep customers aware of environmental issues

Participate in discussions with the public and welcome advice and suggestions from persons in communities near our facilities

Participate in relevant community activities and in the development of responsible legislation, regulations, standards, and technology

Participate with government, industry, and professional institutions and associations in the development of reasonable safety and environmental legislation and regulations

Publicly report progress and challenges

Publish report on social responsibility program in 2001

Strengthen communications activities aimed at harmony with society

To build collaborative relationships with external shareholders

To build mutual understanding and respect through open communications with our stakeholders

Understand and consider the viewpoints of stakeholders in the development of environmental and safety policy and guidelines

We will inform in a timely manner everyone who may be affected by conditions caused by our company that might endanger health, safety, or the environment

We will not take any action against employees for reporting dangerous incidents or conditions to management or to appropriate authorities

We will regularly seek advice and counsel through dialogue with persons in communities near our facilities

SUPPLIERS AND CONTRACTORS, ENVIRONMENTAL PERFORMANCE OF

Conduct second-stage in-depth assessment of third-party manufacturers

Each affiliate must ensure that suppliers and contractors understand the potential environmental impact of their operations and work in partnership to identify and reduce any such environmental impacts

*Environmental requirements for dealers shall be drafted no later
than 2001*

Environmental requirements for suppliers shall be met no later than 2003

Increase supply chain cooperation in environmental compliance

Increase the general awareness of environmental requirements among
our associates

Integrated approach throughout the supply chain

*Launch an Environmental Assistance Network online in FY 2001, and
provide more environmental information to dealers by FY 2005*

Promote Responsible Care ethic among major associations,
customers, suppliers, and policy makers to advocate global
regulatory harmonization

Require key suppliers to be compliant with ISO 14001 by December 2003

To apply the group's environmental requirements to suppliers
and contractors

To guide members of business activities to aim for the realization of
eco-friendly business management

SUPPLIERS AND CONTRACTORS, SOCIAL PERFORMANCE OF

Balance costs and other factors to only hire companies with superior
safety records

WASTE DISPOSED OF (LANDFILLS, INCINERATORS, AND SO ON)

Achievement of zero landfill disposal at all business facilities by 2003

By FY 2000, reduce landfilled waste tonnage to one-third of FY 1990 level

By the year 2000, will no longer send waste to landfills

*By year-end 2000, will achieve a 75 percent reduction in RCRA
hazardous waste shipped off-site or managed on-site, 1993 base year*

Look for any viable alternative to storing materials or sending them to
a landfill

Minimize discharge of contaminants into environment

Reduce amount of waste to landfill

Reduce hazardous waste disposal at landfills by 95 percent from base year 1999

Reduce need to place unneeded products in landfills by offering them to facilities that may require them

Reduce waste for disposal

Reduce waste sent to landfill by 15 percent by 2005

Safe disposal—reduce or eliminate the environmental hazard associated with landfilled or incinerated packaging material

To reduce landfilled waste by one third of the FY 1990 total

We will dispose of all wastes through safe and responsible methods

WASTE PRODUCED OR STORED, HAZARDOUS

Ensure the proper handling and disposal of all wastes, and minimize their creation while pursuing opportunities to recycle and reuse waste materials

Implement solvent recovery systems to reduce the generation of hazardous wastes

Reduce the generation of hazardous waste

Reduce waste volume by more than 95 percent by the end of 2000 (based on 1990 standards)

Treat PCB storage equipment to render it harmless

WASTE PRODUCED OR STORED, NONHAZARDOUS OR TOTAL

Continue reducing general waste

Establish and monitor appropriate targets for continuous solid waste reductions by January 1, 2001

Improve waste management

Minimize or prevent the generation of waste

Prevention of pollution

Prevention of pollution and evaluation of potential risks

Reduce amount of waste produced

Reduce manufacturing emissions and waste

Reduce nonhazardous waste generation through source reduction and
pollution prevention

Reduce the creation of waste and dispose of such waste safely
and responsibly

Reduce the quantity of waste and use renewable raw materials

*Reduce the volume of internally generated waste 50 percent in 2000
compared to 1990 level*

Reduce waste by quantitative management of office supplies

Reduce waste from our production processes and consider the waste
implications of new processes as early as possible

WASTE REUSED, RECYCLED,
OR TREATED

Achieve 64 percent recycling of effluent water

Actively work to further curb waste generation and promote waste
reduction and recycling

Adopt processes that reduce industrial waste through recycling

Adopt production processes that reduce industrial waste through recycling

All waste will be handled and disposed of through safe and
responsible methods

Continue to reduce waste through source reduction and recycling
techniques, handling waste in a safe and responsible fashion in
accordance with regulations

Develop the reuse of waste

*Expand and improve recycling so as to reduce waste by more than 66
percent by 2000*

Find new ways to capture waste products for beneficial use

Implement a separate collection of used paper for recycling

Implement a waste minimization project to recycle as much
as possible

Improve recycling rate up to 90 percent for all industrial waste in the
near future

Improve treatment of pollutants and waste

Recycling—divert waste from disposal by reusing it in another form

*Reduce total water usage by 15 percent per unit of production from the
2000 base year by the end of 2005*

Roll out a program of waste management and communication to improve
current recycling rates and introduce new initiatives

Systematically review how waste is managed across the group and
identify any new areas for reduction, reuse, and recycling

Systematically review management of waste and identify any new areas
for reduction, reuse, and recycling

To recover and use as resources more than 90 percent of the metallic
waste and more than 75 percent of the slag generated within the
entire company

We will reduce and where possible eliminate waste through source
reduction and recycling

WATER SOURCES AND CONSUMPTION

Environmental protection of water sources, centralized data system for
monitoring environment related systems

Optimize water consumption and the use of chemical raw materials
as part of its process development efforts, thus also reducing
the groupwide costs associated with water treatment
and purification

Preserve water quality

Reduce and conserve amount of water used

Reduce water intake

Strive to eliminate any unnecessary use of water and improve quality of water discharges

To define the water imprint on a regional and product category basis and use this in developing partnership programmes for clean water stewardship

Appendix F

Corporate Environmental and Sustainability Reports

The chapter(s) in this book in which the reports are discussed are in parentheses.

CHEMICALS SECTOR

Akzo Nobel 1999 Annual Report on Health, Safety, and Environment (6)

Asahi Kasei 2001 Edition Environmental Preservation, Product Safety, Operational Safety, and Health Responsible Care Report (6, 12)

Bayer 2001 Health, Environment, and Safety at Bayer (6)

BASF 2000 Environment, Safety, Health (8,9,12,15)

Clorox Company and the Environment, 1999 (12)

Dow Public Report—2000 Results (6, 7, 11, 13)

DuPont 2000 Sustainable Growth Progress Report (6, 7, 11)

Henkel 2000 Sustainability Report (6, 11)

ICI 2000 Safety, Health, and Environment Web pages (6, 15)

Norsk Hydro 2000 Annual Report (6)

PPG 2001 Environment, Health, and Safety Progress Report (6)

Rohm and Haas 2000 EHS Sustainability Annual Report (6)

ELECTRONICS SECTOR

ABB Group 2000 Annual Sustainability Report (8, 9, 12)

Apple Computer 2000 environmental Web pages (5, 9)

Canon 1999 Environmental Report (5, 7)

Canon 2001 Environmental Report (7, 10)

General Electric EHS focus Web pages (8)

Hewlett-Packard environmental Web site (9)

Intel 2000 EHS Performance Report (12, 15)

Lucent 2000 environmental Web pages (5)

Matsushita Electric Works 1999 Environmental Report (5, 7, 9)

Matsushita Electric Works 2001 Environment Report (6, 9)

Mitsubishi Electric 2001 Environmental Sustainability Report (6, 13, 14)

Motorola 2000 Global Corporate Citizenship Report (12)

Siemens 2000 Environmental Report (12, 15)

Sony 2001 Environmental Report (6, 7, 9, 14)

Toshiba 2000 Environmental Report (6)

FOOD AND BEVERAGES SECTOR

Coors 1999 Environmental, Health, and Safety Progress Report (11)

Danone Group 1999 Social Responsibility Report (8)

Diageo 2000 Environmental Report (11)

PepsiCo 1999 Environmental Commitment Report (11)

Unilever 2000 Environmental Performance (15)

FOREST PRODUCTS SECTOR

Boise Cascade Corporation 2000 Environmental, Health, and Safety
Report (6, 12)

Georgia-Pacific Corporation 2000 Environmental and Safety Report (6, 11, 12)

International Paper 1999–2000 Environment, Health, and Safety Annual Report (6, 9,12,13)

Kimberly-Clark 2000 Environmental Report (6)

Kimberly-Clark Europe 2000 Environmental Report (6)

Louisiana-Pacific 2000 L-P Clear Results (6)

Mead 2000 Sustainable Development Report (6, 8, 13)

Oji Paper 2000 Environmental Report (in Japanese) (6)

Stora Enso 1999 Environmental Report (7)

Weyerhaeuser Company 1999 Annual Environment, Health, and Safety Report (6, 11)

Weyerhaeuser Company 2001–2002 Citizenship Report (6, 11)

METALS SECTOR

Alcoa 2000 Annual Environment, Health, and Safety Report (12)

Corus Group 2000 Environmental Report (12, 15)

Nippon Steel 2001 Environmental Report (5, 10, 12, 14, 15)

NKK 2001 Environmental Report (8)

Phelps Dodge Mining Company Environmental Inventory Web pages, accessed 12/2/2001

POSCO 2001 Environmental Progress Report (8)

MOTOR VEHICLES AND PARTS SECTOR

BMW 1999/2000 Group Environmental Report (5)

BMW's 2001/2002 Sustainable Value Report (6, 11)

Bosch 1998 Environmental Report (6)

DaimlerChrysler 2001 Environmental Report (5, 9)

DENSO Corporation 2000 Environmental Report (14)

DENSO Corporation 2001 Environmental Report (14)

Fiat 1999 Environmental Report (11)

Ford 2000 Corporate Citizenship Report (6, 10)

Toyota 2001 North America Environmental Report (6, 7, 12)

Volkswagen 1999/2000 Environmental Report (5, 7, 8)

Volvo: 1999 Environmental Report (5, 7)

Volvo Car Corporation: Environmental Product Declarations (5)

PETROLEUM REFINING SECTOR

British Petroleum 2000 Environmental and Social Reviews (6)

Chevron 1997 Protecting People and the Environment (12)

ExxonMobil 2001 Safety, Health, and Environment Progress Report (5, 9, 12)

Phillips Petroleum 1998 Health, Environmental, and Safety Report (8, 10, 12)

Total Fina Elf 2000 Environment and Safety Report (10)

PHARMACEUTICALS SECTOR

Abbott Laboratories 1999 Environmental Health and Safety Report (6)

American Home Products Corporation 2000 Environmental and Safety Report (6)

AstraZeneca 1999 Safety, Health, and Environment Report (6)

Baxter 2000 Sustainability Report (5)

Bristol-Myers Squibb 2001 Sustainability Progress Report (5, 6, 9, 10, 13)

Eli Lilly and Company 1999 Environmental, Health, and Safety Report (6, 11)

Johnson & Johnson 1999 Environmental, Health, and Safety Report (6)

Merck & Company 1999 Environment, Health, and Safety Progress Report (6)

Novartis 2000 Health, Safety, Environment Report (6)

Pfizer 1999 Environmental Health and Safety Report (6)

Procter & Gamble: 2000 Sustainability Report Executive Summary (5, 7)

Roche 1999 Safety and Environmental Protection at Roche: Group Report (10)

RAILROADS SECTOR

Burlington Northern Santa Fe 1999 Providing Environmentally Sound Transportation (11)

East Japan Railway Company 2001 Annual Environmental Report (11, 15)

TELECOMMUNICATIONS SECTOR

Swisscom 1998 Systematic Environmental Protection report (5)

UTILITIES, GAS AND ELECTRIC SECTOR

AEP System Environmental Performance Report 1997–1998 (12)

Centrica environmental Web pages, accessed 1/29/01 (6)

Chubu Electric Power 2001 Environment Report (Web pages) (11, 15)

DTE Energy environmental Web pages, accessed 2/26/01 (6)

Dominion environmental Web pages, accessed 2/26/01 (6)

Duke Energy 2000 Progress Review: Environment, Health, and Safety in Action (6, 9)

EDF 1999 Environment Report (6)

Entergy 2000 Focus on the Environment (6, 11)

First Energy Corporation environmental Web pages, accessed 8/23/2000 (6)

FPL Group environmental Web pages, accessed 2/26/01 (6)

Kansai Electric Power 2001 Global Environmental Action Report (6)

Kyushu Electric Power environmental Web pages, accessed 1/29/01 (6)

Northeast Utilities 1999 Environmental, Safety, and Ethics Performance
    Report (6)

Pacific Gas & Electric Corporation 1996 Environmental Report (5)

Pacific Gas & Electric Corporation 2000 Environmental Report (5, 6)

Reliant Energy environmental Web pages, accessed 11/16/2001

RWE 2000 Environmental Report (6)

Tepco environmental Web pages, accessed 11/12/01 (6)

Tohoku Electric Power Company 2000 Summary of Global
    Environmental Action Report (6)

TXU U.S. 2000 Environmental Report (6)

Bibliography

Ball, A., D. L. Owen, and R. Gray. 2000. External Transparency or Internal Capture: The Role of Third-Party Statements in Adding Value to Corporate Environmental Reports. *Business Strategy and the Environment* 9, no. 1: 1–23.

Block, M. 1999. *Identifying Environmental Aspects and Impacts*. Milwaukee: ASQ Quality Press.

Block, M. R., and I. R. Marash. 2001. *Integrating ISO 14001 into a Quality Management System*. Milwaukee: ASQ Quality Press.

Bongaarts, J. 2002. Population: Ignoring Its Impact, *Scientific American* (January): 67–69.

California Environmental Quality Act (CEQA). 1983. Sec. 1508.27 Significantly, *CEQ—Regulations for Implementing NEPA*. 43 FR 56003, November 29, 1978; 44 FR 874, January 3, 1979.

California, state of. 1994. *Thresholds of Significance: Criteria for Defining Environmental Significance: CEQA Technical Advice Series*. Governor's Office of Planning and Research.

———. 2001. *Guidelines for Implementation of the California Environmental Quality Act*. Web page http://ceres.ca.gov/ceqa/guidelines/index.html .

Coalition for Environmentally Responsible Economies (CERES). 1999a. *1998 CERES Report Short Form*. Boston Coalition for Environmentally Responsible Economies.

———. 1999b. *1998 CERES Report Standard Form*. Boston Coalition for Environmentally Responsible Economies.

———. 2000a. *1999 CERES Report Electric and Gas Industries Form*. Boston Coalition for Environmentally Responsible Economies.

————. 2000b. *1999 CERES Report Financial Services Form.* Boston Coalition for Environmentally Responsible Economies.

————. 2000c. *Web site* www.ceres.org .

CEFIC. 1998. *Responsible Care Health, Safety, and Environmental Reporting Guidelines.* Bruxelles: CEFIC, the European Chemical Industry Council.

Cerin, P., and P. Dobers. 2001. What Does the Performance of the Dow Jones Sustainability Group Tell Us? *Eco-Management and Auditing* 8: 123–33.

Davis-Walling, P., and S. A. Batterman. 1997. Environmental Reporting by the Fortune 50 Firms. *Environmental Management* 21, no. 6: 865–75.

Deloitte Touche Tohmatsu. 1999. *Corporate Environmental Report Score Card.* Web pages www.teri.tohmatsu.co.jp/services/Scorecard_E.html .

Diltz, D. 1995. The Private Cost of Socially Responsible Investing. *Applied Financial Economics* 5, no. 2: 69–77.

EMAS. 1993. *Text of Council Regulation 1836/93-EMAS: Eco-Management Audit Scheme.* Brussels: European Council.

Graedel, T. E. 1998. Life-Cycle Assessment in the Service Industries. *Journal of Industrial Ecology* 1, no. 4: 57–70.

GRI. 1999. *Sustainability Reporting Guidelines—Exposure Draft for Public Comment and Pilot Testing.* Boston: Global Reporting Initiative.

————. 2000. *Sustainability Reporting Guidelines on Economic, Environmental, and Social Performance.* Boston: Global Reporting Iniative.

Hamilton, S., H. Jo, and M. Statman. 1993. Doing Well While Doing Good? The Investment Performance of Socially Responsible Mutual Funds. *Financial Analysts Journal* (November/December): 62–66.

Hart, S. L., and G. Ahuja. 1996. Does It Pay to Be Green? An Empirical Examination of the Relationship between Emission Reduction and Firm Performance. *Business Strategy and the Environment* 5: 30–37.

Hawken, P., A. Lovins, and L. H. Lovins. 1999. *Natural Capitalism: Creating the Next Industrial Revolution.* Boston: Little, Brown and Company.

Holdren, J. P. 2002. Energy: Asking the Wrong Question. *Scientific American* (January): 65–67.

ISO. 1999. *ISO 14031 environmental management—Environmental performance evaluation—Standards and guidelines.* Geneva: International Organization for Standardization.

Jaffe, A. B., S. R. Peterson, P. R. Portney, and R. N. Stavins. 1995. Environmental Regulation and the Competitiveness of U. S. Manufacturing: What Does the Evidence Tell Us? *Journal of Economic Literature* 23: 132–63.

King, A. A., and M. J. Lenox. 2000. Industry Self-Regulation Without Sanctions: The Chemical Industry's Responsible Care Program. *Academy of Management Journal* 43, no. 4: 698–716.

King, A., and M. J. Lenox. 2001. Does It *Really* Pay to Be Green? An Empirical Study of Firm Environmental and Financial Performance. *Journal of Industrial Ecology* 5, no. 1: 105–16.

KPMG. 1997. *International Survey of Environmental Reporting.* Lund, Sweden: KPMG.

————. 1999. *KPMG International Survey of Environmental Reporting.* The Netherlands: KPMG Environmental Consulting.

Lober, D. J., D. Bynum, E. Campbell, and M. Jaques. 1997. The 100 Plus Corporate Environmental Report Study: A Survey of an Evolving Environmental Management Tool. *Business Strategy and the Environment* 6: 57–73.

Lomborg, B. 2001. *The Skeptical Environmentalist: Measuring the Real State of the World.* Cambridge, England: Cambridge University Press.

Lovejoy, T. 2002. Biodiversity: Dismissing Scientific Process. *Scientific American* (January): 69–71.

Maxwell, J., S. Rothenberg, F. Briscoe, and A. Marcus. 1997. Green Schemes: Corporate Environmental Strategies and Their Implementation. *California Management Review* 39, no. 3: 132.

Morhardt, J. E. 2001. Scoring Corporate Environmental Reports for Comprehensiveness: A Comparison of Three Systems. *Environmental Management* 26, no. 6: 881–92.

Morhardt, J. E., S. Baird, and K. Freeman. (submitted for publication) Scoring Corporate Environmental and Sustainability Reports Using GRI 2000, ISO 14031, and Other Criteria. *Corporate Social Responsibility and Environmental Management.*

National Academy of Engineering. 1999. *Industrial Environmental Performance Metrics: Challenges and Opportunities.* Washington, DC: Committee on Industrial Performance Metrics, National Academy of Engineering, National Research Council, National Academy Press.

Niskanen, J., and T. Nieminen. 2001. The Objectivity of Corporate Environmental Reporting: A Study of Finnish Listed Firms' Environmental Disclosures. *Business Strategy and the Environment* 10: 29–37.

Pimm, S. L. 2001. *The World According to Pimm: A Scientist Audits the Earth.* New York: McGraw Hill.

Porter, M. E., and C. van der Linde. 1995. Toward a New Conception of the Environment—Competitiveness Relationship. *Journal of Economic Perspectives* 9, no. 4: 97–118.

Public Environmental Reporting Initiative. 1993. *PERI Guidelines.* Web pages www.ibm.com/ibm/environment/initiatives/peri.phtr .

Reinhardt, F. L. 1999. *Down to Earth: Applying Business Principles to Environmental Management.* Boston: Harvard Business School Press.

Rennie, J. 2002. Misleading Math about the Earth. *Scientific American* (January): 61.

Russo, M. V., and P. A. Fouts. 1997. A Resource-Based Perspective on Corporate Environmental Performance and Profitability. *Academy of Management Journal* 40, no. 3: 534–59.

Schneider, S. 2002. Global Warming: Neglecting the Complexities. *Scientific American* (January): 62–65.

Social Accountability International. 1997. Web pages
www.cepaa.org/introduction.htm .
Stanwick, P. A., and S. D. Stanwick. 2001. CEO Compensation: Does It Pay to Be
Green? *Business Strategy and the Environment* 10: 176–82.
SustainAbility/UNEP. 1996. *Engaging Stakeholders: Volume 1: The Benchmark
Survey.* London: SustainAbility/UNEP.
————. 1997. *The 1997 Benchmark Survey: The Third International Progress
Report on Company Environmental Reporting.* London: SustainAbility/UNEP.
————. 2000. *The Global Reporters: The 2000 Benchmark Survey.* London:
SustainAbility/UNEP.
Turban, D. B., and D. W. Greening. 1997. Corporate Social Performance and
Organizational Attractiveness to Prospective Employees. *Academy of
Management Journal* 40, no. 3: 658–72.
United Nations. 1992a. Report of the United Nations Conference on
Environment and Development, Rio de Janeiro. Annex I: Rio Declaration
on Environment and Development.
————. 1992b. *Agenda 21 Earth Summit: United Nations Program of Action
from Rio.* Geneva: United Nations Publications.
————. 1992c. Report of the United Nations Conference on Environment and
Development, Rio de Janeiro. Annex III: Non-Legally Binding Authoritative
Statement of Principles for a Global Consensus on the Management,
Conservation, and Sustainable Development of All Types of Forest.
Vervaillie, H. A., and R. Bidwell. 2000. *Measuring Eco-Efficiency: A Guide to
Reporting Company Performance.* London: World Business Council for
Sustainable Development.
Waddock, S. A., and S. B. Graves. 1997a. The Corporate Social Performance-
Financial Performance Link. *Strategic Management Journal* 18, no. 4:
303–19.
Waddock, S. A., and S. B. Graves. 1997b. Quality of Management and Quality of
Stakeholder Relations: Are They Synonymous? *Business and Society* 36, no.
3: 250–79.
————. 2000. Performance Characteristics of Social and Traditional Investments.
Journal of Investing 9, no. 2: 27–41.
WBCSD. n.d. *The Greenhouse Gas Protocol: A Corporate Accounting and
Reporting Standard.* Geneva: World Business Council for Sustainable
Development and World Resources Institute.
WCED. 1987. *Our Common Future.* Oxford: World Commission on Environment
and Development.

Company Index

A

ABB Group, 89, 93–95, 125
Abbott Laboratories, 70
AEP, 128–29
Alcoa, 127
Apple Computer, 65, 92–93
Asahi Kasei, 124–25
AstraZeneca, 77

B

BASF, 89, 96, 125, 154
Baxter International, 52–53
Bayer, 76
BMW, 53–55, 74–75, 82, 85, 120–21
Boise Cascade Corporation, 126
Bosch, 71, 76–77
BP, 75
Bristol-Myers Squibb, 23, 55, 70, 73, 74, 77, 96–97, 109, 133–36
Burlington Northern Sante Fe, 121

C

Canon, 55–56, 80–81, 84, 111
Chevron, 13, 128
Chubu Electric Power, 121–22, 157

Clorox Company, 125
Coors, 119
Corus Group, 127, 155–56

D

DaimlerChrysler, 65, 96
Danone Group, 89
DENSO Corporation, 149, 150
Diageo, 119
Dow Chemical Company, 85, 118, 141
Duke Energy, 95
DuPont, 76, 82, 84, 118

E

East Japan Railway Company, 121, 156–57
Eli Lilly and Company, 114–15, 132, 156
Entergy, 122
ExxonMobil, 65, 97, 128

F

Fiat, 121
Ford Motor Company, 75, 109–10

Subject Index

GRI 2000, 168
ISO 14031 Annex A, 168
Pacific Sustainability Index,
171–78
reporting environmental topics,
163–65
SustainAbility/UNEP, 166, 167
voluntary environmental
disclosures, 162–63
significant impacts, 104
performance indicators for, 115
site remediation, definition, 123
The Skeptical Environmentalist:
Measuring the Real State
of the World, 18
Social Accountability International
(SAI), 35
SA800 standard, social aspects,
35, 101
social policy statement, 93–95
spider web graph, 141, *142*
stacked bar chart, 139, *140*
stakeholders, 41, 87–88
identifying, describing, and
consulting stakeholders,
88–90
as target audience, 12
use of stakeholder information by
company, 90
standards of conduct, 97–98
Statement of Principles . . . on the
Management, Conservation,
and Sustainable Development
of All Types of Forests, 6–7
sustainability reporting guidelines, 4
and potential aspects, 101
sustainability reporting, expansion
factors of, xxv–xxvi
SustainAbility/UNEP scoring system,
44, 45, 166, 167
and potential aspects, 101
sustainable development, definition,
5, 6
sustainable development of forests, 8
sustainable forestry, 7
sustainable yield, 5

T

transparency, of performance
indicators, 122
trend data, 132
trend line over filled area, 139, 141

U

United Nations
Conference on Environment and
Development (UNCED), 6
Environmental Program, 4
principles for sustainable
development of forests, 8

V

vertical bar chart, 138, *139*
vision and commitment, 41, 79–80
commitment to minimize
consumption, 83–84
commitment to minimize environmental and social impacts, 84
executive statements, 80–81
impediments and challenges,
84–85
sustainability themes, 85
visionary statements, 81–83
voluntary certifications, 98
voluntary disclosure, 162–63
voluntary regulations, 97–98

W

waste reduction strategies, 21–22
The World According to Pimm: A
Scientist Audits the Earth, 18
World Business Council for
Sustainable Development
(WBCSD), 35–36
World Commission on Environment
and Development (WCED), 6